WWII at Our Front Door

Maria Gargano Jackson Mauck

BookLocker
Trenton, Georgia

Paperback ISBN: 978-1-64719-721-6 I
Hardcover ISBN: 978-1-64719-722-3 I
Ebook ISBN: 978-1-64719-725-4 I

Published by BookLocker.com, Inc., Trenton, Georgia.

Printed on acid-free paper.

BookLocker.com, Inc.
2021

First Edition

Library of Congress Cataloguing in Publication Data
Mauck, Maria Gargano Jackson
WWII at Our Front Door by Maria Gargano Jackson Mauck
Library of Congress Control Number: 2021919646

DEDICATION

I dedicate this book to my family.

To my parents: Agatina Pistone and Michael Gargano, with a special emphasis for my wonderful mom whose incredible strength and courage, in enduring those horrific war years, still amaze me. She always kept her faith, a faith which sheltered and nourished her four young children.

To my three great siblings: Ina Gargano, Vario Gargano, and Gianni Gargano. "We all held in there, together, through thick and thin!"

To my three wonderful sons: Ian Jackson, Lloyd Jackson and Mark Jackson. With a special thanks to Mark whose talent helped me cope with my computer's problems.

To the 'Mauckers' and Stephanie Mauck, witnesses to some of our life's best laughs together.

SPECIAL THANKS

Special thanks to Linda Payne Smith, instructor at the Creative Writing Class, and Lenore Wade who encouraged me and my story.

A very special thanks to April Beltz, author of *All about Ilyas*, and *Letters Across the Pacific*. She encouraged me to publish and told me people would be amazed in learning about this little known, horrific chapter of WWII history.

Finally, a big thank you to Cindy Desmet, my formatting helper and advisor, who – when suddenly confronted with a unique task – beautifully reinstated the integrity of my story. Thanks so much! I couldn't possibly have done without her!

About the Story and the Author

This story is *not* fiction.

The first part of the story is a true recollection of World War II, 1939-1945, told by *Cettina Gargano as a 5 to 10-year-old child. The whole story is told in the first person, present tense. Only two chapters, entitled *Remembering Life in Tripoli, Libya* and *Remembering Life in Catania, Sicily* – where Cettina reminisces back to when the war was just articles mentioned in newspapers – are told in the past tense.

As the eve of the war lingers a little longer, she observes the carefree life of young people exulting with songs to life and love, dancing frenetically to the latest fashions, still unaware of the danger closing in on them.

As a child constantly under foot of grown-ups, Cettina describes people's behaviors, their conversations and imprecations. The child remembers vividly the eventual horror of the war as expressed by people's fear, their desperations, their rage at the cause of so much destruction, and their hatred.

The family, the neighbors, the tenants of the same apartment building – they all make up the experiences as related in these chapters.

In the second part of the book, Cettina is a teenager in school, in Florence, where the severe grading system in Italy still follows the fascist doctrine, which aims to reduce availability of places of higher learning. Italian parents take matters in their own hands and hire and pay extra teachers to prepare their students.

Cettina is then a young girl working as an *au pair* in London, England, and Juan Les Pins on the French Riviera, with the firm goal to continue her education.

She meets a young G.I. in France, moves to California and marries him, and continues her education at San Diego State University.

Cettina was the author's nickname when she was a child.

"We do not argue with those who disagree with us, we destroy them."

- Benito Mussolini

Contents

Chapter 1:

Florence, Italy | Spring 1943

"Let's leave the kids home. There are Nazi-Fascist snipers everywhere. The radio has been warning people all morning."

"No," insists my mother. "If we die, we die together. We must go. We don't have a drop of water left."

My sister, Ina, and I are carrying two empty coffee cans each, with wires across the tops as handles. My cans are much smaller than hers. She is two years older, much bigger, and can carry bigger cans. Uncle Frank and my mother, with my younger brother in her arms, follow closely, carrying an assortment of empty containers and bottles.

We leave the apartment building where we were staying on via Oriani in Florence, Italy. We make a left and then a right on via Massaia. There are unkempt fields in some sections of via Massaia. We walk through the fields until we reach two farmers' wells about 100 feet apart from one another.

"Let's stop here. The group is much smaller," says my mother.

Lots of people are standing around the wells, especially the second one further away, where lots of children are playing and running around. Finally, our turn comes, with Mom and Uncle Frank standing opposite me and Ina, on the other side of the well. We fill all the bottles and containers when a sudden, loud *whizz* sound flies by my face, between me and mom. I extend my hand toward that whistling thing, as if to grab it, when a second, louder *whizz* flies by.

"What… was that?" I giggle.

"Don't do that!" my mother screams.

At that instant we hear an explosion of loud, frightened shouts. People are yelling. Piercing screams and cries are coming from the group at the second well. A woman has fallen to the ground. Men and women are kneeling around her. Someone is crying hysterically.

"Let's go! Now!" *Dear, Dear God…Dear, Dear God*, Mom is praying quietly over and over, as we hurry back home.

"Mom?" I ask, trying not to spill the water from my cans as I run after her, "Mom? What happened? Mom?"

We make a left onto via Oriani and up to the second floor of our apartment building.

"Mom, what happened?" I ask quietly.

"Don't you ever understand anything?" Ina shouts at me angrily. "A woman's been shot by a Nazi-Fascist sniper! And she's dead!"

We have lived in Florence for 2 years since 1941 and on via Oriani for the last few months. My family is among the refugees the Italian government has ordered to repatriate from overseas at the start of WWII. Dad, a Marshal Major in Mussolini's army, remained in Tripoli. I liked it there. It was happy, and we didn't have snipers.

Chapter 2:

Remembering Life in Tripoli | 1939

Our house in Tripoli, Libya (1939). The nasty rooster in the background.

I loved our house in Tripoli. It was all white with a nice white fence. It had a nice garden and fluffy little chicks running around the courtyard. I liked to run after them and pick them up when the hens were not around. If the rooster saw me, he would come screeching and flapping his wings and I would run away. The problem got so bad that he would dash after me and peck at my clothes and legs. I would run screaming back into the house. The rooster never seemed to bother my sister, only me. My father decided that he had had enough of all that screeching. He took a garden rake and slammed the rooster down, together with a hen that got too close. My mother heard all that commotion and was protesting vehemently.

"Look Mom... Mom, look at the chickens!" I said, looking at the frightening sight. "They are running in circles without their heads!"

Benito Mussolini, Adolph Hitler
Berlin | September 1937

***

The fights between my mother and father were getting louder. After an argument louder than usual I saw my mother crying. She was combing her hair at the bathroom window.

"Mom," I asked very quietly, "Why are you crying?"

"Because there is going to be a war," yelled my mom as if to continue the ongoing fight with my dad.

"I'm in the Army! Il Duce* is declaring war!" my father snapped right back. It was the beginning of WWII. I was four years old and my brother, Vario, was just a few months old.

As we prepared to leave our home in Tripoli forever, the house seemed in constant turmoil. Mom, when she was not fighting with Dad, packed all day and cried often.

We finally sailed from Tripoli, Libya to Sicily, Italy. The sea was very stormy. I felt terribly sick and I yelled at everyone who was listening that I wanted to get off the ship!

(*Il Duce, "the leader", was Mussolini's common moniker)

On the right, my dad as a Marshall Major in Mussolini's Army

Chapter 3:

Remembering Life in Catania | 1940

We disembarked at Catania, on the island of Sicily, and went straight to my grandmother's house. The turmoil in my family's life disappeared. Everything was so calm and beautiful at my grandma's house! My mom reconnected with her friends as soon as they heard we were back in Catania. It was comforting to see my mom happy and laughing again. Life was wonderful; nobody mentioned a word about the war that was raging around us.

Most afternoons Mom and her friends got together at the Al Fresco Café-Restaurant for ice cream and danced to the music of a live band. Uncle Frank was always part of that happy crowd. He was the loudest and happiest of the people there, making everybody laugh with his impersonations and his very own version of American tap-dancing.

I loved that café place. It looked like a large garden. It had tall shade trees, long tables and fine bluish gravel on the ground. When the music stopped, we could hear the rhythmic swelling and splashing of the Mediterranean Sea just in front of and below us. A gentle breeze made the leaves rustle softly. I loved Catania. We had so much more fun in Catania than we would have in Florence. Sicily was a beautiful island, especially in the summer.

The live band at the Al Fresco Café had a young lady who sang sweet, love songs:

No, Cara Piccina no,
cosi non va. Diam un addio
all'amore se nell'amore'
l'infelicita.

No, dear little girl, no.
This way won't work. Let's say good-by
to love if in love there's unhappiness

Cara Piccina, lyrics by Libero Bovio (my translation)

I leaned forward as much as possible with my elbows on the table to be part of all that fun, watching people dance. Uncle Frank noticed me and gestured with his hand, 'come here.' I went to the dance floor.

"You are going to learn the tango," he said. "Draw a square with your feet, like this, look. One-two-three-four. Again, look. One-two-three-four," he said, swaying his body. I followed closely and tried desperately to make my feet draw a square on the floor. After trying for what seemed an eternity, Uncle Frank shouted, "That's it. You got it. Now practice."

My sister joined me on the dance floor. Ina already knew the tango and we danced "one-two-three-four" while she, who like Mom had a beautiful soprano voice, sang the song, *"No, dear little girl, no, this way won't work…"*

Life in Sicily was great. We went to many parties. People were happy and nobody talked about the war. Only the radio kept on mentioning it. When we did not go out for ice cream at the Al Fresco Café, Mom's friends gathered at someone's house. The children always went along.

The best of times was when we went to Dr. Cicero's home. Everyone danced to the music of an old phonograph that needed to be cranked by hand. As soon as the song started to go slower and deeper, Dr. Cicero ran to crank the handle until it sounded normal again. The phonograph played the song *Vivere!* (*To Live!*) over and over. Uncle Frank loved that song and he sang it with gusto, making grand gestures with his hands.

Vivere senza malinconia…	*To live, without sadness…*
ridere finche c'e joventu'	*to laugh as long as there is*
Perche' la vita e bella e la	*youth, because life is beautiful*
voglio vivere sempre piu!!	*And I want to live it forever more!*

Vivere! by Cesare Andrea Bixio (my translation)

The song finished, and someone turned on the radio.

> "**…first casualty of war …the Italian destroyer Espero, after hours of fierce fighting against seven Allied cruisers and sixteen destroyers, sunk at 20:45, June 28, off the southwest coast of Crete… The high speed Espero with a convoy of three warships and two smaller escort vessels was headed to Tobruk, Libya …Espero was carrying antitank army unit …110 tons of ammunitions and 162 soldiers… The Espero was first spotted by enemy airpower based at Malta, at noon, on June 28, 1940…**"

The war! The war! Everyone had forgotten about the war…

Battle of Cape Passero (1940)

Part of the Battle of the Mediterranean World War II

Battle of Mediterranean

Part of the Mediterranean and Middle East theatre of World War II

The destroyer *Espero* at anchor

British light cruiser HMS *Ajax*

Battle of Taranto

Part of the Battle of the Mediterranean of the Second World War

Part of the Battle of the Mediterranean of World War II

Aerial view of the inner harbour showing damaged Trento-class cruisers surrounded by floating oil.

"…Captain Enrico Baroni bravely kept the Allied enemy destroyers at length… Even with high speed of 36kn, Captain Baroni was hopelessly outnumbered… The Espero used smoke screen and evasive maneuvers that allowed the rest of the convoy to continue the journey to Tobruk… After expending 5000 tons of ammunitions the British squadron first hit the Espero at 19:20… after a fierce battle the Espero sunk at 20:45… Captain Baroni died aboard his ship… Fifty-three Italian soldiers were rescued from the Mediterranean. Il Duce praised the heroic patriotism of the captain…"
Wikipedia: Battle of the Espero Convoy

TORINO
Anno 74 - Num. 140
Ogni numero 30 centesimi

LA STAMPA

MARTEDI'
11 Giugno 1940-XVIII
Edizione MATTINO

IL DUCE HA PARLATO

La dichiarazione di guerra all'Inghilterra e alla Francia

"Scendiamo in campo contro le democrazie plutocratiche e reazionarie dell'occidente "
Svizzera, Jugoslavia, Grecia, Turchia, Egitto, per quanto dipende da noi, non saranno coinvolti nel conflitto - "La parola d'ordine è una sola: vincere. E vinceremo "

Ecco le parole pronunciate ieri dal Duce in Piazza Venezia

« Combattenti di terra, di mare, dell'aria, Camicie Nere della Rivoluzione e delle Legioni, uomini e donne d'Italia, dell'Impero e del Regno d'Albania, ascoltate!

« Un'ora segnata dal destino batte nel cielo della nostra patria, l'ora delle decisioni irrevocabili.

« La dichiarazione di guerra è già stata consegnata agli Ambasciatori di Gran Bretagna e di Francia.

« Scendiamo in campo contro le democrazie plutocratiche e reazionarie dell'occidente, che in ogni tempo hanno ostacolato la marcia e spesso insidiato l'esistenza medesima del Popolo italiano.

« Alcuni lustri della storia più recente, si possono riassumere in queste frasi: promesse, minacce, ricatti, e alla fine, quale coronamento dell'edificio, l'ignobile assedio societario di cinquantadue Stati.

« La nostra coscienza è assolutamente tranquilla. Con voi, il mondo intero è testimone che l'Italia del Littorio ha fatto quanto era umanamente possibile per evitare la tormenta che sconvolge l'Europa, ma tutto fu vano.

« Bastava rivedere i Trattati per adeguarli alle mutevoli esigenze della vita delle

braccia contro gli affamatori che detengono ferocemente il monopolio di tutte le ricchezze, di tutto l'oro della terra.

« E' la lotta dei popoli fecondi e giovani contro i popoli isteriliti e volgenti al tramonto; è la lotta fra due secoli e due idee.

« Ora i dadi sono gettati e la nostra volontà ha bruciato alle nostre spalle i vascelli, io dichiaro solennemente che l'Italia non intende di trascinare nel conflitto altri Popoli con essa confinanti, per mare o per terra. Svizzera, Jugoslavia, Grecia, Turchia, Egitto, prendano atto di queste mie parole e dipende da loro, e soltanto da loro, se esse saranno o no rigorosamente confermate.

« Italiani!

« In una memorabile adunata, quella di Berlino, io dissi che, secondo le leggi della morale fascista, quando si ha un amico si marcia con lui fino in fondo.

« Questo abbiamo fatto e faremo con la Germania, col suo Popolo, con le sue vittoriose Forze Armate.

« In questa vigilia di un

evento di portata secolare, rivolgiamo il nostro pensiero alla Maestà del Re Imperatore (la moltitudine prorompe in grandi acclamazioni all'indirizzo di Casa Savoia) che, come sempre, ha interpretato l'anima della patria, e salutiamo alla voce il Führer, il Capo della grande Germania alleata (il popolo acclama lungamente all'indirizzo di Hitler).

« L'Italia proletaria e fascista è per la terza volta in piedi, forte, fiera e compatta come non mai (la moltitudine grida con una sola voce: Sì). La parola d'ordine è una sola, categorica e imperativa per tutti.

« Essa già trasvola e accende i cuori dalle Alpi all'Oceano Indiano.

« Vincere! (il popolo prorompe in altissime acclamazioni).

« E vinceremo! per dare finalmente un lungo periodo di pace con la giustizia all'Italia, all'Europa, al mondo.

« Popolo italiano, corri alle armi e dimostra la tua tenacia, il tuo coraggio, il tuo valore ».

(Stefani)

La comunicazione agli ambasciatori

ROMA, 10 giugno

Oggi, alle ore 16,30, il Ministro degli Affari Esteri, conte Ciano, ha ricevuto a Palazzo Chigi l'Ambasciatore di Francia e gli ha fatto la seguente comunicazione:

« Sua Maestà il Re e Imperatore dichiara che l'Italia si considera in stato di guerra con la Francia a partire dalle ore 11 giugno ».

Alle ore 16,45 il conte Ciano ha convocato l'Ambasciatore di Gran Bretagna, e gli ha comunicato in termini identici che l'Italia considera lo stato di guerra contro la Gran Bretagna

Telegrammi di Hitler al Sovrano e al Duce

BERLINO, 10 giugno

In lotta a fato dei Germani sta ...

HITLER.

In seconda pagina:

Le dimostrazioni in tutta Italia

In terza pagina

IL GOVERNO FRANCESE HA LASCIATO PARIGI

LA STAMPA | June 11, 1940 (Torino)
IL DUCE HAS SPOKEN
Declaration of war against England and France
We are taking up arms against the plutocratic reactionary democracies of the West,
Switzerland, Yugoslavia, Greece, Turkey, Egypt, who depend on us shall not be involved -
There is only one watchword: win. And win we shall.
Article: "Fighters of the land, sea, and air, Camicie Nere [armed squads, "Black Shirts"]
of the revolution and of the legions…"

"Il Duce! Il Duce *un corno*!" shouted Uncle Frank.

Dr. Cicero said, "Shhh!"

"Fancies himself emperor and declares war on France and England just like that! The 10th of June he declared war! All by himself!" said Uncle Frank.

"King Vittorio has given him all the powers," said Giovanna, Mom's closest girlfriend. People started talking all at once, sounding angry.

"…and makes laws all by himself! That *cornuto*! (an insult, a cuckold)," Uncle Frank said. Everybody was shouting and I couldn't hear 'un corno' anymore… Everybody was angry. It was no use. Uncle Frank stopped singing *Vivere!* (*To Live!*).

This cartoon from Germany, after the 1929 Lateran Treaty with the papacy depicts the King, Victor Emmanuel III, begging Mussolini for some restoration of authority such as that accorded to the Pope

A German cartoon. The Italian King who relinquished all powers to Il Duce.

***

Mom's friends met once more, at Giovanna's apartment, in the fall of that year, 1940. Grandma hadn't been feeling very well, and we were all very sad.

Uncle Frank, instead of being sad, danced and sang along to *Vivere!* (*To Live!*), which had climbed the charts to number one.

Everyone was dancing to the up-tempo beat of that song in Giovanna's apartment, except Mom and Dora, who were sitting close by. Dora got very close to my mom and whispered, "That poor Giovanna." She was watching Giovanna dancing with Uncle Frank. "She is so beautiful! How did she lose her arm?"

"I told you. The whole balcony fell down to the second-floor balcony and that fell down to the first," my mom whispered back.

"She should have sold this old, decrepit place years ago," said Rosalia who heard the whispering. "It's almost two centuries old, for heaven's sake! With the outhouses still on the balconies!"

"Yes," agreed my mother. "The owners are retrofitting this whole building after the accident. Yes, Gio is very beautiful."

"Well, if you ask me," said Rosalia, the oldest lady there, "that doctor who amputated her arm, that Doctor Cicero, could have saved it. If only he knew what the heck he was doing! The least he could do now is marry her. The poor girl!"

"Shhh!" Dora whispered.

Before leaving, Mom helped Giovanna carry the cups and glasses to the kitchen. Giovanna had taken her prosthetic arm off and prepared to wash the glasses. She didn't seem to mind at all that she didn't have her left arm. I got very close and looked up at her, fascinated. It was so clever the way she held down, with the stump of her arm, the glass on a folded dish towel over the kitchen counter. With her right hand she swirled a soapy dishcloth inside the glass. Yes, my mom was right: Giovanna was the second most beautiful lady in the world, after my mom.

***

Two months passed and my grandmother still wasn't feeling any better. Nonna wanted to know about the war because her next-door neighbor said the Italian Navy was doing very badly, that the British had sunk many Italian ships and lots of soldiers were dying. Also, because of the bombing in the Port of Catania, her neighbor said we might have to evacuate. Mom answered that it was not as bad as that.

"Well," asked Nonna point blank, "I want to know how many Italian ships have sunk!"

"Well, you already know about the destroyer Espero, then there is the cruiser Colleoni that sank this last July. Five hundred fifty Italian soldiers were rescued from there. But one of the British cruisers was also hit." Mom kept silent for a little while to see if Grandma was satisfied.

"What happened right here, right behind us, at Cape Passero?"

"A British cruiser sank the Italian destroyer Artigliere and two Italian torpedo boats. Two hundred Italian soldiers died."

Nonna wanted specific answers and wanted to know why. Mom tried to explain that it was all because of the Mediterranean supply routes.

"I don't understand, *un corno*!'" Nonna sounded really irritated now.

Using that same sweet, low voice as when she sang *Good night, dear Jesus* to us at bedtime, Mom explained to Nonna and to me and my sister:

"You see, Italian supply convoys go from Genoa in the north of Italy down to the south, here to us in Sicily, and then continue to meet our soldiers in Tripoli. If the Anglo-American and the Axis navies (Italo-Germans) meet in the Mediterranean, they fight."

Nobody really knew why all these terrible things were happening, except maybe Uncle Frank, who kept on telling everyone how that *cornuto* of Mussolini got us into a war without knowing what the heck he was doing.

"He decides to go to war with Britain, that bastard! Without thinking! We are not ready for a war! With the United States! Our Navy has no air support. Our ports are not adequate. He has no brains!" kept on shouting Uncle Frank, his neck bulging with veins. Dr. Cicero also said the same things, but without shouting.

LA STAMPA | Friday December 12, 1941 (Torino)
The declaration of war on the United States
announced to the Axis Nations by Il Duce and the Fuhrer
Mussolini speaks to the passionate assembly in Rome
The tripartite becomes a military alliance that aligns around his flags
250 million men resolved to everything for victory.
We shall win!

***

I looked at my Nonna who had fallen asleep and I felt ashamed of myself because days earlier we had behaved badly towards her. Mom had told my sister and me to go and apologize to Grandma -- but neither I nor my sister budged. Finally, Mom said we were not getting any ice cream until we apologized to Nonna. My sister said sorry and she got her ice cream. I didn't apologize. I waited until the ice cream cups were all gone, then I went up to Nonna and gave her a hug and a kiss. Mom didn't say a word to me at the time but I knew I was wrong because she told the same story of the ice cream, and me refusing to apologize, over and over, to everyone.

***

Mom didn't even want to see the neighbor anymore because she didn't want to worry Nonna, but the neighbor rushed right in and started reading the newspaper about the Battle of Taranto.

"Listen to this, Agatina" the neighbor was reading to my mom.

> **"On the night of November 11, 1940, at 23:00 hours, the Royal British Navy launched an aerial assault from the aircraft carrier, HMS Illustrious. Eleven Swordfish biplanes, in two waves, torpedo bombed the Italian Regia Marina battle fleet still anchored in the harbor of Taranto... The attack on the Italian Navy came completely by surprise, causing heavy losses. 59 sailors were killed and 600 wounded. Three Italian battleships sank, one cruiser and two destroyers were damaged, two aircraft were destroyed on the ground. The British lost two Swordfish aircrafts, 2 dead soldiers and two prisoners."**

Wikipedia: Battle of Taranto, precursor of the attack on Pearl Harbor

"Dear God, help us," said Mom. "Frank keeps on saying how criminal this war is, and how we are not prepared for it! The Italian Navy does not even have radar like the British do. He says Mussolini is going to be the death of Italy. The military was already suffering, the food was scarce, and now we are going to lose it with the convoys at sea!"

"Half of the Regia Marina was destroyed. The British can now go back and forth in the Mediterranean as they please," said the neighbor. "It will be easier for them to destroy our convoys sailing to Tripoli. Mark my words."

Mom did not say a word to Nonna about all this. She tried to convince my grandma to leave Catania and go to Florence with us, but my sweet Nonna died late that week.

***

The radio was announcing that Il Duce was giving a speech to the nation, his voice thundering and frightening through the air waves.

Benito Mussolini's Speech at the Teatro Adriano in Rome | February 1941

> **"Camicie Nere Dell'urbe (Black Shirts of Rome), I come among you to look you firmly in the eyes, feel your temperature and break the silence which is dear to me, especially in wartime... From November 7th to when English torpedo planes hit us in Taranto, as we have already admitted, we have met adversity in the war. We have had dark days... But the morale of the Nations of the Axis is infinitely superior to the morale of the British people...The fact that Fascist Italy dared to measure herself against Great Britain is a matter of pride that will live through the centuries. Nations become great by daring, risking, suffering!!"**

Once more we were packing. I was sorry to leave Catania. I would have liked to still have Nonna with us. I would have liked to go to the *plaia* (beach) one more time.

Catania had white-golden beaches, and the sand was very fine and soft under your feet. Laying down on it seemed like being on air, and if you snuggled your body a little bit left and right, the sand would hug you all around. My sister and I were dreaming about going to the *plaia* again, especially because Mom said 'there are no beaches in Florence'.

News of Mediterranean battles of convoys at sea was getting more and more worrisome. Uncle Frank came to the house with a newspaper in his hands and more bad news.

> **"The battle of Cape Matapan, off the coast of Greece, a tremendous loss for the Axis forces of the Regia Marina Italiana (Royal Italian Navy) and the German Air Force, dashes the Luftwaffe's hope of dominance in the Mediterranean... It's a decisive victory for the Allied forces of Great Britain and Australia...**
> **On the morning of March 28, three British battleships, one carrier and nine destroyers left Alexandria, Egypt to hunt for the Italian fleet that had departed from their bases in Italy. At 06:35 hours, three Italian cruisers moved to engage in combat joined by the battleship Vittorio Veneto. The Italian Fleet damaged all four Allied cruisers...**
> **Without air cover from the Luftwaffe, and without German Navy support, the Italian Admiral Iachino was aware of the disadvantage of lack of radar. He ordered his fleet back to port.**
> **At 23:30 hours three British battleships, undetected, attacked the Italian Regia Marina. Two Italian cruisers, the Fiume and the Zara and two destroyers, the Alfieri and the Carducci, were sunk. 905 Italian soldiers were rescued. At the end of the battle at Cape Matapan, 5 Italian warships were lost and 2303 men died."**

Wikipedia: The Battle of the Mediterranean, The Battle of Cape Matapan, 1941

"Do you see what I mean? We are fighting a war with our hands and feet tied. We have no business fighting a naval war without radar! That clown, that pompous ass, that lowlife Duce! Why not declare war on the whole damn world?!" said Uncle Frank.

"Shhh!" said my mother. "Walls have ears. We have to move as soon as we can, before the war spills over on land."

"We can start tomorrow!" Uncle Frank sounded angry still. "If you're ready. How much more do you have to pack?"

"Not much, just the kids' clothing. Everything else is in the trunk."

"My toys are all packed too," said my sister. I didn't have anything to pack.

"We will take the Cyclops Riviera all the way to Acireale and from there to Guardia Mangano. You can leave your heavier baggage and the trunk with the farmers in Guardia Mangano. We can stay overnight with them and then get back on the road to Messina. I'll get the tickets," said Uncle Frank.

***

We were ready for our trip. Uncle Frank had a passion for cars. He and his father owned a garage with cars they rented out to wealthy people. Sometimes they would chauffeur their customers themselves.

It was fun to be in Uncle Frank's car. It was much better than the bus. We could enjoy the trip and the view from the windows all along the Cyclops Riviera. When I asked, "What's a cyclops?" my sister immediately said, "Don't you know anything? The Cyclops was a giant monster."

My brother, Vario, had fallen fast asleep with the gentle roar of the car. The open windows brought a gentle breeze and the smell of the sea.

"The Cyclopes are a race of giant people," said my mother, who used every opportunity to teach us about Sicily. "The ancient Greeks believed that the Cyclopes lived here, in those caves that you see all over the coast. The most famous Cyclopes was Polyphemus. He was huge and had only one eye in the middle of his forehead. He was so strong... do you see those big, huge rocks right in the middle of the sea that look like narrow pointy mountains?"

"He threw those mountains in the middle of the sea, with his own bare hands," said Uncle Frank, "because he was mad at Ulysses."

"Polyphemus saw Ulysses and his sailors steal his sheep. So, he closed the cave with a big boulder with the sailors inside," said my sister. She, too, knew the story.

"Because nobody else could remove the boulder, Ulysses gave Polyphemus bottles and bottles of good strong Sicilian red wine to drink until the giant fell asleep," Uncle Frank said.

"While he slept, Ulysses and his men blinded the only eye he had. When Polyphemus removed the boulder to let his sheep go by, the sailors escaped, making fun of the giant. Finally, in a rage, the giant threw those big boulders that you see out there, in the middle of the sea. He sank the sailors' ships right there," said Uncle Frank pointing at a spot in the sea, "and killed many of them."

We all kept silent for a long time. There were only a few cars on the road, and the sea looked so peaceful and so blue.

We arrived at Guardia Mangano at two in the afternoon just in time for lunch. After lunch my sister and I went to see the fields. I had never been to the country before. I just stood there looking at the fields and the trees. It all seemed so big and peaceful until we got to the animal pens where a couple of men and ladies were taking care of the animals. I ran straight to the chicken coop where lots of fluffy chicks were running around. Seeing me so delighted, one of the ladies picked up two chicks. She handed one to me and the other to my sister. I held my chick close to my chest and ran to show it to my mom. I played with my chick the whole afternoon watching it peck the ground close by the outhouse. When I saw it run all the way through the open door of the outhouse, I ran after it and tried to grab it. But the chick stepped up, and then up again and disappeared into the bowl. I looked at it in a state of shock. My mom came running when she heard my screams. We could hear the chick chirping frantically but could not see anything. Mom got a long wide plank and tried to lift the chick up, but every time we thought the chick was almost at the edge of the bowl, it would fall right back in. A lady from the fields looked at my mom and smiled. We could hear the chick's desolate cry. Mom wouldn't give up, but every time the chick sounded close to the edge it would fall right back in. It finally stopped chirping. I was devastated. There wasn't anything Mom could say or do to cheer me up.

***

We left Guardia Mangano for the port of Messina to get the ferry. Uncle Frank had to get back to work and left for Catania. There were lots of people at the dock waiting for the ferry. They were saying the ferry was late and we might not be able to embark that evening. Suddenly people started running away from the port. "Run! Run! They are bombing," everybody was shouting. "Come Signora, run!"

A man picked up my little brother, Vario, from Mom's arms and we all followed him along the coast and up the Christo Re hill. We stopped halfway up a little bluff. On the left, a deep gorge carved into the hill, opening up the view to the Port of Messina. I looked down the steep gorge at the sea right below us; from that height a Regia Marina's ship looked very small in the waters below. The ship was maneuvering back and forth, trying to make itself an unsteady target. Bombs from a British airplane were falling all around the ship in what looked like little geysers of water splashing up from the sea.

We finally departed late that afternoon from the dock of Messina. My mom was still shaken from watching that warship being bombed. Since our departure from the Christo Re hillside, she had been quietly praying, "Dear God" and "Dear Jesus…" I wished I could comfort my mom somehow and I wished Dad were there with us.

"Signora, are you travelling all alone with three little children?" a lady sitting close by remarked. My mom answered that we were going to Florence and that my dad was going to join us there. She hoped that Florence would be safer because it was declared *Citta Aperta* (Open City). The lady told my mom that no one was safe when the enemy used strategic bombing. She then reminded Mom about the bombing of Turin, Milan and Genoa and many other cities around the world after the Axis' declaration of war in 1939.

"Words cannot express the feeling of profound horror with which the news of these raids has been received by the whole civilized world. They are often directed against places far from the actual area of hostilities. The military objective, where it exists, seems to have a completely secondary mission. The main object seems to inspire terror by the indiscriminate slaughter of civilians…" - Lord Cranborne

Wikipedia: Strategic Bombing During World War II

The lull of the ferry helped my brother go to sleep but my sister and I were not tired or sleepy at all. From the deck of the ferry, Mom pointed out the famous Charybdis whirlpool some 150 feet out to sea. It was shimmering in the late afternoon sunlight and looked like a small circle of water slowly dancing around and around over the shallow water of the Strait of Messina.

"Sometimes, when the sea is very rough, that small whirlpool is very dangerous to the ships," said Mom, "but sailors know Charybdis is there, so they steer away from it. The story says even Ulysses lost some ships in that whirlpool."

We arrived in Villa San Giovanni on the Italian mainland and the train station was just at the end of the pier. Many Italian and German soldiers were walking up and down the sides of the train. It was very dark already and I was glad we didn't have to walk far. I was happy to get into one of the compartments of the train and settle down. We slept most of the time until we arrived in Florence the next day.

Chapter 4:

Florence 1941 | via Giusti

Everything is so different here in Florence! The Central Station is huge and very noisy. On the loudspeaker a lady's voice in German directs passengers to the train platforms. There doesn't seem to be too much news about the war.

We take a taxi and go to via Giusti. The apartment is one of the apartments offered by wealthy Italians to military families like us who are repatriating due to the war. The place is beautiful and we settle in very comfortably. It has a playroom with a nice triangle-shaped cabinet in a corner. My sister goes right to it, opening the glass doors of the cabinet and arranging her doll furniture on the shelves. I keep waiting, very patiently, for her to finish so we can start playing but by the time she finishes rearranging the doll's furniture it's time to go to dinner.

***

School has already started in Florence. Because of the war and our traveling, we have missed a couple of months of the school year. My sister is enrolled in third grade and I am going to start first grade.

I am completely transfixed by the experience of school. I have never seen a classroom before. Everything is so drastically new to me. Mrs. Ballotti is my first-grade teacher. I am totally fascinated by Mrs. Ballotti. Rather than paying attention to what she is teaching, I listen to her sweet voice, the way she speaks, and the way she looks. She has a nice round face, soft brown hair and a gentle manner when she talks to the kids. I like her a lot.

The classroom desks filled with children I've never seen before amazes me too. There is a particular girl, taller than most, who wears a pretty hat over her light brown curls and has a beautiful dress. She looks and behaves so grown up every time she gets up from her desk to talk to Mrs. Ballotti.

***

I am failing first grade. Mom has a conference with my teacher and is unhappy at my failing the class.

"What do you think the problem might be, Mrs. Ballotti?" asks my mother anxiously.

"I can't tell," answers Mrs. Ballotti, "she seems intelligent and she understands things but when I ask her questions, she doesn't have the answers."

I am sorry that my mom and Mrs. Ballotti are so unhappy with my performance but I really do not know how to improve. Halfway through the end of the school year my mother decides to teach me how to read herself.

Her method is very simple. First, she reads with me, twice, a page from the children's version of the book *Pinocchio*. Then she tells me to go to the kitchen table and reread the page by myself, loud enough so that she can hear me. I have to circle all the words that I don't recognize right away. If there are only two words I don't recognize, I have to reread that same page twice. If there are three words, I have to reread the same page three times. My mother used this same method with my sister.

Neighbors and friends criticize my mom for this strange method of teaching and tell her that I am only going to learn by parroting the words and not understand a thing. But my mom rejects all the criticism thrown at her. She has a very clear, personal opinion about "critical thinking" and the different methods of teaching, and she does not hesitate to tell her critics about it.

"She doesn't need to understand at the moment. She's in first grade!" Mom answers, quite irritated at times. "At this point she needs to recognize, pronounce, and read all words without hesitation. How can children follow the meaning of a story if they have to stop every minute because they cannot read and recognize words and phrases?"

My mom studied to become a teacher but never had the chance to get her final credentials. She also plays the piano beautifully and tells us that if we want to play the piano well, we first have to practice on the keyboard, just to learn by heart where the keys are located and find them with our eyes closed. The same rule goes for learning how to read!

At first, it's hard to sit at the table for two hours in a row, but then it gets easier. I don't dislike this exercise anymore because it's starting to become more like a game. After reading a page more than once, I like to guess what comes next. I am even learning some passages by heart and I love it! It is the end of fall semester and I am reading well. I can understand everything that is happening to poor Pinocchio. Mrs.

Ballotti is flabbergasted. I have become one of the fastest readers in the class and I am passing first grade with flying colors. As always, Mom is right.

***

This winter we are all happy because Dad is coming to Florence for Christmas. In January he has to go back to his unit of the Regia Marina in Tripoli. But while he is with us we make the most of it, constantly badgering him and listening to every word he says. Our next-door neighbors came over to meet Dad; they want to know how badly the war is going in the Mediterranean and in the southern mainland.

"We cannot win this war," says Dad. "Actually, from March to August of this year, 1941, the Regia Marina has had some success. We attacked four British convoys, sank 4 destroyers and damaged as many cruisers. There were casualties and 216 prisoners taken, but it's not going to last. We cannot win this war," repeated Dad. "Mussolini gets angry with Italian people who are defeatists, but we also have to be realistic. Milan, Turin, and Genoa have been bombed mercilessly. The Tuscan countryside has been attacked. We need to stop this war." The man next door agrees and tells him that he has heard about the disaster of El Alamein.

"He should have never declared war!" Dad sounds almost desperate. "We do not have the equipment we need; we do not have supplies, we don't even have enough fuel for our troops, or our ships. We are not even equipped with radar. Mussolini was lucky in WWI. Hitler does not seem to be able to concentrate; he is fluttering about all over the world, from one war to another, from France to England, to Egypt to Russia!"

"What are we going to do?" asks Mom.

"Stay here until the war is over. I have to go back to my unit, but what worries me," says Dad, talking to the neighbor, "is that the patience of the Italian people is stretched to the limits. They are suffering and very unhappy. An underground movement has started already in the north and it's not just Italians. Other Europeans are part of it…" Suddenly my dad turns to my sister and me, "Do not repeat a word of what I am saying, do you understand? Not a word. Never, never. Promise? Or bad things will happen to people." Both my sister and I are startled at Dad's severe tone of voice and solemnly promise not to say a word to anybody.

"What is going to happen?" our neighbor asks Dad.

"I do not know, Signora. I am a Marshal Major in the Italian army. But I assure you that the soldiers are praying that this war will end soon and hope that… I can't say any more…" Dad makes a gesture with both his hands towards the floor.

***

FIRENZE LA SEDE DEL PARTITO FASCISTA REPUBBLICANO
IN VIA DEI SERVI

"La città italiana che preferisco? Firenze.
Perché lì gli Italiani ci hanno accolto sparandoci addosso."
(Gen. H. Alexander)

Florence, the headquarters of the Fascist party on Via Dei Servi.
"The Italian city I prefer? Florence. Because there the Italians have greeted us shooting at us."
Gen. H. Alexander

Dad has to go to a meeting at the Fascist headquarters in Florence and wants to take my sister and me with him. Mom refuses to let my sister go but allows me because, she says, I am "still a very young child." The headquarters are full of officers like Dad. There is a picture of Il Duce on the wall, the fascist logo – the Fascio – and posters on the tables around the room.

The Fascio. The weapon of the ancient Roman Littori. The rods tied together by leather straps symbolizes all
Roman citizens united for the state and the state for all Romans. The Fascio became the
logo for Mussolini's fascism.

My dad, never letting go of my hand, takes me to a table where an officer gestures to me: "Come here."

A young lady, also in uniform, picks up some clothes from the table and with a smile says to me, "This should fit you beautifully." She takes me into a big dressing room with lots of young girls. The lady helps me put on the Fascist uniform of the *Piccola Italiana* and says, "Look at yourself. You look beautiful."

The uniform has a light grey pleated skirt, a light blue blouse, and two white, wide bands that make an X across the chest. After years of wearing my sister's hand-me-downs, this uniform looks absolutely gorgeous to me!

My Dad is waiting right outside the door. He helps me put my coat on, takes my freezing hands in his and rubs them briskly. "Why on earth does this child have such freezing hands all the time?" he asks himself aloud.

When we get home, I can't wait to show Mom my beautiful uniform but I can't tell if she likes it or not. She looks at the uniform and then at my dad. He shrugs his shoulders and leaves the room.

***

In September, Dad takes me to the Fascist headquarters office to receive gifts for me and my siblings, compliments of Il Duce. I have my Piccola Italiana uniform on. Up in the sky, Allied airplane formations are thundering by with a frightening, deep-to-high-pitched roar. The first time we heard the British RAF my sister, Ina, said they sounded like live, angry monsters.

"Are they Italian, Dad?" I ask.

British airplane formations over Florence.

"No, they are the Allies," he answers.

"Where are they going?"

"I do not know."

After an hour-long conference with the officers at the headquarters, we are ready to leave. Our apartment on via Giusti is an easy walking distance. We are almost home when suddenly the military sirens pierce the afternoon silence and keep wailing for what seems like an eternity.

Dad grabs my hand and we start running. People are coming out of their apartment buildings and running towards the shelters. After a few minutes we arrive at the underground refuge of via Giusti.

Total chaos reigns in the refuge; lots and lots of people are shouting, some calling last names. Everywhere one can hear children crying. Dad spots Mom and my siblings in a corner by the wall. He yells something to my mom but the noise and the voices are too loud in that dark, closed-in space.

A sudden, deafening explosion shatters the air. That loud metal sound leaves me stunned, as if I have been forcefully slammed on each side of my head. A brief silence falls in the shelter and then the screams and cries start again. Men are speculating as to where the bombs have fallen, all agreeing that it must have been very close – right there on via Giusti. More explosions follow. The sound reverberates against the walls, so intensely that my head throbs painfully inside the closed-in refuge.

Dad finally reaches Mom and tells her that he is taking me home and that she should wait there until the sirens sound the all-clear.

He takes me by the hand, we climb up the steps of the shelter and, finally, we are out on the street. "*Niente paura, niente paura*! (Nothing to fear, nothing to fear)," Dad keeps saying to me. "*Niente paura! Niente paura*!" We walk until the end of via Giusti. He rubs my hand and gently taps it. "See? There is nothing to be afraid of. It's safer here."

As Dad and I walk down the street there is an eerie, reddish fog everywhere. At the end of via Giusti, on the opposite side from our apartment, the garden structures of Giardino della Gherardesca have been hit by the bombs and so have the gardens of the Horticultura. A mountain of debris is crushing all the shrubs and flowerbeds of the garden. A building that was part of the Cimitero degli Inglesi, opposite our apartment on via Giusti, has also been hit and reduced to rubble. Piazza d'Azeglio, situated at the other end of via Giusti, has also been hit.

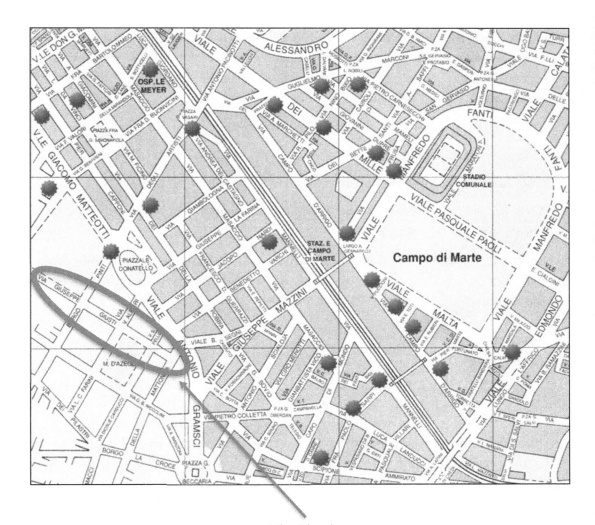

Via Giusti

The red round targets on the right-side of via Giusti, and Piazza d'Azeglio shows the most destructive bombs in Florence. - C, September 25, 1943.

The British RAF has targeted the marshalling yards of Campo di Marte to destroy German supplies, but the pilots missed the target. Some bombs fell on the yards with little damage. The rest of the bombs fell in a direct, northerly direction without touching the historic center of Florence. Besides Piazza d'Azeglio il Cimitero degli Inglesi, Piazza Cavour and the Giardini della Horticultura have also been hit.

Two hundred seventy-five people died this night, some of them as they were running trying to reach the shelter Radiocorriere. - I bombardamenti di Firenze, 25 Settembre 1943.

I am still clutching that little bag with the gifts, compliments of Il Duce, that I received at the Fascist headquarters, and I hand it to Dad.

When Dad and I get back home, we find our next-door neighbors in a frantic state. They did not have time to run to the shelter and the whole house shook when the bombs hit. When Mom gets home from the shelter, she asks the neighbors to please put on the radio. Mom's radio was among the things we left in Tripoli.

Our next-door neighbor's hands are visibly shaking.

"What's happening? What is going to happen, Michele?" she asks Dad.

"We have to pray that we can stop this war soon, Signora."

Mom is also badly shaken by the bombing. She wants to get away from via Giusti and move to the outskirts of Florence.

Before going to bed that night, I fold my Fascist uniform neatly on a chair. That is the last time I see it. Any time I ask Mom where my uniform is, she always answers, "in the laundry."

***

Christmas is a quiet time at our house. Our Nativity scene, with shepherds and sheep made of china, was left in Tripoli. But Dad has bought a beautifully painted popup Nativity scene complete with wise men and camels. He puts it on a low table and arranges it so we can see it only if we stand right in front of it. That way the perspective is very realistic and we only have to dim the light to make those figures come alive. I like to get on my knees to be on the same eye level with the shepherds and pretend to be part of them.

With the New Year, my mom is determined more than ever to move away from via Giusti. She keeps looking for an apartment to rent in the outskirts of Florence. It's decided we are going to stay on via Giusti until the end of the school year.

It is early January, and Dad is preparing to go back to his unit in Tripoli. He goes next door to say good bye to the elderly neighbors since he is leaving very early the following morning.

"Seriously, Michele, what do you think is going to happen? What do you expect will happen?" asks the neighbor.

"I do not know, Signore. I am only a Marshal Major in Mussolini's army, and I have no way of… but Italian soldiers are praying for this war to end soon. Personally, I'm hoping for…" It is very hard to understand what Dad is saying. He and our neighbors say good bye, hoping to see one another soon.

That evening I hear Mom and Dad in their room, arguing until late into the night but I still only hear pieces of their conversation.

"What is it that you are hoping for, Michele?" asks Mom.

"It's impossible… a kind of an accord with the Anglo-Americans," Dad says in a low voice. "An armistice. Il Duce and Hitler would consider it high treason. Generals would be shot on the spot…"

The argument between Mom and Dad continues until the early hours of the morning, sometimes getting loud. In the morning Dad leaves for Tripoli very early and I do not get up in time to kiss him goodbye.

"Mom, why were you and Dad fighting," I ask.

"It's nothing, don't think about it."

"Mom, what's an 'arms-tice?'"

"It's very complicated, I will explain later," she answers.

***

British airplane formations keep flying low over Florence for weeks at a time, towards the northeast of the city. People say the targets are two small villages in the countryside vineyards of Tuscany – Compiobbi and Pontassieve. The Allies want to destroy the main railroad from Rome and stop the Nazis, our neighbors say.

My sister and I see airplanes every morning on the way to school. It seems they are taunting us and chasing us with their loud roar and deep angry rumbling. Ina is very sad thinking about those poor villages being hit by the bombs every day. When we get home, Mom is at our next-door neighbor's, listening to Radiocorriere broadcasting the news about the war in North Africa:

> **"During the celebration of the Twentieth Anniversary of the Italian Armed Forces, Il Duce, pleased at the calm demeanor with which the Italian People have received the news of the invasion of 'our Libya' by the enemy, passionately promises: "There, (in Libya) when we once were. There, where our dead wait for us! There, where we have left powerful and indestructible footprints of our great Civilization. There, we shall return."**

> Radiocorriere, no. 5 and no.6, January 14, 1943

"Delusional or crazy. He is crying because we lost Libya!" says our neighbor.

"Both," says Mom.

On the 22nd of January, Radiocorriere announces that Libya's capital, Tripoli, has fallen to the enemy and many Italians have been taken prisoner. Many soldiers have died in the fight to save 'our' Libya! After days of frantic search to find out about Dad, we are finally notified that Dad repatriated with the very last retreating hospital ship of the Red Cross and is now at its base in Naples.

During the weeks that follow, we often go to our neighbor's house to listen to the news but also to listen to the fun programs like the singing concerts, competitions, and Comedy Hour with my favorite comedian, Macario.

> **"In February, Radiocorriere announces that Il Duce and the German minister Von Ribbentrop met...and reaffirmed the decision of the two countries, Italy and Germany, to conduct the war with all the energy necessary until the complete annihilation of the enemy forces and the elimination of the deadly danger of the Bolshevization of Europe."**

> Radiocorriere, February 1943 no.10

The 9th of April, Radiocorriere reports:

> **"...the conclusion of the dialogue between Mussolini and Hitler in Klessheim castle, where they reaffirmed the intention of continuing the fight until the definitive victory and the complete elimination of any future danger to the Euro-African Land."**

> Radiocorriere, April 1943 no. 16

The 13th of May the radio announces:

> **"...The Anglo-American Allies have inflicted a massive defeat to the Axis troops (Italian and German) in the North African campaign... totally annihilating all hopes for the Axis powers... to regain any African Territory..."**

> Wikipedia: North African Campaign

***

As springtime approaches, the sun gets warmer in Florence and the *ginestre*, the most beautiful Tuscan wildflowers, burst into bloom. On our way home from school, we see lots of people on the street, gathered in groups sitting in front of the open doors of the café. They are sharing the news of the latest bombing. We go in to get a newspaper for Mom.

A man by a table says, "The British are still bombing Campiobbi and Pontassieve to oblivion. They are destroying the Gothic railway line from Bologna to Rome. They want to stop the Germans; instead, they are bugging the Italians to death, those cornuti!"

A woman next to him says the bombs have reduced those villages into a mountain of rubble. The Allies are bombing the railways to stop the lines of communications. Her cousin, who lives in Pontassieve, told her that the villages are completely unprotected. "Where are the Axis forces? There's no protection from the Italian military, the Air Force, or the Germans." She says, "People are being massacred by the hundreds, those disgraziati!"

Chapter 5:

Florence | via Oriani

Mom has finally found an apartment in the outskirts of Florence, on via Oriani, N° 17, and our neighbors are sorry to see us go. We are also very sorry that we will miss Radiocorriere and the songs and jokes of Macario from our neighbor's radio.

We do not have much to pack except clothes, mattresses, and kitchen things but we need a cart or something to transport our stuff. Our neighbor knows someone who owns a cart with a donkey and he is willing to rent it out for an afternoon.

"Everybody is trying to move away to someplace else," our neighbor says. "The people by the River Arno think the Nazis are going to blow up the bridges of Florence. Everybody is looking for a cart or a wagon. They are even looking for hand carts or barrows. It's incredible what's happening to Florence!"

We make two trips. On the first trip we throw our clothes, kitchen appliances, ourselves, and everything else that fits into the cart. On the second trip we go back to get the mattresses and whatever else is left. Our neighbor is driving the cart.

The apartment building on via Oriani is newer than the one on via Giusti. It has huge entry doors as tall as the ground floor. It has a large, square foyer in front of the stairs that lead to the upper floors.

The neighbor parks the cart on the opposite side of the street, parallel to the walls. Mom, my sister, and the neighbor are all carrying things to the second floor, to our apartment. My brother, Vario, who is a toddler, is also carrying something. Mom tells me to stay down here and watch the donkey while they are going up and down the stairs with our stuff. My sister remains in the apartment with my brother.

A little apprehensive, I look at the cart and the donkey and stand by them in silence. Suddenly, the donkey starts to move towards the wall of the building. I pull on the reins as hard as I can to make the donkey stop but he continues forward at a very good clip. I plant my feet firmly on the pavement and pull. However, I am the one being pulled instead. "Oh no!" I say out loud and keep on pulling, but the donkey does not stop. "Ooh no!" I yell again in a panic. A man who is standing by the door of the building next to us sees me frantically pulling on the donkey and says very calmly,

"It's okay, little girl. He is not going anywhere. See? He just wants to eat those weeds by the wall. Not to worry!"

Mom and the neighbor are going back to get the rest of the stuff and I am relieved to go upstairs to see the new place.

Via Oriani is a short street lined with apartment buildings, all attached to one another and all three stories high. Our second story apartment has two bedrooms, a kitchen with a balcony, a bathroom, and a long corridor that spans the full width of the building. One bedroom has a window that overlooks the main street on via Oriani. The other bedroom window and the kitchen balcony, both at the very opposite side of the corridor, overlook the interior gardens and courtyards. These small, fenced gardens belong to the apartments on the basement floors.

My favorite place is the kitchen balcony overlooking the gardens. From there I can see the interior high walls of the building directly facing ours. It, too, has similar little gardens and balconies with luscious potted plants of red geraniums.

I like to watch the well-kept little quadrangles for hours, with their flowers and laurel plants that go in double rows all the way to the very end of the complex. Sometimes I can catch glimpses of the people, some 70 feet across from us, going about their own apartments, doing chores, cooking dinner. It is like a completely different world, hidden from the streets and totally enclosed by the apartment building's high walls. It feels like I'm in a secluded, secret place, remote and peaceful. I want to ask Mom if we can have geraniums on our balcony too.

***

We soon make friends with all the neighbors. They seem amazed that the Italian government has repatriated so many families from Tripoli because of the war. They all want to know about Dad in the Army. I chime in and volunteer to say that my brother, Vario, was born in Tripoli but nobody seems interested. Mom tells them about the white little house we had in Tripoli with a garden and a white fence all around, and how we had to leave most of our belongings there. The government will ship everything back to us in Italy, but what we miss the most, Mom tells them, is the personal little things, like our radio. The lady that lives right across from our apartment invites Mom to come listen to the radio as often as she wants to. I think that is exactly what Mom was hoping to hear.

One of the most listened-to programs of Radiocorriere is the *Nightly News with Mario Appelius*. He is a broadcaster very loyal to Il Duce and a strong propagandist of his Fascist ideas. Like Mussolini, he fiercely believes in the total, absolute victory of fascism. But very few people have faith in him because they cannot tell the 'false' news from the 'real' news, the fascist propaganda from actual news about the war.

"Il Duce says we will defeat the enemy!! We'll chase the enemy until the end, until complete victory!!" mocks la Signora Daccanto, our neighbor. "Meanwhile Pontassieve and Compiobbi hardly exist anymore! Torino and Milano keep getting bombed over and over again, completely unprotected by the Axis air forces. They are lies, all lies! The Phantom Voice was right."

Listening to the Phantom Voice is the best part of the *Nightly News* program; it is the voice of a man that has infiltrated the airwaves and is interfering with Appelius' news program. The voice sounds far away, intermittent and sinister. While Appelius talks about the great defeat the Axis forces have inflicted on the Allies, the voice of the *Specter* (Phantom) abruptly interrupts and says,

**"It's not true... You are a liar...
You are deceiving the people of Italy ..."**

Quello Spettro alla radio che sbeffegiava Il Duce, by Vindice Lecis-Edizione Sassari
Article by Constantino Cossu

Nobody knows how the *Specter* has infiltrated the radio waves and the *Nightly News*. "Il Duce is livid about the *Specter*. He can't handle this problem anymore," Mom says. "He thinks the *Specter* is a friend of reporter Appelius', and has become a traitor to the Regime."

It's fun to listen to the *Specter*. Any time Appelius speaks, the *Specter* immediately denies what he says. It's a muffled voice and it seems to come from nowhere, spooky and dangerous. Finally, not being able to find out where the *Specter*'s voice comes from, Mussolini fires Appelius. The *Specter*, though, is still there:

**"Italiani, here speaks the voice of truth! The voice of free Italy! The
voice of antifascist Italy!"**

Constantino Cossu

***

Florence smells very sweet in June. By the beginning of July, the hills surrounding Florence are blanketed with *ginestre* and in the orchards the trees are laden with fruit. via Massaia, which intersects via Oriani, is an old, wide country road. Half of the road is paved, the other half has fields with long, swollen ears of wheat.

My siblings and I use a little stretch of road in via Massaia and a little angle of street right in front of our apartment for our very own backyard. We run up and down the streets, we chase one another, and I chase Vario until he falls down with laughter. We make a ball with an old t-shirt and use that to play ball games but it gets destroyed very fast. We soon find the lid of an old can, that doesn't feel sharp, and throw that to one another. Suddenly Vario's head, above his left eyebrow, is bleeding profusely and I am terrified. We rush upstairs and Mom, after a big scream, cleans and disinfects Vario's forehead, putting a big band-aid above his left eye. Then she lets me have it. "You could have blinded him! You would have been destroyed for the rest of your life. He could have blinded you! And he would have been destroyed for the rest of his life…" Mom is always right. At night I can't sleep at the thought of what could have happened, like mom said, "for the rest of my life!"

***

By the end of July airplane formations are still flying every day over Florence and we are not allowed to play out front anymore. Mom and a few neighbors are huddled at Mrs. Daccanto's place listening to the latest news of the war.

The cities in central Italy have been bombed again by the Anglo-American air forces, in an effort to get to the Nazis.

> **Livorno, Civitavecchia, Pisa…Casualties are in the thousands, with up to 50% of the cities destroyed…**
> **On the 10th of July 1943, the Allies land in Sicily under the command of the British General Alexander. There was hardly any opposition from German or Italian troops. The casualties are great…3000 civilians dead…**
> **…on the morning of July 19th, the Anglo-Americans, with six hundred Allied aircraft bombers, attack Rome, the Eternal City… 700 civilians are killed…in the afternoon Pope Pius XII goes to visit the San Lorenzo zone devastated by the bombing…The Pontiff writes a letter to Roosevelt requesting that Rome… be spared as much as possible, from further injury… and shield the many treasured shrines from irreparable ruin."**

The Origins of the Radio diffusion in Italy

The bombing of the Italian capital, housing the King's residence, has deeply shaken the people of Italy. Mussolini has become the most hated man in the Country, and everybody wants him out; "Fuori Mussolini!"

Everybody is consumed by the need to know. They are glued to the radio, sharing information and newspapers, hungry for 'real' news, not the Regime's news. The national radio broadcasts have been suppressed by the Fascist regime and so have all newspapers. The only way to get the truth is through Radio Vatican, Radio Alger, or Radio London. On July 25, 1943, the headlines of the *Corriere Della Sera* and the Radiocorriere announce:

CORRIERE DELLA SERA
Le dimissioni di Mussolini
Badoglio Capo del Governo
UN PROCLAMA DEL SOVRANO
Il Re assume il comando delle Forze Armate - Badoglio agli Italiani: "Si serrino le file intorno a Sua Maestà vivente immagine della Patria,,

Dismissal of Mussolini
Badoglio Head of the Government
A proclamation of The King

The king resumes full command of the Armed Forces. Badoglio to the Italians: "Lets close ranks around His Majesty, living Image of our Country." - Corriere dell Sera

In our building and all across via Oriani, people from window to window all shout with joy! They are happy because they believe, with Mussolini dismissed by the king, that the war will end soon.

But the following day, July 26, consternation grips the neighborhood. Curses and damnations are flying from every door and window, from neighbor to neighbor.

"Mussolini has ignored the King," they say. "That *disgraziato* has gone back to work at the Grand Council, as usual… as if nothing happened, that *maledetto*! Italian Generals have lost all confidence in him."

No more news is heard on the radio that day to calm the nation – not even propaganda – until finally late that evening at 10pm Radiocorriere announces that Il Duce, as he left the royal palace soon after the conference with the King,

"...was arrested by order of his Majesty, King Vittorio Emanuele. Prime Minister, Marshal Badoglio, new head of the Government, declares [however] the war will continue in alliance with Germany."

The transmission lasts only 42 seconds but people are hungry for more news. All the window lights are on, on via Oriani. Nobody is going to sleep on that hot July night, all wondering how the Italians and the Germans can continue to be allies.

The following day the Partito Nazionale Fascista Italiano, Mussolini's party, is dissolved by Marshal Badoglio. The Italians who were ecstatic about the news of the end of fascism are shocked to find out that not all of their neighbors are happy about that. The Italians loyal to Mussolini are furious and ominous brutal fights, ending in deaths, break out in the neighborhoods of Italy.

***

The carpet-bombing of Italy continues without respite into late August. La Signora Daccanto and the upstairs neighbor, Signora Fanetti, come in to see Mom with sad news, something that happened two weeks before. The ladies are frantically waving a newspaper. "Leonardo da Vinci's painting was destroyed! Those *disgraziati*," the ladies say. "They bombed the Santa Maria Delle Grazie Convent with an incendiary (fire) bomb! The British have destroyed the walls of the refectory!"

As soon as the neighbors leave, Mom reads the newspaper carefully. During the night of August 13th, five hundred and four British bombardiers dropped bombs on Milano, Genoa, and Torino, which are the centers of Italy's industrialized zone – the worst concentration of incendiary bombs ever unleashed. The destruction of the cities is estimated to be 40%. Casualties are in the thousands. The Convent of Santa Maria Delle Grazie has been badly hit. Mom continues reading.

The Bombing of the Santa Maria Delle Grazie Convent, Milano, Italy
The Last Supper, just a few years before the bombing of August 13, 1943.
Leonardo had finished the painting in 1495.
Wikipedia: The Last Supper (Leonardo)

"Luckily, a protective structure had been built in front of da Vinci's wall fresco of *The Last Supper*..." Deeply moved, Mom stared at the destroyed building for a long time. Then, almost inaudibly, she murmurs, "like a miracle..."

That same day, August 13th 1943, Rome is declared *Citta Aperta* (Open City).

***

It is the month of September and school starts soon. September 7th is a very important day in Florence; Signora Fanetti tells Mom that we celebrate an old festival that originated in the Middle Ages and is called The Festival of the *Refricolone*. *Refricolone* are paper lanterns that farmers use to light up their country roads at night. Centuries ago, every fall, hundreds and hundreds of farmers used to walk down from the surrounding hills, with fancily adorned, colored paper lanterns, as they made their way to the markets of Florence to sell their produce. The festival usually ended with a religious procession.

The *Refricolone* tradition still lives on in Florence, and it is now just an excuse to fill the resplendent markets with delicious delicatessen foods.

A market up the street sells *Refricolone* and some parents are taking their kids to the procession. My sister and I immediately ask if we can go too.

"But isn't it dangerous, with the bombings and all?" asks Mom.

Signora Fanetti suggests going up the street to Piazza Viessiex, buying an ice cream, and coming right back. That is what most of the parents are doing. We buy three beautiful paper lanterns adorned with bows and silver ribbons and we wait until dusk. We light the candle inside and the *Refricolone* sparkle delicately through the beautifully colored designs. We hold the lanterns by the little rod attached to it and we go outside. via Oriani looks amazingly charming, all lit up with hundreds and hundreds of trembling lights moving slowly towards the Piazza. On the way back home, in the dark of the night, the hundreds of *Refricolone* seem to magically hover freely, unattached to anything, their flickering lights looking like enchanted fireflies, as we walk up the stairs to the apartment.

***

September 8th 1943 dawns on Florence like thunder. After wild speculation about secret negotiations with the Allies, the voice of Marshall Pietro Badoglio, through Radio-Alger, announces at 7pm "that an armistice was sought and granted by General Eisenhower, commander-in-chief of the Allied Forces."

Corriere della Sera, 1943
Armistice
Ceased the hostilities between Italy, England and the United States.
The Message of Badoglio:
The Italian government realizing the impossibility to continue the unequal fight against the overwhelming power
of the adversary, in trying to save more and more grievous misfortunes to the Italian nation has asked for an
armistice from General Eisenhower, Commander-in-Chief of the Anglo-American forces.
The request has been accepted.
Consequently, all acts of hostility against Anglo-American forces by Italian forces must cease everywhere.

Most Italian Generals are relieved to hear this and tell the army to go back home.

When the Germans intercept Badoglio's speech about the secret armistice, way ahead of its radio announcement, the Fuhrer's reaction is immediate and ferocious against the Italians. Determined to stop the advance of the Allies at all costs, he invades all of Italy. He disarms the Italian forces and sinks the battleship, Roma. As the Nazis marched on to invade Rome, Italians watch Marshal Badoglio, the King, the Crown Prince and all the Royal household, run away from Rome to southern Italy.

With Badoglio and the King fleeing, Italy is in chaos and anarchy reigns. Italian armed forces are left with no instructions. They are forced to surrender to their former German comrades. When Italian soldiers resist, 1500 of them are slaughtered. If they surrender, 5000 of them are shot. Many are taken prisoner to work in labor camps in Germany.

Italia va Alla Guerra - Franca Lanci

Finally, high-ranking Italian Generals take command, declare war on Germany, and set up a new antifascist government in Salerno, south of Rome. Many other Italian Generals, however, remain loyal to Mussolini's fascism and to Hitler.

***

It's the second week of September and school has started in Florence. We are busy getting a coat and shoes for my sister. I'm getting my sister's hand-me-downs and I'm very glad because some of her stuff is really pretty. I am happy to see some of my old classmates from the previous year, except for one big bossy girl, Anita, who keeps on asking questions about Dad: "Is he a traitor? Is he a Fascist?"

"Never let anyone lock you into a corner with questions. Just answer them with another question." I usually listen to Mom and Dad's advice but that day, after class, I tell Anita to get lost and run like the wind to join my sister. Together we walk back home.

At home we find Mom at Signora Daccanto's place listening to the radio with other neighbors. "This is really very bad news," I hear Mom saying.

"Mom, what happened?" asks my sister. "What's going on?"

"Hitler sent a German commando to free Il Duce from prison a week ago," answers Mom quietly. "Mussolini has renamed the Italian government, *Governo Fascista Republicano*. He has taken the seat of power away from Rome, into German territory in northern Italy."

The lady from upstairs adds, "He is furious as hell! He's going to execute all the Italian Generals that have put him in jail, including his own son-in-law! We are trying to get Radio Monaco. Mussolini is now giving a speech to the Italians."

"Mom, didn't the armistice mean that we were going to stop fighting?" I was totally confused. I don't dare ask my sister because she is already looking at me with her you-never-understand-anything expression.

Mussolini's unmistakable voice comes through angrily, pompous, thundering as usual and stressing every single word.

Camicie Nere! Italiani e Italiane!
[Black Shirts! Italian Men and Women!]

After a long silence, again comes to you my voice… It is the voice that has called on you before, to rally around in the most difficult times… and that has celebrated with you the most triumphant days of our nation.

It has happened before, in peace or war, that a prime minister has been dismissed, or disgraced…but never in the history of mankind has happened that a man… such as the one talking to you now, who has served the King for twenty-one years with absolute, I say absolute loyalty, was enticed and arrested at the very King's home threshold… The word loyalty has a profound, irrefutable, eternal meaning in the German soul…It was the Monarchy that has betrayed the Regime with the signing of the armistice. It has been the King who has advised his accomplices to betray our German allies in the most ignominious way …a deception reinforced by deadly and vicious bombing by Anglo-American forces. Even our enemies do not hide their scorn toward our disgraceful capitulation.

Camicie Nere! Faithful from all Italy!

It's imperative to reorganize our armed forces… to eliminate all traitors, especially those who have gone to the enemy.

I call on you again to take up arms… together with the great empires of Germany and Japan who will never capitulate.

You, infantrymen, reconstitute your battalions…

You, young Fascists, be part of the divisions that must renovate the glory of our nation's past.

You, aviators, get back next to our German comrades at your posts as pilots. Your will, your courage, your faith will give back to Italy its own soul, its honor, its future and its place in the world. More than hope, it has to be for you an absolute certainty!

Viva l'Italia! Viva il Partito Fascista Republicano!

Translation. Speech of Benito Mussolini, September 18, 1943- Fondazione della R.S.I.

The neighbors remain in astonished silence by the radio for a long time.

"Dear God, protect us! Mussolini is inciting a war among Italians. A civil war!" exclaims Mr. Daccanto. "He is instigating hatred in young Italians' minds… those who have not accepted the armistice."

"We already have the Germans and the Anglo-Americans against us. Now we will have our own Fascist sons and daughters against us too," says the lady from upstairs.

"Florence has been spared a lot. Look at the immense destruction of Sicily and our cities in the north. I hope our enemies will respect Florence as Open City," says Mom sounding worried.

***

One day, Mom has some incredible news to tell us! We are going to have a new baby sometime in February in the coming year. My sister, Ina, is so happy that she jumps up and down with joy but I am not quite sure what that means just yet. My brother, Vario, who is only four doesn't seem to care at all.

The cold months of October and November go by rather calmly in Florence. The big difference is that now Germany has taken over Italy. German soldiers patrol everywhere. There is even a German commando unit that has taken up residence in one of the villas on via Massaia. Mom does not allow us to go play down in the street in front of our building anymore.

Dad is coming home for Christmas and I am very happy. He will be in Florence by the second week of December, in time for my 8th birthday. He will then return to his unit in Naples by mid-January.

When he arrives, he has a gift for me; a pair of beautiful, soft, woolen gloves 'to warm up those little hands that are always so freezing' he says.

The next day, he tells Mom that he is going to take me Christmas shopping. Ina is needed at home with Vario. The Mercato Centrale is all lit up in soft Christmas lights and decorations. Meats, poultry and all kinds of cold cuts are beautifully laid out on beds of red lettuce and it all looks very tempting on the low marble counters. Everything looks very festive but this year there are very few people out.

"I am surprised there is any food at all," says Dad. "Everything is so expensive. Many other cities have almost nothing." He buys a few things: cheeses, fancy cold cuts and the Christmas cake, *panettone*. Florence is below zero degrees (centigrade) in winter, and even with my new gloves my hands feel like ice.

Dad feels that my hands are very cold. He puts my left hand in my pocket. He holds my right hand tightly in his hand and stuffs them both in his big coat pocket. His hands are always warm. Suddenly I feel so much better. It seems like warmth is enveloping me all over. I walk with my hand in Dad's pocket all the way home.

***

The neighbors are anxious to talk to Dad. They corner him every way they can. Mr. Daccanto, our elderly neighbor, comes to see Dad. Both are veterans of WWI, except that Dad was only eighteen in that war.

"Was the armistice a cowardly thing to do, Michele? We didn't show enough stomach to continue fighting? That British General seems to think so."

"What does he know? He doesn't have a clue! Nobody has a clue," bursts out Dad.

I have never heard Dad sound so angry. "Our soldiers have been starving for years – no food, no medicine, their boots in shreds, for years! No adequate weapons, non-existent Axis air-defense. The Anglo-American Allies themselves have no clue! They are needlessly bombing totally defenseless cities. Our casualties are immense and believe it or not so are theirs. Do I think the armistice was a good idea? You bet I do. We need to fight the wars that we can win for the country, not satisfy one's dreams of fame and glory! Badoglio just behaved like a cowardly imbecile, keeping the signing of the armistice secret for so long!"

"There is going to be a civil war, isn't there, Michele?"

"I am afraid it has already started, Mr. Daccanto," answers Dad. "Even before the bombing of Rome, from Sicily to the northern Italy, men have secretly banded together to fight the German and the Italian Fascists. The real betrayal is Badoglio letting the Germans believe we are still fighting next to them!"

Listening to Dad is very upsetting. Everything is so confusing. Now I understand why bossy Anita asks so many questions about Dad. That afternoon, thinking about my beautiful, Fascist uniform of the Piccola Italiana, I ask, "Dad, how come it's a bad thing now to be Fascist?"

"It's a bad thing because some Fascists have become criminals," says Dad. "They only think about themselves, not about all the citizens and the country. You do know what a *fascio* is, don't you?"

I pucker my lips and shrug my shoulders to convey a 'no'.

"Fascio was the weapon that the *Littori*, the ancient Roman soldiers, used in battle. It's a bundle of rods tied together with a weapon inserted on top," Dad continues, "and

from *fascio* comes the word fascism. Like the rods tied together, it means the union of all citizens for the good of the State, and the State for the good of all citizens."

***

Dad has made the Nativity scene in a corner of the kitchen using the same pop-up Nativity from the previous year. Late on Christmas Eve, in complete darkness, Dad lights up two candles that he has smartly hidden behind a small potted plant. The candles shine brightly on the shepherds and the three wise men. There is something magical about those figures casting long flickering shadows and when I stare at them long enough, they seem to move in earnest toward the manger.

December 25th dawns with a beautiful clear sky and very cold weather. Dad built a beautiful wooden truck for Vario that he keeps dragging all over the place with a thunderous noise. We all try to help Mom with the Christmas meal. Suddenly we hear a great commotion up and down the stairs. The neighbors are yelling; "The Allies are bombing the marshaling yards again!"

For months, the Anglo-American forces have been trying to drive back the Germans and the pro-Mussolini Italians from Tuscany, the Axis' strongest line of defense against the advancing Allies from the south. Just five months before, Pisa was devastated by the bombs, and its railway station razed to the ground. Two thousand people died that day in August 1943.

The following day, December 26, 1943, there is another commotion in the building. At 13:30 (1:30pm) the Allies start bombing the railway tracks of the Tuscan cities of Pistoia, Prato, and Empoli. Of the 210 bombs dropped over Empoli, only 40 hit the intended railway tracks. The rest fall on city blocks. There are 123 deaths and many injuries.

All three cities are within nineteen miles of Florence, and Prato, the closest, is only eleven miles northwest from us. From our home we can hear the deep rumbling of the Anglo-American airplanes flying low over the valley between Florence and Prato. We hear the bombs exploding, one after another, like continuous loud thunder in the distance. Two hours later, the marshaling yards of Prato are destroyed. No casualties are being reported. Mom is seven months along and extremely unnerved by these loud explosions.

"*Niente paura, niente paura*," says Dad. "Have no fear, have no fear! Nobody is going to bomb Florence, nobody!"

"But Florence… all of Tuscany, is completely under control of the Nazis!" Mom shouts.

"Niente paura, niente paura," Dad keeps saying.

***

It's the first week of January and Dad is leaving for Naples. He has been very busy this past week in the kitchen building something with slats of wood, knobs, and thin bands of steel. When I ask him what he's doing, he says he's building a radio transmitter. He shows me that by tapping and holding the knob on the steel for different lengths of time, the radio transmits different sounds, the sounds of the Morse alphabet, and so he can communicate with people.

I am sorry he is leaving but he says he will be back soon. Usually, after Dad leaves, I ask Mom why she and Dad fight so much. Today I don't even want to ask Mom a single thing.

The second week of January, late in the evening, we have a big surprise. Mom tells us that Uncle Frank and his brother Santo are in Florence. "They are down in the cellars of the apartment building," she says. "When they come up to see us, do not make noise, keep very quiet. Nobody must know that they are here."

I can hardly wait. When Uncle Frank finally appears at the door, looking very tired and old, his coat collar pulled up around his face. He is not the same laughing, happy person I remember. Mom hugs him in silence. Brother Santo, who is much younger, seems more jovial and smiles without saying a word.

"It's all gone, Titina [my nickname]," says Uncle Frank in a broken voice. "Everything is gone. Sicily is destroyed. But Santo is here! There are many more with him down below."

We all go into the kitchen and Mom closes the balcony doors and shutters. She gives them something to eat that she cooked earlier but they hardly eat anything. They talk for a while and then Mom gives them one of Dad's army blankets and half a glass of wine. After they go back to the cellars, Mom explains to me and my sister that Santo is a Partisan and fought the Nazis in Sicily. He and many others were taken prisoner and sent to a labor camp in Germany. Luckily, some managed to escape and they are here, hiding, waiting to join other Partisans in Tuscany. Uncle Frank came up from Sicily to help them as much as he can. During the night I pray that Uncle Frank and

Santo, together with the others in the basement cellars, will keep safe and well-hidden from the Germans who are outside, patrolling the streets.

Very early the next morning, Mom tells us they were leaving. She keeps the kitchen shutters slightly ajar. It is still dark out and from our second story balcony we can make out seven or more men exiting from the basement's narrow windows and stepping into the enclosed courtyard. Transfixed, Ina and I watch the men jump, one after another, over the small fences of the private gardens and run until they reach the very end of the courtyard. Soon the men disappear inside the last door of a ground floor apartment opposite our building. "They are safe! Thank you...Dear God!" says Mom. I am really surprised to find out that people living in that apartment are Partisans themselves.

***

The OSS and Italian Partisans in WWII

Even before the signing of the armistice on September 18, 1943, the majority of Italian citizens, very impatient with Mussolini and tired of fighting an unequal war alongside Nazi Germany, had formed an underground resistance. Some Italian Generals, believing that all Italian Generals would behave the same, and honor the new Badoglio administration's terms of the armistice, dismissed their troops.

Many soldiers put down their arms and went back home, while many others joined the Partisans' Resistance. The Italian Partisans fought Nazi Germany, the Italian Fascist followers of Mussolini, and the Italian fascists Franchi Tiratori. Inflamed by Il Duce's speech of the 18th of September, Italian Fascists swore loyalty to him and his new government "until the last man standing."

The Partisans fought the Nazis for every inch of Italian soil and proved invaluable to the Allies against the German occupation of Europe. After the invasion of Sicily in 1943, the Partisans helped Anglo-American troops to move up the Italian mainland, to Anzio, Rome, Tuscany, and the north, forcing the Germans to their eventual total collapse.

"The contribution of Italian anti-Fascist Partisans to the campaign in Italy in World War II has long been neglected. These patriots kept as many as seven German divisions out of the line... They also obtained the surrender of two full German divisions... in and around Genoa, Turin, and Milan... The Partisans' success was largely due to the arms and supplies parachuted to them by the British SOE [British Special Operations] and the OSS [U.S. Office of Strategic Services] and to the brilliance of the intelligence network developed by members of the Resistance keeping in constant touch... via secret Morse radio, with the Fifteenth Army."

For example, the very accurate intelligence collected by the Partisans from the Nazi headquarters itself was crucial information about the German troops' whereabouts and was received instantly by the OSS, on the very day of the battle of Anzio on January 1944.

From: https://www.cia.gov/static/fcbf4625e96eea6207373743c0dffcc9/oss-italian-partisans-ww2.pdf

The Anglo-Americans were thus favored with the element of surprise that January 12th, and upon their landing in Anzi, they encountered no resistance, and immediately gained three and a quarter miles of beach head with no problems. A single jeep even made it all the way to Roma.

Lo Sbarco di Anzio - by Giuditta Mosca

The Partisans got better and better organized, and the names of some of them became well known throughout Italy. As the American Generals needed more intelligence further north, the OSS infiltrated, by submarine, Italian Partisans behind enemy lines. One such agent was 20-year-old Mino Farneti who sat at the foothills of an Apennines mountain with his secret radio to pinpoint parachute drops of arms and supplies while his colleagues managed to smuggle back five Allied officers captured by the Germans.

Another Partisan, Riccardo Vanzetti, who served as an Air Force engineer, set up his radio in an active beehive of a farmhouse that was also used by the unsuspecting Germans. Well hidden, he transmitted until the end of the war and trained saboteurs to disrupt German communications. He also formed new mobile brigades of Partisans, first with bicycles only, then with cars, trucks, and finally tanks, all taken from the Germans. Many more names of Italian Partisans will become well known throughout Italy.

From: https://www.cia.gov/static/fcbf4625e96eea6207373743c0dffcc9/oss-italian-partisans-ww2.pdf

Chapter 6:

Florence | February 1944

Italy is still calm the first months of 1944. Mom needs to go to the hospital for the baby's birth. She puts my brother, Vario, under the care of the Franciscan orphanage, my sister with a neighbor, and I must go to a school which is also a convent of nuns. Mom tells Vario and me that it's only going to be for a few weeks and that she will come see us every Sunday. I really, really do not want to go with the nuns and ask, "Why can't I stay with Ina at the neighbors?" Vario starts crying. Mom tells me to be strong, for Vario.

At the convent Mom hugs me and says she will be back on Sunday. A Sister takes me by the hand and says, "Just in time for dinner!"

Inside a big hallway I join about 100 girls and, in a line, two by two, we go to the refectory. The sisters introduce me as the "new girl."

The convent building is two or three centuries old. It belonged to a rich, noble family and was donated to the city of Florence. It has magnificent marble stairways and a huge rectangle ballroom. In the center of the ballroom, a large basin, beautifully carved on the outside, stands four feet tall and is filled with small hot lumps of coal that spark and sizzle upwards to the roof of the basin – an interesting heating method that has come to us through the centuries. This tub is completely surrounded by a balustrade that makes it impossible to get close to it. Colonnades run the length of the walls and, along the colonnades, there are two long rows of small beds. This magnificent room is our dormitory. I stand in a corner feeling very lonely when a group of older girls, 12 to 13 years old, come to my corner.

"Are you Jewish?" asks a girl who seems to be the head of the group. She wears brown tresses down to her shoulders.

Am I Jewish? Nobody has ever said anything to me about that. Mom's words come to mind: never let anyone back you into a corner with a question. Just answer them with another question.

"Why?' I answer.

"Because your last name is Gargano," continues the girl with the tresses. "That's the name of the spur in the Boot of Italy. Jewish people take their last names from places. Do you understand what I am saying? The Boot? The geographical shape of Italy… it's a boot!" It felt like she was saying *Are you stupid or what?*

"How can she be Jewish with a first name like Maria?" says a girl that is part of the same group. She has blond, short, curly hair around her forehead. She is very pretty. She looks like the faded painted angels on the chapel's ceiling where we go to say prayers. One of the sisters claps her hands and we all go to the foot of our assigned bed to say our prayers.

I feel very homesick. I think of home, with Mom and Vario, in the kitchen, balcony, and the gardens of the courtyard.

The following day passes quickly, with prayers in the chapel, classes, lunch, and dinner. Soon we are back in the dormitory waiting in line to go to the foot of our beds. The older girls are in line in front of me and tower over me. I am the very first in the line of younger girls. I feel a sudden push from the back and a shove from the front.

"Stop pushing me!" says the tall girl in front. I say sorry and with my index finger I point to the girl behind me. Again, there is another push from the back and a shove from the front. "Stop pushing me, I said! Do you hear me?" Oops! That is the same girl with the brown tresses and the question about my last name. I move sideways, completely out of the line and out of her reach, as she argues and yells and tries to shove me again. Finally, I angrily slap the column with my right hand, I smack my left fist on my hip, and I cross one foot over the other, as if to say, *So, what are you going to do about it?* In this very instant something really strange happens. As I slap the column, all the lights go out in the dormitory and all the girls cry out in unison. At the same instant, lots of fiery sparks from the hot coal explode loudly in one long flame upward, to the grate of the basin.

"She's a wiiitch!" shrieks the girl with the tresses, causing panic in the line.

When the lights come back on and the Sister claps her hands, ready for the prayer, the girl that looks like the painted angels on the ceiling walks closer to me.

"Are you really a witch?" asks the girl with the curly hair.

I am still terrified. I think I might actually BE a witch. The light turning off at the very moment I slapped the column, the coal sizzling and crackling loudly at that very instant as if I had caused it… it is just too much for me! More of Mom's words come to mind: Sometimes it's better to be feared than to be loved. (From Machiavelli's *The Prince*.)

"Yes, I am a witch!" I scream with a voice that cannot not hide my true fear.

At night, in bed, I feel like crying. I want to go home. Finally, as I am about to fall sleep, a rustle by my neck startles me. I turn my head and find myself nose to nose with a head staring at me. I am ready to scream in fear when, "Shhh!" a voice says. "You are not really a witch, are you?" It is the blond, curly-haired girl. Still shaking from the fright, I answer that I am not.

"Good! Don't tell anyone. We are going to have some fun!" she says, and crawls away to her bed. I have found a friend.

However, it isn't meant to be, having fun pretending to be a witch. Mom has sent word to the Sisters that I have a baby brother and she will come see me the following Sunday. Also, Uncle Frank is back in Florence and brother Santo is safe in Sicily.

The following Sunday finally arrives and the sister tells me that Mom, Uncle Frank, and Ina are in the reception hall. Mom is sitting on a sofa holding a bundle from which a couple of little arms are sticking out and waving about. I feel like crying as I kiss Mom and Ina and Uncle Frank. I look at my new brother, Gianni, and he looks as if he couldn't care a fig whether I am there or not. The baby has curly, reddish hair like Mom had when she was young. Ina talks to me quietly while Mom and Uncle Frank are chatting.

"Cettina," she says in a begging voice, "why don't you tell Mom that you want to come home! Even Uncle Frank is here!"

I am supposed to stay in the convent one more week but Ina's suggestion is too tempting and I follow her advice. I can't believe it when Mom says I can go home. I go with the Sister to the dormitory, take my uniform off and grab my few belongings.

"Sorry," I tell my newfound friend, "I will not be able to be a witch anymore. I am going home."

***

Everything is normal on via Oriani. The neighbors don't seem to have missed me very much. They had eagerly waited for baby Gianni who is "adorable, like a little angel with a head full of curls."

Florence is straining under the repression of German occupation. All apartment buildings on via Oriani are counting the hours until the Allies break through the enemy line.

"What is taking them so long? It has been months," says Mr. Daccanto. The Anglo-Americans are stuck in a ferocious war against the Nazi-Fascists south of the city.

All Florentines, especially the people in our building, know that Anglo-Americans and Nazis alike are well aware of the importance of Florence in the world. "It's a special city full of art. It's the jewel of Europe," says our next-door neighbor. From the Cupola of Brunelleschi to Michelangelo's David and the rest of his famous statues, (Dawn, Night, Day and Dusk,) to the Doors of Paradise, to Giotto's Bell Tower, to Botticelli paintings, to the magnificent Renaissance palaces – they are all precious works of art.

The Anglo-Americans, as well as the Germans, know the world is watching, and they will avoid destroying Italian artistic heritage as much as possible. In fact, Mr. Daccanto says that the German Consul himself, Mr. Wolff, will do everything to avoid much damage. The Consul is especially concerned about the thirteen-century-old bridge, the Ponte Vecchio, that he has admired since he was a young man studying in Florence.

"At this moment though," says Mr. Daccanto, "it's the Italian Fascists, more than the Germans, that are afflicting Florentines. They are criminals! Some of them even belong to the fascist band of Mario Carita and are determined to viciously get revenge for the betrayal to Mussolini."

On the 21st of March, an Italian Fascist tribunal rounds up, at gunpoint, five young men in their twenties; they are made to march against the fence of the stadium and wait until dawn. In the early hours of the 22nd of March, as punishment, a large group of young draft dodgers, who refuse to enlist in Mussolini's army, are forced at gunpoint to watch the execution of the five young men who had been standing all night by the stadium fence. The news of this horrific act rages like wildfire throughout Florence. This medieval city is small, only five miles long and four and a half miles wide, and the news of this Fascist cruelty reaches fast-as-lightning to every corner of every district, compelling hundreds of Florentines to join the antifascist Partisans; their main objective is to help the defenseless.

This starts a desperate search for arms. Nobody knows where they can be found. Not even Mr. Daccanto knows. In an address to the Italian Senate in 1931, Il Duce gave the "categorical order to confiscate the largest possible number of weapons of every sort and kind." Even the urban police are forbidden to carry weapons; "For law and order, we have the military," Mussolini declared. The newly-formed Florentine Partisans steal arms from wherever they can: from the Italian King's Army, from the pro-Mussolini army, from the civilian Fascists, and even from the German Army, if they can manage it.

(https://americainchains2009.files.wordpress.com/2010/01/mussolini_antigun1.jpg)
Benito Mussolini - Promoted Gun Control

"The Measured adopted to restore public order are: First of all, the elimination of the so-called subversive elements. ...They were elements of disorder and subversion. On the morrow of each conflict I gave order to confiscate the largest possible number of weapons of every sort and kind. This confiscation, which continues with the utmost energy, has given satisfactory results."
__ Benito Mussolini, address to the Italian Senate, 1931

The most foolish mistake we could possibly make would be to allow the subject races to possess arms. History shows that all conquerors who have allowed their subject races to carry arms have prepared their own downfall by so doing. Indeed, I would go so far as to say that the supply of arms to the underdogs is a sine qua non for the overthrow of any sovereignty. So let's not have any native militia or native police. German troops alone will bear the sole responsibility for the maintenance of law and order throughout the occupied Russian territories, and a system of military strong-points must be evolved to cover the entire occupied country."
– Adolf Hitler, dinner talk on April 11, 1942

From 1930 to 1945, 13 million Jews were exterminated with no possibility to protect themselves

The people on via Oriani are outraged about the massacre at the stadium. From every floor of our building come shouts of anger. It is no use trying to get to the radio; Signora Daccanto tries but there is only Fascist propaganda. We can't even get *La Voce della Verita* from the Phantom Voice, who infiltrates the radio programs. We cannot get Radio London or Radio Roma. We are completely censored, silenced, and isolated.

Chapter 7:

The Battle of Piombino, Nazi Atrocities

The following day, March 23rd, is a very cold day in Florence. I keep covering Gianni's arms because they constantly stick out from the blankets of his crib. He looks at me, smiles and in a frenzy of hand waving uncovers his arms again. Vario talks to his baby brother and laughs.

Suddenly at 11am the sirens of the Florentine alarm system pierce the air with a loud, prolonged wail all over the city. Uncle Frank takes the baby, grabs blankets and the baby's bottle, and opens the front door.

"Run, run, run," Mom shouts to us. Ina takes Vario's hand and we all run down the stairs, jammed with screaming neighbors. We are barely downstairs, in the underground cellars, when there is an immense explosion that resounds against the walls of the building, followed by other even louder, unrelenting explosions in rapid succession. In the cellars there is chaos and silent screams – the noise of the blast shuts out human voices. I think about Dad's words: *niente paura, niente paura.*

After a long silence, the alarms sound the all-clear signal. Piazza delle Cure, a few blocks from via Oriani, has been heavily bombed and so has Viale dei Mille. The target was still the marshaling yards of Campo di Marte but many buildings along the railroad have also been hit. On via di Credi, which is just behind the train station, many houses have collapsed and there are many casualties.

Even in the historic center of Florence a bomb has exploded, barely missing the Basilica of Santa Croce, the burial place of Michelangelo and Galileo.

> **"In all these bombings, so far, not a single Axis plane has tried to protect the city of Florence or, for that matter, tried to down an Allied airplane."**
>
> Wikipedia: Florence, the Bombing

After the alarm sounds the all-clear, Mrs. Fannetti, who lives one flight up, remains to talk to Mom and help with baby Gianni. Mrs. Fanetti is very agitated.

"These bombings make me crazy. I hate this war. I hate the Germans. But most of all, I hate the Fascists. I think about those young kids executed in the stadium! Oh please, Dear Jesus, protect us. Dear God, help us. I have nightmares! In Piombino these 'porci' (pigs) Fascists… monsters… they are not even Italians anymore…" Mrs. Fanetti is crying and sounds incoherent. She has lost close relatives in the battle of Piombino, and most of her relatives still live in there.

"The biggest torture is not being able to know, not being able to turn the radio on and get the news," Mom tries to comfort her.

"It happens that, from time to time, powerful forces of evil seem to obscure the whole earth under a toxic cloud determined to destroy all life on the planet. In such instances, since ancient times, history records the horrific cruelty of man against man: from the primitive Assyrians skinning their enemies alive, to the ferocity and spectacle of ancient Romans, to the barbarity of the Dark Ages. In Modern Times we witness the inhumanity of World War II."

Wikipedia: Inhumanity of Man against Man

***

Piombino is a city of Etruscan origin situated on the Tuscan coast. The Etruscans were the ancient people who lived in the region and predated the ancient Romans by thousands of years. This city was of great importance to the Romans for its polymetallic ores which contained copper, lead, zinc, iron, silver and tin. Copper slags, carbon dated from the 8th and 9th centuries BC, were still found on the beaches together with shreds of Etruscan artifacts along the ancient roads of Populonia and Volterra. The Etruscans became wealthy as their beautifully ornate funerary urns and sarcophagi from their necropolises attest to this day.

After the signing of the armistice, the proud city of Piombino refuses to accept Mussolini and his new government. On September 10th 1943, when a German flotilla demands entry to the harbor, the city's Port Authority, aware of the Germans intentions to occupy the town, denies it access. The Italian Fascist General De Vecchi, however, orders the city to allow the Germans in. The local population sides with the Port Authority and the whole city revolts in a furious insurrection that demands the Italian forces to stand up to the German army. An Italian senior officer orders an open fire on the defenseless civilians to disperse the crowd. General De Vecchi, at the same time, forbids any action against the Germans. Outraged by the killing of Italian civilians, Italian junior officers act against their generals' orders and start arming the citizens of Piombino who are only too happy to join the sailors. A tremendous battle breaks out. On one side the German forces and the senior Fascist Italian officers, on the other side the antifascist Italian junior officers, sailors, and the whole citizenry of Piombino. The battle ends with heavy damage to the Germans; 120 killed and 300 captured. The Partisans win. General De Vecchi, infuriated by the insubordination of his sailors, orders German prisoners released and their weapons given back to them.

> **As another more ferocious civilian insurrection erupts against General De Vecchi, Fascist Italian senior officers flee the city while heavy bursts from German machine guns pan in all directions over Piombino, causing a massacre. With the city under solid German control, citizens, sailors, junior officers, and anyone else who survived the battle against Nazi Germans, flee to the woods and the hills. There they start a formidable anti-Nazi, anti-Italian-Fascist movement and call themselves the Partisans.**

Wikipedia: Piombino | The Battle of Piombino

***

Mrs. Fanetti confides to Mom that she, too, has relatives who are Partisans. I notice a difference in the way the people of via Oriani talk with their neighbors. There is a reticence even in greeting one another.

"Mom, is Dad still a Fascist, or a Partisan?" I ask and immediately realize my stupid question by looking at my sister's rolling eyes; she always knew everything.

"Of course not. Dad is in the Navy, part of the Red Cross of the Regia Marina. Anyway, never, never, talk to anyone in the neighborhood about Dad, about Partisans or Fascists," Mom says.

"I think I feel pretty safe with the people of this building," says Mrs. Fanetti. I like Mrs. Fanetti. She is often down in our apartment talking to Mom and helping her. Uncle Frank will soon leave for Sicily and I am glad that Mom has a good friend in our neighbor.

Mrs. Daccanto has terrible news and comes over to talk to Mom and Mrs. Fanetti about it.

> **The Comando Generale of CVL (Corpo Volontario della Liberta) announced that on the 23rd of March, the very same day of the recent bombing of Florence, the tragedy of the Fosse Ardeatine took place in Rome, still under the yoke of German occupation. A group of 16 Italian Partisans attacked a column of 32 German SS and killed 28 of them. Hitler ordered an immediate reprisal of ten Italian men for every German killed and needed to be carried out the very next day. Three hundred thirty-five Italian civilians were rounded up from the streets,**

from houses, from prisons, and taken into the ancient caves next to via Ardeatina, in Rome. All of them were ordered to be shot in the back of the head and allowed to fall into piles, each one a meter high.

The Tragedy of the Fosse Ardeatine. Rome WWII

Mom thinks that perhaps we should not talk about the war in front of Mrs. Fanetti because she gets very emotional and starts crying. Mom tries to comfort her but it is impossible to keep the news of the war quiet while all the neighbors on via Oriani are talking about it. It is impossible not to hear about the atrocities that are happening all around us. People talk constantly about Fascists and Nazis everywhere we go whether we stand in line with Mom and Uncle Frank at the bakers for bread or at the farmers to buy 'cheese-water', the leftover water from cheese production, because milk is too expensive, or to get water at the street fountains.

People waiting in line for bread are saying that we are lucky in Florence. In the Casentino Valley, located between Florence and Arezzo, the Nazis, led by an Italian Fascist officer, rounded up all the people inside the main church. They were looking for Partisans and it seems someone ratted them out. They found and shot the Partisans, then burnt them in their own homes.

The stories people tell seem to get more and more gruesome. In the village of San Polo, in the Arezzo region, 48 men, mostly Italian Partisans, were rounded up by the Nazi and Italian Fascists. Tubes of tritium were tied around some of the men, each connected to electric wires. The men were told to dig deep in the ground, and then were buried alive. Only the men with the tritium were left with their heads above ground. An electrical signal from the Germans reached the tritium, which in turn ignited all others and exploded underground. I told Mom that this was probably the worst, most horrible story I had ever heard.

In the village of Bucchio, close to Florence, two Nazis were killed. The Germans reacted ferociously. Guided by the Italian Republichini, (Mussolini's Italian army), they went from house to house, and they ended up rounding up 108 people. Some of them were women, some were babies as young as three months, some were teenagers. Complete families were destroyed. At the end, incendiary bombs were thrown in the houses to incinerate the bodies.

Firenze Va Alla Guerra, by Franca Lanci, pp 106/117

People waiting in line with us and listening to these stories are appalled! Disgusted! Men curse, "*Vigliacchi cornuti*, bastards!" People are having a very hard time comprehending all of this and they are afraid. They say there is no Italian army, there is no urban police. There are no armed civilians to protect the people. There is no protection from anywhere against the enemy. Finally, it is our turn in the baker's line and we buy two loaves of bread. We go back home with jugs of water, bread and cheese water.

***

When we get home, Ina is glad to see us because baby Gianni was getting fussy. He needs changing. He needs a bath and food. Mom does wonders using as little water as possible for everything. The aqueducts of Florence were damaged by the bombings and water is scarce. The faucets in the house let out only a fine drip of water at a time, and then stop. Sometimes it doesn't reappear for days.

Mr. and Mrs. Daccanto come to visit Mom. Mrs. Daccanto has extra water to give Mom for baby Gianni. Our neighbors have already heard about the atrocities happening in Bucchio. Mr. Daccanto tells us the same thing is happening in Germany. The SS are rounding up Jews by the thousands, often helped by young Jews, traitors to their own kind.

"Filthy scum, vile, young Jew who rats… who discloses to the Nazis where Jews live, about their jewelry, their precious things, their precious family… just like Italian Fascists who helped the Nazis round up the people of Casentino, and the people of Bucchio." Mr. Daccanto sounds very sad and furious at the same time.

This is the second time that I hear the word Jewish and I make myself a note that I need to ask Dad about that. I need to tell him that a girl at the Sisters' convent asked me if I was Jewish because of our last name. I also have to ask Dad why being Fascist is so bad now! I remember I used to love to wear my Fascist uniform of the *Piccola Italiana*!

Uncle Frank tells our neighbor about the terror he felt when brother Santo was taken prisoner to Germany. Partisans from Tuscany helped him and many other prisoners to escape to Florence.

Uncle Frank has changed a lot since the very beginning of the war when Mom and us children were still in Sicily. Those months, just before we left for Florence, were a lot of fun. Mom and all her friends had lots of parties and Uncle Frank was always so much fun to be around. He was the life of the party, singing and dancing with Mom's friends. He made everybody laugh with his pretend American-tap-dancing and his impersonations of famous people. He used to sing at the top of his lungs that beautiful song, *"Vivere!"* (*To Live!*). "I want to live as long as there is youth, because life is beautiful and I want to live it for-ever mo-o-ore!" He would end the song with arms stretched wide open and an adoring look at the sky.

At night, after we repeat with Mom the usual prayer, for Jesus to "Please, bless baby Gianni, and Vario, and Cettina and Ina, and Dad and…" Mom added a very special prayer: "Please, Dear God, protect us and give us Your Peace, so much needed in this world!"

***

Since the beginning of this terrible war, Florentine schools have mostly been open because parents need to go to work, however painful that might be. My sister and I go to school on and off because Mom is worried, even though Dad says that schools are safer than apartment buildings and cellars. The mornings when we do go to school, we hear the constant rumble of the airplanes above us. When Mom needs to go to the Commander of the *Corpo D'Armata Militare* for Dad's papers, she asks me to stay home with Gianni. She prefers that Ina not miss too many school days. She feels it will be easier for me, being younger, to catch up with my schoolwork when this nightmare of a war is over.

Baby Gianni, added to the family. From left to right: Ina, Gianni, Mom, Vario, Dad, Maria.

I like to babysit for Gianni. It is very easy. I just talk to him while he sits in his highchair in the kitchen waving his arms excitedly and laughing. Once in a while I offer him his bottle and a spoonful of baby food. Mom usually takes only a little over an hour for this task but today Mom and Uncle Frank are very late, and Ina is at school. On her way home, Ina picks up Vario from kindergarten.

I start getting a little panicky because I know that pretty soon Gianni is going to get fussy. He will need changing and will roll around on the blanket on the floor. I stop talking to him and try not to make him laugh because it excites him even more. I move farther away; I sit down by the table and do not look at him. I hope he falls asleep. After five minutes, no such luck. He starts squirming and fussing in his chair. I tell myself that if he starts crying, I will have to take him out of the high chair.

"The problem is I am still too small to lift you up, see?" I tell him. I put my hands under his arms and try to lift him up. My head is at the same level as his, when I stand up next to him, and the arms of the high chair do not lift open. He gets excited and opens his arms, expecting to be picked up. I put my hands under his arms again, lift him up a little, and let him back on the seat. Gianni laughs. We do this over and over again. He thinks we are playing a game. I decide that even if I cannot lift him high enough to clear his feet from the chair, I can always drag him out if I can topple the chair and Gianni on top of me. I try to get enough courage to think about doing it when the front door opens and Mom and Uncle Frank walk in. I breathe a sigh of relief when suddenly the military alarm wails long and strident, sounding like an animal howling in pain. Mom easily lifts Gianni off the chair, takes the bottle and blanket, and we all run down the stairs. Ina and Vario, just home from school, join us in the underground cellar. Our neighbors are already there. The siren continues on for a long time and makes Gianni cry. The horrendous noise of the siren and the blasts of exploding bombs have a strangling effect on the hearts and souls of the people. The scene in the cellar is always the same: confusion, cries, and shouts that nobody can hear because of the uproar.

The consensus of the neighbors in the cellar is that the Allies are bombing Campo Di Marte marshalling yards again. The rumbling of the airplanes continues for two hours and the sound of bombs exploding close-by startles everybody into more screams and imprecations. The train station of Porta al Prato is destroyed. The offices of the station and the Teatro Comunale nearby are also hit by incendiary bombs and are all in flames. Houses on via San Jacopino are hit too and there are casualties.

After the all-clear, we go back upstairs, spiritually exhausted. The grownups are hysterical, cursing and shouting. Mrs. Fanetti is crying. Ina seems very frightened. She holds Gianni tightly and that night we all go to sleep in Mom's big bed and say the prayer, "Please dear Jesus, force these people to stop this war..."

***

Mom has decided that nobody is going back to school until the war is over. Ina and I are very happy.

The very next day, the 2nd of May, 1944, late in the morning, the siren wails once again. It is long and loud and reverberates all along the walls of via Oriani and into our building. We have grown so tired of this. We feel as if we have just walked down from a high mountain and then, exhausted, we have to climb it again. The siren's piercing sound hurts our ears just as much as the exploding bombs. We move like robots. Mom, Uncle Frank, and the four of us children run down into the cellar. I think about Dad and wonder what he is doing right now. I know he prefers to remain outside. He says if a bomb hits our building, we will be buried alive but he truly believes there is nothing to be afraid of. The bombers are trying to hit places like the marshaling yards. He is right and I keep saying, "*Niente paura, niente paura.*"

The blasts of the bombs feel like a hard punch on the side of the head and the young children and babies in the cellars scream with pain. The bombs seem to have fallen very close, as if via Oriani itself has been hit.

When the siren sounds the all-clear, like robots, again, we go back upstairs. The neighbors yell, "Finally! They managed to hit the marshalling yards of Campo di Marte! Finally!" The Rifredi train station was also destroyed. With the marshalling yard finally destroyed, Florentines believe the bombing will stop.

Chapter 8:

Bombing Campo di Marte, Florence

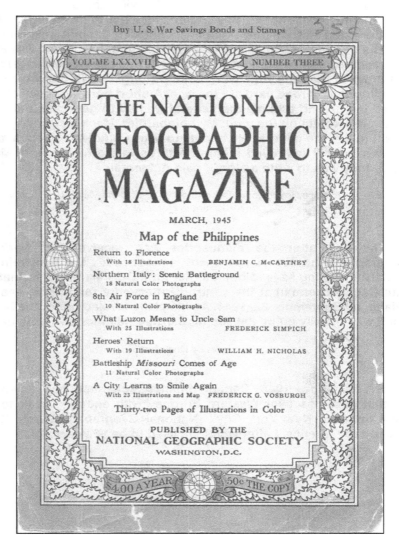

Benjamin McCartney's account of his and Captain Stanley Ackerman's B-26 bombing of the marshaling yards in Florence appears on the March 1945 issue of the National Geographic

"Captain Ackerman was Executive Officer of the 320th Bomb Group, 12th Air Force flying out of Sardinia, Italy, with a squadron of B-26 attack bombers. He was in his mid-twenties during WWII. By far

his most famous bombing mission was the one his group made to knock out the railroad yard at Campo di Marte, Florence, on the second of May 1944. Florence, 'The Jewel of the Renaissance,' was declared an Open City, meaning both sides agreed not to bomb it or fire their artillery into the city. But the railroad yard, used by the Germans, on the city outskirts, was fair game: "They sent us up to do the job because they didn't want the heavies, the B-17, B-24, or B-25 bombers, to attempt it. They couldn't hit a bull in the backside with a fiddle at the altitude they bombed," chuckled Captain Ackerman.

The heavies flew at 20,000 feet according to the captain. His B-26 "Marauders" bombed low, at 12,000 feet. It was extremely dangerous, but most of the time they were dead on target. "We did a nice job bombing the railroad yard at Florence. A short time later my colonel called me up and told me the general wanted to get some publicity on the job we did on the yard. My bombardier, Mack McCartney, and I went to see the general. He told us to take a flight to Florence, take pictures of the destroyed railroad with us in the foreground. Mack McCartney was to write a story," said Ackerman.

The story McCartney wrote appeared months later as the lead story in the March 1945 *National Geographic*, titled "Return to Florence"

The day after the manuscript was received by *National Geographic*, the War Department announced: "Lt. Benjamin C. McCartney, flying as lead bombardier for a B-26 Marauder formation with Capt. Ackerman at the controls, attacked a rail bridge, east of Milano, on September 22, 1944. As his plane leveled off for the bomb run it was heavily hit by flak. Lt. McCartney was mortally wounded."

War Tales by Don Moore

By December 1944, Captain Stanley Ackerman had flown 66 combat missions over Western Europe "with enough credit to go back home to New York City" (National Geographic March 1945, "Return to Florence") after which he lived to be 96 years old.

Bombardier B 26 Marauder over Campo di Marte, Florence, May 1944

With the total destruction of the railroad yards of Campo di Marte on the 2nd of May, 1944, the Allies eliminate the major means of cargo transport for the Germans. The neighbors on via Oriani start to believe there is nothing in Florence that needs bombing, so the bombing should stop.

***

Instead of bombs, the Allies start throwing messages out of their airplanes. They fill the sky with thousands of *volantini* (leaflets) that drift and dance in zigzag waves slowly to the ground, to the delight of everyone. The kids in the neighborhood run to gather them. When a sudden updraft of air steals the *volantini* out of their hands and lifts them up again toward the clear May sky, the children roll with laughter. They think it is a game.

"Mom, I'm going downstairs to get the *volantini*," yells Ina. She comes right back with a few of them. "I got one for you, too, Signora Fanetti, and you, Signora Daccanto," says Ina. Our two neighbors are often here to help Mom with extra water and stuff for baby Gianni.

"It's a message from the Allies. It's the British General Alexander," says la Signora Daccanto, reading from the *volantino*.

"SPECIAL MESSAGE TO THE CITIZENS OF FLORENCE.
General Headquarters of General Alexander

The Allied armies are getting very close to Florence. You, citizens of Florence, must be united to preserve your city from destruction and defeat our common enemies: the Germans and the Fascists... Allow free passage of military vehicles in the roads and city's squares. It's vital for the Allies to cross Florence without wasting time to complete the destruction of the German armies that are retreating to the North. Citizens of Florence! This is not the time to make demonstrations. OBEY these instructions and continue your work. Florence is yours! Your task is to save the city. Ours is to destroy the enemy.
Citizens of Florence, these are your instructions.
THE FUTURE OF FLORENCE IS IN YOUR HANDS"

The Germans and the Fascists are also reading the *volantini*! As the Germans are forced to retreat street by street, they become more and more belligerent towards civilians. People's irritability in Florence gets more intense.

***

Mom and Signora Fanetti are often at la Signora Daccanto's to listen to the radio.

The broadcasts from Florence are very few and far between and people are thirsty for news. On May 10th, a short radio bulletin says that EIAR, the Italian National Organization for Radio Broadcast is being moved from Florence to Torino.

"Torino! Oh great!" says Mr. Daccanto, "The seat of power of Mussolini! That means in Florence there will be a total blackout."

On June 4th, a short bulletin on the radio announces that "Allied troops have entered Rome, freeing it from the Germans already in retreat for the last two days."

Later, in the evening of the 6th of June, la Signora Daccanto shouts for Mom and Signora Fanetti to come and listen. We all go to listen, with Gianni in Mom's arms.

"This might be the last day for a long time we can hear the news," says Mr. Daccanto. The broadcast, in progress, is from the forbidden BBC, Radio Londra:

"...in the very early hours of today, the 6th of June, the Americans have landed in Normandy. D-Day has begun... 150,000 Americans, British, and Canadians have landed on five beaches along the coast of Normandy in France... General Eisenhower's messages were delivered to the Allied forces and the people of Europe.
Sailors, soldiers and airmen of the Allied Expeditionary Forces: you are about to embark upon the Great Crusade, toward which we

have striven these many months. The eyes of the world are upon you. The hopes and prayers of liberty-loving people everywhere march with you… You will bring about the destruction of Nazi tyranny over the oppressed people of Europe…

I have full confidence in your courage, devotion to duty, and skill in battle. We will accept nothing less than full victory!

Good luck! And let us all beseech the blessing of Almighty God upon this great and noble undertaking.

People of Western Europe: A landing was made this morning on the coast of France by troops of the Allied Expeditionary Forces. This landing was part of a concerted United Nations plan for the liberation of Europe… I have this message for all of you… the hour of your liberation is approaching. All patriots, men and women, young and old, have a part to play in the achievement of final victory…

As Supreme Commander of the Allied Expeditionary Forces, it was imposed on me the duty and responsibility of taking measures necessary to the prosecution of the war… Those who have made common cause with the enemy and so betrayed their country will be removed. I assure you that I shall do all in my power to mitigate your hardship… Great battles lie ahead… Keep your faith staunch; our arms are resolute… together we shall achieve victory."

Dwight Eisenhower, BBC London

"… In Italy at 13:00 hours on June 6th, Radio Roma opened the new transmissions announcing the newfound freedom of the broadcasting agency now under control of PWB (Psychological Warfare Broadcast). The retreating Germans have dismantled the radio systems. Radio Roma manages with what was left… the transmitter of Monte Mario was still operational."

Wikipedia: Le origini Della Radiodiffusione in Italia, Cronistoria

As the Germans are forced to retreat, street-by-street, block-by-block, the repression and raids on the civilian population get more ferocious. The seventh of June, the Germans arrest the people of a clandestine radio, called Radio CORA, at its headquarters on Piazza d'Azeglio. There end up being eleven people there that get arrested. The news of the arrest spreads immediately through the neighborhood.

"They are finished! They are well-known, good people – even their elderly parents. They are finished," says Signora Daccanto in a mourning voice. Mom gives a big sigh and says a prayer to herself, "Dear God, protect…"

Radio CORA maintains contact between the Partisans and the Allies. The Germans hand over the prisoners to the Italian Fascists. "The most cruel, sadistic band of Italian

Fascists in all Italy! They call themselves *La Carita* (charity). "*Vigliacchi*," says la Signora Fanetti. "*Miserabili Vigliacchi*."

***

Uncle Frank leaves for Catania to help brother Santo with their car rental business. Travelling towards the south of Italy is quite safe and free of the Germans. Just a few kilometers south of Florence is the same but just south of the River Arno, at walking distance from via Oriani, the Anglo-Americans are waiting. In the meantime, Florence itself is watching this war rage with a cruelty and ferocity that seems to strangle the very soul of the city. Mr. Daccanto says that German troops and *Republichini* (Italian Fascist soldiers in Mussolini's army), patrolling the streets with their tanks, continue to make raids on civilians at gunpoint, with the aid of Italian and Jewish informants. People from the small Hebrew community that have been hidden by Italian Catholics are shoved into trucks in route to Germany. Young Italians are forced to enlist in Mussolini's army. Those who resist are machine-gunned on the spot.

From Mr. Daccanto's tone of voice it is clear that he hates informants and traitors to their own kind. "*Maledetti assassini*!" he says.

***

Scarcity of food and water is getting very critical. We go in groups to the two farmers' wells on via Massaia but Fascist snipers from the buildings' windows are shooting at people gathered by the wells. Since the day a woman was shot to death by a Fascist sniper right in front of us, Mom does not like to go to those wells anymore. She prefers going to Farmer Neddi's, who has a water fountain right in her front yard by a beautiful vegetable garden. Also, it is located on via Vannucci, closer to our house. All other fountains in the street of Florence have long queues in front of them and the same danger of Fascist snipers. Very long lines are also at the baker's and at the *Frutta e Verdura* (fruit and vegetables) store. "We are luckier than most. We have Dad's money from the military. Some people don't have any and can't even go to work because of the war," Mom says.

Even with some money, though, there isn't much to buy at the stores. Besides, the stores are mostly shuttered. Mom and Signora Fanetti hear that some men in the neighborhood are selling food on the black market. They both go out late at night and find the man who is selling meat out of a suitcase. When they get home, at about one in the morning, Mom and Signora Fanetti cook the meat in Mom's kitchen with the few lumps of coal that we have left. I join them and while everybody else in the house sleeps, we eat steak, leaving the rest for the kids the next day. I do not remember what meat tastes like but I don't like it very much.

"Is she always awake this late at night?" asks Signora Fanetti, pointing at me.

"Yes," Mom answers. "For as long as I can remember. She is worse than I am. She is a night owl."

***

The 17th of June, as predicted by Mr. Daccanto, the radio announces, "EIAR Station of Florence will stop all transmissions as of today. All the guidelines that were expressed during the Fascist governing body are upheld."

"We are completely silenced by the Fascist regime," says Mr. Daccanto. "This means there will be a blackout. We won't be able to tell what's going on at all." Weeks later, another set of *volantini* graces the late July sky. They are from the American, General Eisenhower, to the people of Italy on July 29th, 1944. Mr. Daccanto reads:

"YOU CAN OBTAIN AN IMMEDIATE PEACE WITH HONORABLE CONDITION

We address a word of praise to the Italian people and to the House of Savoia (King Vittorio Emanuele of Italy) for having known how to remove Mussolini from power, the man who pushed them to war to serve Hitler and almost sent them to the edge of disaster.

The most serious obstacle that separated the Italian people from the United Nations has been removed by the Italian people themselves. The last obstacle on the road to peace was the German aggressor, who was still on Italian soil.

You want peace. You can obtain an immediate peace with the honorable conditions that our governments have offered you. We come to you as liberators. From your part you have to immediately stop giving any help to the German military forces in your country. If you do that, we will free you of the Germans and we will save you from the horrors of war...

ITALIANS! If you want peace, act immediately and help us to free Italy from the Nazis.

In the back of this volantino you will find instructions regarding the way in which you can help Italy to obtain peace."

General Eisenhower. July 29, 1944

"*Perbacco*, (good heavens!)," says Mr. Daccanto to Mom after reading the *volantino*. "Michele was absolutely right! What do they know about what's happening in Italy! These people don't have a clue!"

The following day Dad is finally home and we are all on top of him, talking, hugging, and bugging him. We are telling him all about the bombing and the *Franchi Tiratori* (Italian civilian Fascist snipers) shooting at the crowd in line by the water wells.

Nobody, though, is happier than the gentleman next door to be able to talk to Dad. Mr. Daccanto tells Dad about the German commando's order to clear all the houses that line the River Arno. People have to leave their homes by the following day, July 31st.

"Are the Germans thinking of blowing up the Bridges?" asks Dad.

"I really hope not. These people have to move out by tomorrow. Where are they going to go? Do they have to take their belongings with them? Nobody seems to know anything. Some say that it's only for a few days," says Mr. Daccanto.

It is really nice to have Dad home, even if I hear Mom and Dad arguing until very late at night. People in our neighborhood do not know what to think of Dad. The Partisans are afraid that he might be part of Mussolini's army. The Nazis and the Fascists think that he might be from the King's army. In our own building, though, people know Dad well and are very friendly, except the lady on the very last floor. She doesn't like Mom very much because she keeps referring to her as, "the woman with all those children."

***

The morning of August 3rd 1944, dawns hot and bright in the Florentine sky.

"I have used too much water to change Gianni," says Mom to Dad. "I hate to ask Signora Fanetti, again. I need more water for the baby's food."

"Mom, I can go get water for you," I volunteer. "I have gone many times by myself to farmer Neddi's."

"Is it far?" asks Dad.

"No. A little over a hundred yards," says Mom. "She has a water fountain right in her front yard."

After a while, I grab my pail and make a left out of the building's big entrance doors until I reach the end of via Oriani. I then make another left on via Massaia. It is early afternoon and there isn't a soul about. It feels like a Sunday. The silence and the calm are very pleasant. I continue on via Vannucci for a little while and cross the street right in front of Signora Neddi's place. That part of the street is still unpaved with lots of vegetation surrounding the farm. She sees me crossing the street and comes out of her front door.

"Cettina! What are you doing here?" Signora Neddi sounds alarmed.

"We need water for baby Gianni's food," I tell her.

"Quick, give it to me," she grabs my pail, fills it up and says, "Run! Run home now, quick!"

I cross via Vannucci and walk toward home when suddenly two German soldiers emerge from the corner of via Oriani and walk towards me. They are involved in an animated conversation and are not aware of me. I look at them with great apprehension and continue to walk slowly. The sidewalk is very narrow and I think, maybe I should step down and let them go by. They finally see me and stop walking. The soldier on the left removes the strap off his shoulder, slowly raises the rifle up and points it at me. I look up at him. Dad's words come to mind: "*Niente paura, niente paura.*" I stop walking and I stand, silently, a few yards away from his rifle. A violent jerking of the head coming from the soldier on the right gets my attention. A terrified look on his face frightens me; his eyes, wide open in horror, bulge out of his head, his mouth seems about to scream as his right elbow strikes his companion's left arm. The soldier with the rifle almost staggers from the blow on his elbow. With a nasty laugh he puts the rifle strap back on his shoulder and the two walk by.

In a daze and still terrified by the look of the other soldier's eyes, I continue my walk home and turn the corner onto via Oriani. The street is completely deserted except at the very end on the opposite side of the road. There, in front of me, an incredible sight is taking place. A German armored truck is parked by the last building, with German soldiers standing on each side of the entrance. Many Italian civilians are filing out of the building and forced into the truck, at gunpoint. They are men and teenage boys.

Nobody is aware of me. I realize I am witnessing one of those German raids that we hear so much about. I am frightened and want to go home but as I arrive in front of my apartment building, I am shocked to find the tall, heavy entrance doors locked.

Those two huge doors are always, always open. I start getting panicky: I am locked out of my home and I am in the street with the Germans. I start crying.

I bang on the doors and yell, "Mom! Mom!" At that very instant the doors open and Mom pulls me inside. She falls on her knees, holds me tightly to her bosom and starts sobbing uncontrollably. There is a commotion up the stairs. The neighbors want to know what is going on. Signora Fanetti tells them, "Cettina is back."

"Back? From where?" They all talk at once. "Why? Where did she go? This is the most irresponsible..."

I am overwhelmed. Mom hardly ever cries. I know Mom loves me very much but I can hardly breathe. I twist my head hard to the side and I am careful not to tip the pail of water that I am still holding.

"Mom, careful, you are spilling the water for the baby's food," I whisper.

The neighbors are still yelling, especially the lady who doesn't like Mom. She says that letting me go get water was just the most criminal and irresponsible thing she had ever heard.

"We received the ordinance LATE!" shouts la Signora Fanetti angrily back at her.

Dad comes downstairs and takes me and Mom back to the apartment. Mom is still hysterical and keeps thanking God over and over again. "I prayed...I prayed so hard..."

"Dad," I say, "a German soldier pointed his rifle at me on via Massaia. His friend looked scared and pushed him with his elbow. The guy with the rifle almost tripped and started laughing."

Dad has huge tears in his eyes. I have never seen Dad crying. Mom, still shaking, goes to the kitchen cabinet and pours a spoonful of something out of a bottle for me.

"No, no, no! What are you doing? She is fine. She is just fine. She just saw a stupid, drunken German soldier and got scared a little bit. That's all." Dad takes my hands and rubs them between his own hands. "See? *Niente paura*!" says Dad quietly to Mom. Ina and Vario hug me and are very supportive of me.

It is only 2 o'clock in the afternoon and Mom has enough water to make Gianni's food. The ordinance from the German Command, received just after I left to get water, reads:

Firenze Citta Aperta by Ugo Cappelletti p. 38

Ordinance
For the Security of The Population, We Order:

1. **Starting from this moment it is forbidden to anyone to leave their homes and walk about the streets and piazzas of Florence.**
2. **All windows, even those of the cellars, as well as all entrances and doors of private homes and apartment buildings, must be shut, night and day.**
3. **We recommend the population to go in the cellars, or where these do not exist, to go in churches, or other public buildings.**
4. **TROOPS OF THE GERMAN ARMED FORCES HAVE ORDER TO SHOOT ON SIGHT THOSE FOUND ON THE STREET, OR THOSE WHO WATCH OUT OF WINDOWS.**

Il comandante Della Citta' di Firenze, 3 Agosto, 1944, proclama lo stato d'Emergenza, English translation

Mom makes baby food and Gianni seems very hungry. Ina and I take turns spoon feeding him and he is delighted.

Chapter 9:

The Bridges of Florence | Aug. 3-4, 1944, the

Two Worst Days in the History of Florence

News circulates all day that the Germans are mining the bridges over the Arno River to stop the advance of the Allies.

The news is confirmed. The Florentines are very angry. The renaissance-era mansions that line the Arno River have to be abandoned as of noon today, by order of the German command. It is now past two in the afternoon. Florentines found out only yesterday that they would have to leave their homes.

"They have no place to go," Mr. Daccanto almost screams, exasperated. "Where in the hell are these people supposed to go so suddenly?"

The City of Florence opens courtyards, offices and government rooms of Palazzo Medici, the offices of Palazzo Pitti, all public galleries, government archives, hospitals and churches for the suddenly homeless – five thousand of them.

Some people still wander around the city trying desperately to go back to their houses just to retrieve that precious "something" they left behind, but they are forbidden to walk about in the streets and *piazzas* of Florence. The German armed forces have orders to shoot on sight, and they do.

***

It has been a long, emotional day for us with my encounter with the German soldiers and Mom and Dad crying. We are locked in our building and we can only remain in contact with our closest neighbors.

The sun goes down but it is still very hot and humid. The city seems very calm and our building is silent. Florence has all doors and windows shut and all streets are deserted. Once in a while on via Oriani we hear the sound of machine guns directed at windows with open shutters. The people in our building immediately share the news to everyone as soon as they hear something: five brave Partisans tried to disentangle the fuses under the bridges but the mines did not forgive and all five lost their lives. Others were met with rounds of machine guns.

At ten o'clock at night we hear a terrific roar and a tremendous explosion. The first bridge has blown up. After an hour or so, another bridge explodes like thunder, hurling fragments and massive pieces of stone far and wide onto city streets and buildings.

The bridge of Santa Trinita, "the most beautiful bridge in the world," after many explosions, still refuses to give up.

"They are destroying Santa Trinita, the bridge of love!" la Signora Daccanto explains to Mom. "What a tragedy for Florence! Those bastards!"

Florentines have a particular affection for this bridge. First built in 1252 and restructured after a flood in 1566, based on a design by Michelangelo, Signora Daccanto tells us, "On this bridge, circa 1280, the Florentine poet Dante Alighieri, famous for his voyage through *Inferno*, was said to meet his Beatrice for the first time."

After the fourth explosion, the bridge of Santa Trinita finally surrenders. The terrific explosions continue throughout the night. Six medieval bridges are destroyed. With the bridges also go all the renaissance homes and medieval streets by the sides of the river. The only bridge standing is the famous Ponte Vecchio built in 1325. It is being saved from destruction by Hitler's order; he admired the bridge during his youth while in Florence.

"Those *maledetti, cornuti*!" explodes Mr. Daccanto to Dad. "They are destroying so much, for what? The Allies are already here. Someone should explain to those illiterate *cafoni* about the historic bridges..."

"Someone has," says Dad. "The City of Florence and the clergy tried to save the bridges. They talked to the German command... but these people are tone deaf about art. The Swiss Consul himself tried to save the four renaissance statues on the bridge of Santa Trinita..."

In Piazza Santa Trinita rises the most grandiose medieval Florentine palace, the SPINI-FERRONI PALACE, built in 1289, with 3 stories of windows and an imposing projecting battlement.

Two of the four statues seen at the entrance of the Santa Trinity Bridge.
In the background, the famous Ponte Vecchio.
(Loretta Santini - Giusti di Becocci - via Canto de Nelli, Firenze, p 66)

The fragments of the statue *Winter* (by Landini), those of *Summer* and *Autumn* (by Cacini) and *Spring* (by Francavilla), as they were recovered from the River Arno. Some Florentines, after the bridge was reconstructed, did not want the statues put back, as they considered them not good enough to adorn the "the most beautiful bridge in the whole world." But Florence decided they all had to go back exactly as before, even if *Primavera*'s head was still lost in the Arno.
The 7th of October 1961, *La Nazione* announced T. Lucaroni had found the head 50 meters from the bridge, as he was maneuvering a dredge on the bank of the river.
Primavera, all complete, had returned to Florence!
Firenze- Gli Anni Terribili-Testi di Piero Pieroni- Bonechi, p 92

One of the monuments is severely damaged. Sections of the frescoed ceiling of the world-famous Uffizi Gallery, badly shaken by one of the bridges' explosions, has fallen to the ground.

"They have completely destroyed the aqueducts and the *Centrale Elettrica*. Florence and all the villages north of Florence, for miles, are without electricity or water," continues Mr. Daccanto. He is extremely upset and so is everyone in the building.

It is past three o'clock in the morning and we go to bed with the light of one candle but nobody can sleep because of the recurrent explosions of the mines. The candle flickers, creating grotesque shadows on the wall and on our faces.

At this point, I have forgotten my encounter with the German soldier's rifle. The explosions are less frequent and finally the wonderful scent of the burning candle seems to calm everyone to sleep.

***

Very late that same morning, August 4th, lots of *volantini* fall from the sky with a message from the German command. The Germans are accusing the Anglo-Americans of the destruction of the Florentine bridges.

"*Ma va*! (You are kidding!)," say the neighbors, but it's true. The message reads:

Firenze
OPEN CITY

So, this was how the Anglo-Americans respect the international laws of war! Every Italian knows Florence has been acknowledged, for months, as "open city." Every Italian knows how the German armed troops have scrupulously pledged to recognize to the city of Florence all its qualities of an "Open City." But General Alexander sent, on the 29th of July, an appeal to the Florentines inciting them to fight for the Allied cause. In it he says, among other things:

"It's vital that the Allied troops pass through Florence without wasting time." If the German command, as a consequence, found itself forced to take preventive action to impede the advance of the enemy

THROUGH THE CITY

the fault falls exclusively on the Anglo-Americans. They are the violators of every international law, and, therefore not even the population of an "Open City" can be safe in front of their criminal attitude.

The Germans justify their destruction of the bridges and attribute all responsibility to the Allies. Ugo Cappelletti - Firenze Citta Aperta, p 69, translation

***

We are all reminded of the German orders not to walk around in the streets or *piazzas* of Florence or to look out the windows. The German troops have orders to shoot on sight. This causes great anxiety among the neighbors. "But we need to get provisions. We need food and water," they say and then, starting to comfort each other, say things like, "It's only for a day or two, you'll see. After all, the Allies are already in Florence! The Nazis are leaving."

For months and months, I hear "the Nazis are leaving." But I see they are still here.

We are prisoners in our own apartments with the main doors of the building locked. The windows' outer shutters are closed. The glass windows, opening inward, need to remain open, for the August heat is tremendous. Mom gives us a strict order not to get close to the windows. But, if I keep the shutters' louvers slightly ajar, I can see the armored tanks and the German soldiers patrolling via Oriani.

As the enemy retreat, the *Franchi Tiratori* (pro-Mussolini Italian civilians) form a line of defense behind the Germans. Mussolini's order is to stop the advance of the Allies and obstruct the maneuvers of the Italian Partisans at all cost to the last man standing. The *Franchi Tiratori* obey the mandate and as soon as they notice movement in the streets in the dark of night, they answer with fire. They shoot mercilessly from the rooftops and the high windows of buildings at the people down below. Florentines are risking their lives walking in the streets of the city but the need to get water and food is stronger than fear.

In Borgo San Frediano, which is south of the River Arno, a hand grenade hurled from a rooftop explodes in the middle of a group of people in line in front of a grocery store, the neighbors tell us. Among shouts of horror, adults and children are killed and maimed.

Our neighbors are very upset. "How is it possible?! San Frediano is already free of the Nazis," they say. "The Anglo-Americans are already there in San Frediano! *I Tiratori Sparano da pertutto*! (They are shooting everywhere!)"

Italian Partisans know, first and foremost, they have to eliminate the threat of the Nazi Fascist group *Franchi Tiratori* one street at a time, from every *borgo* (village) and every alley. The Anglo-Americans won't engage in this civil war. They are waiting south of the River Arno.

Most of the Fascist *Tiratori* are very young boys and girls, sixteen to twenty years old.

"It's really heartbreaking to see these young Italian kids believe they are chasing dreams of fame and glory and honor!" says Dad to Mr. Daccanto. "The same goes for these young Germans kids. Their minds have been so twisted by Hitler's and Il Duce's words – they honestly believe they are going to die for the freedom and glory of their country! They believe they are redeeming their motherland from disgrace and dishonor!"

I remember my beautiful Fascist uniform of the *Piccola Italiana* and the meetings at the Fascist headquarters and I ask, "Dad, why is it so bad to be a Fascist now?"

"That's not the problem," Dad seems to hesitate. "You know what the *fascio* is, right?"

"It's a bundle of rods tied together with a leather strap, like the ancient Roman weapon, the Roman *fascio littorio*" I say promptly.

"Exactly," says Dad, "and that bundle of rods tied together symbolizes all Italian people united for the good of the country, and the country united for the good of all Italian people."

"But that's a good thing!" I tell him.

"Of course, it's a good thing! Except," Dad says to Mr. Daccanto, "when military leaders think they are more important than the country and the whole darn world. It's hard to think of Giovanni Gentile's philosophy when we look at the sorry state of Italy right now, isn't it?"

"You are going to be nine at the end of this year, aren't you, Cettina? You are going to learn all this stuff in school. You are going to learn all about Giovanni Gentile and all the things he has done for schools. You are going to learn history, philosophy, chemistry, and Latin."

Dad is, and will always be, my hero! I want to ask Dad one more thing: Dad, why do you and Mom fight all the time? Don't you love Mom anymore? But I don't have the courage. Besides, Mr. Daccanto is listening. I also want to ask Dad why a girl at the Sisters convent thought I was Jewish because of our last name, but I change my mind. I do not want to waste Dad's time. Besides, I think, I already know the answer – a name or surname doesn't have to mean anything.

***

Dad has suddenly been called back and leaves for Naples the same night. Still dark the following morning, someone delivers a package of food. Mom is happy because our provisions are getting very low. There is flour made of dried peas, powdered milk, matzo crackers, an assortment of canned food, and olive oil. There are also little white loaves of bread. Mom says, "It's American bread." She hasn't had it before. It is very different from our Tuscan loaf which is much denser and darker in color. These little bread rolls are white and fluffy. They taste very good. Gianni gulps one down pretty fast. There is also a bag with the word "Sauerkraut" written on it, and Mom doesn't have any idea what that is or what to do with it. She just boils it. It looks like thinly sliced white cabbage in vinegar and it tastes weird but we eat it all up.

***

It is the 10th of August already and the heat is merciless. Florentines, confined to their houses, long for evening walks in the cool parks of Le Cascine. They want to run down to the river or sit by the shade of the trees in the hills surrounding Florence, but no one dares go out. The *Franchi Tiratori* seem to have eyes and ears everywhere and they shoot on sight.

La Signora Fanetti and two other ladies in our building desperately need food and water. Mom offers some food, but it isn't enough. Late that night they walk down to the Arno River, where the Allies are. In that zone the stores are open even if there isn't much to sell and the Anglo-Americans are helping with extra provisions. Mom is very worried about the ladies because we can hear the almost constant gusts of machine-guns. The ladies get back at around three o'clock in the morning. They are laden with packages and they are terrified. Signora Daccanto opens her door to them.

"*Sparano dappertutto, dappertutto*! (They are shooting everywhere!). We saw the men from Pronto Soccorso carry the dead and the wounded to the hospital in wheelbarrows. It's horrible," says la Signora Fanetti. "They are shooting close to us, right here, on via Venti Settembre!"

The ladies tell horrific stories of massacres that they heard from people they encountered during the night. They also heard the CTLN (Tuscan Council for National Liberation) is going to sound the *Martinella* the next morning, August 11th. *La Martinella* is the most famous medieval bell in Italy and is located in the highest arch of Palazzo Medici, in Piazza Della Signoria. Since ancient times, at the sound of that bell, Florentines descend from surrounding hills and farms to answer the call of war against invaders, ready to defend their beloved city. Tomorrow, the same *Martinella* will be the sign for all Partisans everywhere to unite for the Battle of Florence.

The Partisans are from every nationality. They are Polish, French, Yugoslav, Czech, Russian, and Ukrainian. They are from all political parties – communists, socialists, liberals, Christian democrats, republicans, monarchists, and ex-fascists.

There are also many Germans who have rebelled against Hitler and are fighting next to their old comrades, the Italian Partisans. Every Partisan fights for one common cause: the enemy is Nazi-Fascism, whose leaders – Hitler in his Chancellery and Mussolini at Salo – still want to crush the will of their own people.

Firenze Insorge E Si Libera Da Se (Florence Revolts and Frees Herself)
By Sergio Lepri, Correspondent, Essaista

"**Eight days of fear have passed from the third to the eleventh of August with Florentines locked in their houses, without water, without electricity, without food. Bombs fall everywhere and we can hear shootings and gusts of machine guns; jeeps and armored tanks go by. In the city there still remain regiments of German parachutists, a division of anti-partisan, and many dozens of Italian Nazi-fascists. In the streets, women cautiously leave their homes and venture out to get water and food...**
But in the Prefettura and in Palazzo Vecchio, the leaders of the CTLN are already taking care of the city administration and some of them, passing through the Galleria Degli Uffizi and the (secrete passage of) Vasario Corridor, have gone down to the Ponte Vecchio, crossed over the Arno River and made contact with the Allies."

http://www.ticketsflorence.com/blog/wp-content/uploads/2016-/05/Schemata
The Corridoio Vasario was built by order of the Duke Cosimo De Medici in 1565. It's an elevated, enclosed, secret passageway. It connects Palazzo Vecchio (left side of image), the seat of government, to the Palazzo Pitti, the Duke's palace (right side of image).

And then, on the eleventh, freedom! People leave their houses, and young men come out from the cantine. We meet, we hug, we cry, and we laugh. And when -- a week has already passed since the first toll of the Martinella - -the Allies will finally decide to cross the river, they will find a city defended by divisions of partisans who are still fighting against the last German troops and Italian Franchi Tiratori, mostly in the region of le Cure, Rifredi, Piazza Dalmatia, via Vittorio Emanuele, all along via Bolognese, up the hills of Fiesole, Campo di Marte, and the zone of San Gervasio.

Night and day this part of the city was still under fire from German artillery and Franchi Tiratori, but when the Allied commander Edgar Hume will arrive at Palazzo Vecchi, (the administration building), he will realize -- at first surprised and then disappointed -- that the city has already all the administrative structure in place. And when the Allies will suggest that from now on, they will manage the war and will tell the Italian Partisans to surrender all weapons, Aligi Barducci, head of the Tuscan partisans Command will refuse and, he says, he will tell his compatriots never to surrender their weapons under any circumstances.

Firenze Insorge E Si Libera da Se - Sergio Lepri, Giornalista, Essayista (translation)

Chapter 10:

Surviving August | Florence 1944

The southern part of Florence, including all Dila D'arno area south of the River Arno, is mostly free of the Germans, and there the Anglo-Americans are still waiting. However, a new line of "Nazi fire" divides Florence in two again. On the south side are the Partisan formations fighting with little supplies and sometimes very poor-quality weapons. On the north side are Nazi tanks, the anti-tank guns, mortars, and machine guns.

German artillery, from the hills of Fiesole, continues to bomb all over the city. In the historic center, the Duomo, Giotto's bell tower, the Doors of Paradise of the Baptistry, the Logge of Bigallo, San Lorenzo, and Gli Uffizi all suffer damage.

Life in this part of Florence has become painful. The people of our building are getting exasperated. The worst part of it is that we cannot go out to get water or food. Mr. Daccanto is lost without Dad. He could talk to Dad and let go of his anger against the Fascists. He desperately wants to go out, walk about town, stop and get newspapers, stop at the bar for a cappuccino. He gets very annoyed with Mrs. Daccanto, who has absolutely forbidden him to go out, especially at night. The Nazis still have orders to shoot on sight when they find people walking in the streets. I really wish Mr. Daccanto wouldn't get so angry because the veins on his forehead and neck get very red and purple and bulge out. He is always mad about the same thing, how Mussolini and his *cornuti* Fascists have, on purpose, created so much discord and hatred among the Italians and to want to fight to the death.

"Fascist propaganda has destroyed the brains of the young people for years," shouts Mr. Daccanto, "and they believe Il Duce is the absolute God on earth, commanding them to 'eliminate the elements of disorder and subversion' against Italy. Michele was right, these kids are our Florentine kids from San Frediano, from Rifredi. They love Florence and Italy. They are going to die and they know it. That's their mandate."

"Among the Italian Fascists there are also many women. Reuter speaks of 25 girls taken prisoners in Florence alone. In Milano 3 women were executed. Other cities where women, all Franchi Tiratori, are taken prisoners are Parma, Piacenza, and Torino. One of

the strangest episodes was the one registered in Florence. In Borgo degli Albizi, on the last floor of a building the shooter is a young woman. The Partisans cannot identify her. When the Partisans raid the building, the woman hides her gun on a plank in the roof, takes her baby in her arms and opens the door. This happens three times until one Partisan remains hidden in the apartment and finds out the shooting comes from her. Taken prisoner, she is executed later."

Testimonianza: Luca Tadolini, "I franchi tiratori di Mussolini

***

Italian Fascists, shooting from the rooftops, are the main reason we cannot go out of our apartment to look for food. We hear the shooting close by but we can't figure out where it's coming from.

The food we received the day Dad left is long gone, even the last of the sauerkraut. Mom boiled it and drizzled it with olive oil. It didn't taste very good, but hunger is a very powerful bully, so we ate it all up. Hunger makes my stomach hurt and forces me to curl up in pain. It makes me want to slide down on the floor and go to sleep, but I can't fall asleep because my stomach burns.

"It's the gastric juices," says Mom.

We have enough powdered milk for Vario and Gianni. Mom, Ina, and I divide two oranges among us that we got from farmer Neddi. Later we eat the peel of the oranges. Mom and Signora Fanetti go out to the Allied side of the river that night to get food and they have to go through Rifredi. The Rifredi zone is still the target of heavy fire from the Germans shooting at the Partisans who ferociously fight back. We hear the constant sound of machine guns but we have no idea if it is the Germans, the Partisans, or the *Franchi Tiratori*. We wait for Mom in the dark for a long time and Ina and I are getting very worried. Gianni and Vario are asleep.

At about 2 o'clock in the morning, Mom and Signora Fanetti get back with lots of food. Mom gives Ina and me a little roll of white, fluffy American bread. I am starving and chomp down on the roll but I have to stop. My stomach burns and I can't eat.

"It's the gastric juices," says Mom. "Eat slowly."

We are all in the big bed and ready to go to sleep when Mom makes a sign with her finger for me to follow her. In the dark I follow her into the kitchen. She gets an egg from the food she brought back.

"They assure me it's very fresh," says Mom. She takes the egg in her hand and makes a pinhole on one side of the egg with a needle, turns the egg on the other side, and makes another pinhole.

"Here," she says. "Close your lips tightly around one of the pinholes, breathe in hard, with your mouth only, and swallow the egg that flows out." After a few attempts that go nowhere, the egg finally slides slowly into my mouth and feels smooth and soothing going down all the way into my aching tummy.

"*Accipicchia*! (I'll be darned!). I have never sucked out an egg before!" I look at the empty eggshell, perfectly whole, in my hand, and am amazed.

"Don't tell anyone about it," Mom says.

At night, even with a full tummy, I still can't sleep. I keep on thinking that Mom got that egg just for me, not for baby Gianni or Ina, but for me alone, and she said not to tell anyone! I am very moved and wish I had said something. I wish I had said, "Thank you, Mom, for loving me so much."

***

Almost every night, some women from our building go down by the Arno River where the Anglo-Americans are. There, some stores are already open and carry small quantities of food. Looking through the shutters slightly ajar, almost at my eye level, I can make out, down in the street below, silent shadows walking very close to the walls and disappearing off in the dark.

The ladies come back with terrifying stories they saw or heard; a pregnant woman going out for bread was strongly warned by her neighbors about a hidden *tiratore* sniper. She went anyway, as she needed bread for her children. Hit by a blast of machine gun, she lay on the pavement with her abdomen torn apart.

The ladies also tell many heroic stories of doctors and *Crocerossine* (Red Cross nurses) who try desperately to save very ill and horribly injured people, while at the same time facing *Franchi Tiratori* and Nazi-Fascist cannons. The nurses are often too late to save the injured and often pay with their own lives.

"The stench of death is everywhere," Signora Fanetti says. "Dead bodies are not buried right away. The smell of garbage in the streets is very bad in this hot weather. Nobody is picking up the trash. It's a wonder we don't come down with an epidemic, a plague, or something."

Signora Fanetti says she is not going out there anymore.

***

Volantini (flyers) from the retreating Nazi-Fascists cover the streets. The Fascists never forgave the Italians and Badoglio's government for secretly accepting Eisenhower's armistice and betraying the country. The Fascists consider the armistice of October 8th, 1943, highly treasonous to the nation of Italy and to Il Duce, himself, who was arrested the same day and freed later by the Germans.

As the Nazi-Fascists retreat, Mussolini's furious, thunderous voice sends his last message to his faithful, and its last dire threat to the Florentines who have betrayed him:

WE SHALL RETURN!

Soon England will not be able to endure the effects of the newest German weapons! Only a few people already know where and when these powerful weapons, still concealed, will be utilized!

In a little while we will launch the offensive, and it will be in that moment that the Italians faithful to the country will be rewarded, and it will be in that moment that the traitors will have what they deserve. We will not forget any of them! Observe them and remember their names and their treason!

War is getting close to its last and great phase. In a little while we shall return. It will be only then, that Europe shall have its victory and that we will all be secure in our free, native soil.

GOD WILL PUNISH TRAITORS AND COMPENSATE THE FAITHFUL

Ugo Cappelletti- Firenze Citta' Aperta p.43- my translation, Mussolini's speech

This last threat by Nazi-Fascists, coupled with the threat of *Franchi Tiratori*, cowardly shooting from terraces, windows, and rooftops onto defenseless civilians, does not sit well with the Partisans. The leader of the Tuscan Division, *Potente*, sends a message to all his men:

> **"...we observe the substantial difference from the odious retaliation used by the Fascists against the civilian population... These are Fascists who are already guilty... instead of imprisonments or a trial, we will apply capital punishment... a ratio of ten Fascists for every person, civilian, or Partisan, who falls under the actions of the Franchi Tiratori, and five for the gravely injured."**

Luca Tadolini, I Franchi Tiratori di Mussolini (my translation)

"It looks like we are going to have an all-out civil war!" shouts signor Daccanto. He is worried and I feel very sorry for him because of all those purple veins in his neck.

> **"Germans and Mussolini's troops are retreating very slowly, one street at a time, one corner at a time, creating destruction and horror as they leave. Building by building they raid homes for as many Italian men as they can find. Sometimes women and children are caught in the raids, too. Meantime, the Italian Franchi Tiratori Fascists want to believe that they are succeeding in slowing down the advancement of the enemy whom they think to be the Anglo-American invaders! The Partisans have finally forced the new line of German resistance to be moved back again. The Nazi-Fascists have left Florence's historic center and life has come back to the downtown area again. It's another world down there! People are happy. They come and go freely, they go shopping... they have water and food."**

Firenze Citta Aperta- Ugo Cappelletti (my translation)

But in our enemy-occupied area, life is still a nightmare. There are German tanks and cannons in Rifredi to the south, in via Bolognese to the east, in the Mugnone Stream to the south, and cannons in via Vittorio Emanuele to the north of via Oriani, just behind our street and our building. Nobody believes a word about there being freedom in Florence! We are still locked in our apartments in the dark with no food, no water, and completely ignorant of what is happening around us. We only know the terrific sound of machine guns that are almost constant day and night. Signora Daccanto and Signora Fanetti try to keep in contact with the people on via Oriani. They decide they need to go down to the Arno area for water and food.

> **"The Partisans need to get to our zone still occupied by the Nazi-Fascists. But first, they need to dislodge the Franchi Tiratori who, hiding on rooftops, and in windows and terraces, machine-gun anything and anybody who ventures next to the defense line. For weeks the Franchi Tiratori have kept the Partisans at bay, killing dozens of civilians and Partisans. For the first time in this war, the Anglo-Americans back up the Partisans with smoke bombs, armored cars, and mortars. The Franchi Tiratori are then easily dislodged from their hiding places, rounded up, arrested and executed later after a brief trial. One particular case that took many days to identify was that of a sixteen-year-old Tiratori. He would open the manhole of a sewer, pops up, kill tens of civilians and Partisans with his high-powered German machine gun and then disappear into the drain canals again, until he was finally discovered. With the help of the British armored cars and smoke bombs, Partisans cross the Mugnone line, take Piazza Vieusseux and Piazza Dalmatia, shooting at the German tanks and cannons posted in via Vittorio Emanuele."**

Firenze Città Aperta-Ugo Cappelletti (my translation)

The Partisans, with the help of three British armored cars, free the Convento dei Montughi on via Massaia of Italian sniper *Tiratori*, while the Anglo-Americans engage the Nazi-Fascists on via Bolognese.

"It's over. It will be over soon. How long will they last if the Allies are helping?" the neighbors say, but Signora Fanetti doesn't think so.

The Partisans don't have a good supply of weapons with which to protect the civilian population. They have to steal the arms from the Nazi Germans, the Italian Fascist army, and the *Franchi Tiratori* any way they can. Partisans try to find out for the longest time where on earth Mussolini is hiding all those weapons that were forcibly confiscated from the Italian civilian population at the beginning of his dictatorship. Even the old Florentine armory museum has been ransacked. There are no arms.

The neighbors constantly tell sad stories of Italian civilians shot to death by the *Franchi Tiratori*. A furious war is going on in Florence between the Partisans and *Tiratori* snipers. It is what Mr. Daccanto calls the civil war.

"It's literally brother against brother. Family and friends try very hard to save these young kids who are determined to die for Il Duce. These kids shoot from rooftops and windows at anyone walking in the streets of Florence! At anyone looking for food and water," says Mr. Daccanto, getting very angry.

> **"I Franchi Tiratori (14 /17 years-old) are Italian Fascist boys and girls, brought up with Mussolini's ideals, but too young for the army. They follow Il Duce's mandate: ambush and kill all Italian traitors and die in place. They work with the Germans and are procured with German machine guns. They follow Mussolini's: mandate "Believe, Obey, Fight."**

Ugo Cappelletti Firenze Città' Aperta (my translation)

On via Bolognese, a man who is going for water is ambushed and shot as he is trying to jump a fence. The neighbors say that people heard him moaning quietly for hours until he died.

The bad news that goes around is that the Nazi-Fascists are raiding every single street in the area before retreating and will come to via Oriani very soon.

***

"Keep the children tightly next to you," Signora Fanetti and Signora Daccanto tell Mom. Everybody in the building seems to be very worried about us, even the lady on the last floor who doesn't like Mom and still calls her "the woman with all those children." She is old and cranky while Mom is young and beautiful.

"I have to meet this boy tonight. Last time he promised me food and milk," says Mom.

"You are insane!" says Signora Fanetti. "Germans are shooting right behind us, from via Vittorio Emanuele, via Vannucci, from Piazza Viessieux and via Fabbroni. The Partisans are shooting nonstop right back at them from the kitchen balconies, and we see German tanks on via Vannucci."

"I am going to be alright. We need the food."

"I'll go with you," says Signora Fanetti.

"Absolutely not!" says Mom. "I need you to keep an eye on the kids. I have to meet him now." There is no use arguing with Mom. She is always right.

Even with the constant sound of machine guns around us that night, Ina and the boys fall sleep and Signora Fanetti has gone back up to her apartment. Very late at night I hear Mom quietly getting up, opening the bedroom door, and then the front door. I know she is going to meet that boy, and I am afraid about what Signora Fanetti said about the shooting. After a few seconds of hesitation and fear, I get up from bed, open the front door of the apartment, and leave it ajar, just like how Mom left it. Silently and quickly, I go down the stairs and open the big, heavy doors that Mom left ajar.

Via Oriani is in complete darkness. With no electricity, the whole city and streets are black under a leaden sky except for sudden flashes of red lights from machine guns illuminating the area in front of me. The continuous sound of machine guns seems to come from everywhere around me. I venture a few steps on the sidewalk and I strive to see Mom in the dark. The street is deserted. At first, I can't see anything. Suddenly I see her, a dark shadow crossing the street. She walks briskly, hugging the walls closely until the end of via Oriani. I continue following slowly but I dare not cross the street. I see Mom arriving at the end of our road, crossing via Pagnini and making a right. The sound of machine guns is incessant and often startles me. I fly down via Oriani and arrive at the corner of via Pagnini to see Mom continue down the short street until she arrives on via Fabbroni. I follow a few more steps and, at the corner of the street, I barely make her out talking with someone, a young boy on a bicycle. I see her gesticulate at him. The young man hands her a sack and then disappears down via Fabbroni. Mom is coming back very fast towards home. I quickly retrace my steps, stop on via Oriani, and turn around a couple of times to see if she is following. She spots me and, with an imperious gesture of her hand and index finger that means *get back now*, I am compelled into a fast run toward the front doors, flying up the stairs and bolting into bed with the sheet over my head. I know Mom is angry.

After a few minutes, I hear Mom opening the bedroom door.

"Do not ever," Mom starts, and because Gianni is beginning to fuss, she continues with a whisper, "do that, ever again!"

But under the sheets I giggle silently with sheer happiness; Mom is back home safe, and I got away with an incredible adventure! We have food for a whole week and I know Mom is happy.

***

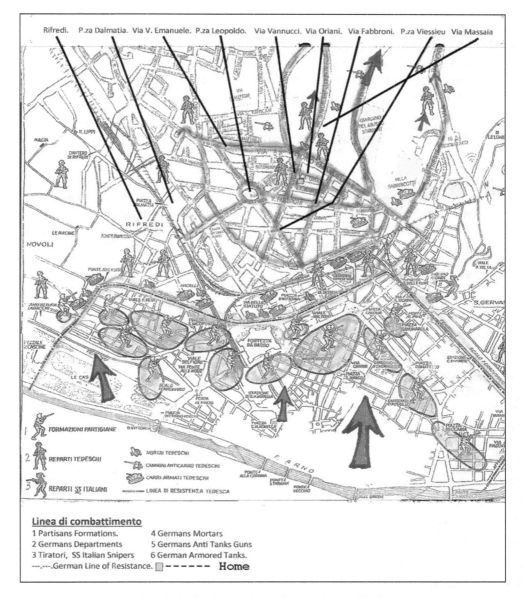

Rifredi.   P.za Dalmatia. Via V. Emanuele. P.za Leopoldo. Via Vannucci. Via Oriani. Via Fabbroni. P.za Viessieu Via Massaia

Linea di combattimento
1 Partisans Formations.	4 Germans Mortars
2 Germans Departments	5 Germans Anti Tanks Guns
3 Tiratori, SS Italian Snipers	6 German Armored Tanks.
---.---.German Line of Resistance.	▣ - - - - - - **Home**

Cronica di Nello Niccoli: la liberazione di Firenze

Combative actions. August 11th through August 27th,
1944 between Partisans and German Units, translation and summary, pp 58-65

"II Sector - During August 18th and August 27th there was strong German artillery and mortar fire against the position held by the Partisans. There are many victims among the civilian population, whether from German actions or Franchi Tiratori.

In P.zza Dalmatia despite the violent clash of fire, Germans resist at first to the Partisans pressure, and then retreat. When Germans try to retake P.zza Dalmatia, Italian patriots hold fiercely to their line, which goes from Piazza Dalmatia, to Piazza Leopoldo to Piazza Viessieux to via Fabbroni; north to via Vittorio Emanuele and to the east to via Bolognese.

There is constant, violent fighting throughout this area. Members of the Partisan Brigata Roselli are cited for their valor.

II Sector: At six o'clock in the evening of 24th of August, German troops initiate the offensive with division coming from the south from via del Romito, and from the north, from via Vannucci. The Germans were trying to retake Piazza Viessieux already held by the Partisans. The Partisan Brigata Rosselli was holding the line fiercely, inflicting at least six deaths, and forcing the enemy to retreat. The Partisan defense allowed a Partisan unit to infiltrate the German division in via Vannucci.

At 20:00, a violent German attack against the Partisans on via Bolognese forced the Partisans to retreat, but at the early hours of dawn on the following morning the Partisans, helped by British armored cars, retook the lost ground while others still under the protection of British armored tanks got as far as via Bolognese - Nello Niccoli —lieutenant colonel, WWII. President CTLN Comitato Toscano National Liberation.

La liberazione di Firenze, 5th of August, 1944

On via Oriani and in all neighboring streets, we are still all locked in our apartments. The sound of machine guns has gone on for weeks, without much respite. The boys seem to be accustomed to the noise, even if they are restless. Mom says we all need to go play in the sun and eat good food and take long restful baths, but no one can walk up the street to farmer Neddi on via Vannucci to get water, and no one knows when the water mains will be restored. The little water we have is needed for drinking. The one who seems to suffer the most is Ina. She is only two years older than I am but she is much taller and looks so much more grown up. Everyone in the building thinks of her as very pretty. She is always absorbed in something far away and she seems very unhappy.

The neighbors in our building are short-tempered and seem unable to endure the confinement anymore. Mr. Daccanto goes on ranting any time he hears about the *Franchi Tiratori*. I think Mr. Daccanto feels very sorry for these young boys and girls deceived by Il Duce's false propaganda and tricked into following his orders. They are 'baby-victims' sacrificed to the pride of the Nazi-Fascists. Mr. Daccanto says the *Franchi Tiratori's* young minds have been poisoned into believing they are giving their lives for the glory of Italy, and that they are saving the nation from dishonor and from the Anglo-American invaders, but Signora Fanetti doesn't buy it.

"They might be innocent victims, and all that," says Signora Fanetti, exasperated, "but surely they must know they are killing Italians, their own brothers! If it wasn't for them, it would be easier to go get water and food!"

Mom agrees with Signora Fanetti. "If it wasn't for them," Mom says, "the war would be over much sooner."

The tens of hundreds of civilians killed by the *Franchi Tiratori* stretch the Partisans' patience. The *Tiratori* are being ferociously hunted down by the Partisans, taken prisoners, sentenced, and quickly executed.

I Fucilati di Firenze (Excerpt, I Franchi Tiratori di Firenze) The Kids Executed in Florence (Reconstructed by Curzio Malaparte, La Pelle)

The Fascists sitting on the steps of the Church of Santa Maria Novella are fifteen and sixteen-years old kids with hair that falls freely across their foreheads, eyes brown and alive on their pale faces. The youngest, dressed in a black t-shirt and a pair of shorts that leaves his skinny legs naked... looks like a little child. There was a girl among them, also very young, sitting... and looking at the summer clouds...

...when we hear the shots, we are half-way in via Della Scala. As we come to the square, we stop the jeeps by the steps of Santa Maria Novella right behind a Partisan officer seated in front of a little iron table... A squad of Partisans with machine guns are aligned on the steps... a trickle of blood runs down the marble steps.

At the noise of the jeep's brakes the Partisan officer at the little table does not move nor turn around. He extends his index finger towards one of the boys and says, "It's your turn. What's your name?"
"Today was my turn," says the boy getting up, "but one day or another it's gonna be your turn."
"What's your name?"
"My name is whatever I want."
"Hey! Why do you answer him for! That muso di bischero! (that muzzle of a dummy!)," a boy sitting next to him says.
"I answer him just to teach some manners to that coso (that thing)," the boy answered, his lips trembling but laughing with boldness.

Suddenly all the other boys started to talk among themselves and laugh. They all spoke with that unique, popular Florentine dialect from Dila' D'Arno (the south side of Arno River). The Partisan officer raised his head and said, "Hurry up. Don't make me waste time. It's your turn."

"Well, if it's a matter of not making you waste time," says the boy, with a sneering voice, "I'll hurry it up right away." Stepping over his buddies he situated himself in front of the Partisans armed with machine guns, next to the mound of corpses, right in the middle of the puddle of blood…

"Careful not to dirty your shoes," shouted one of his buddies, and they all started laughing. In that instant the boy shouted, "Viva Mussolini," and fell riddled with shots."

Curzio Malaparte. Italo-German, journalist, writer, filmmaker. WWII correspondent for Radiocorriere. Member Italian Fascist Party. Exiled by Mussolini for his attack on totalitarianism, he changed his political views from fascism

***

The situation is very bad in our building. Food provisions are nonexistent and we have very little water left. We are drinking water by the spoonful. Mom decides to go with Signora Fanetti and Signora Daccanto the next time they go to the liberated zone of Florence for food but it is still too dangerous to get to the Arno River zone, even though the Allies have been there for quite some time. In our neighborhood, between Piazza Dalmatia, Piazza Viessiex, via Atto Vannucci, and via Fabbroni, we are still under the nightmare of violent clashes between Germans and Partisans.

One afternoon at the end of August we hear a continuous roar coming from via Vannucci, the street right behind our apartment building. The noise comes from a long line of German armored cars making its way toward via Massaia, via Vittorio Emanuele, up via Bolognese, and moving to the north of Florence. The tenants, in the top floor apartment from their open windows, see the German troops marching away, and they yell to each other down the stairwell: "They are leaving! The Nazis are leaving!" However, immediately after comes the bloodcurdling news from Signora Fanetti: "RAIDS! RAIDS! They are making raids!"

A second line of armored cars, trucks, and jeeps is moving slowly from the very end of via Oriani up towards our building. Through the lowered shutters of the bedroom window, we see Nazi and Italian Fascist soldiers go in and out of buildings.

Each time the soldiers are followed by very young Italian civilians who are then shoved onto military trucks.

"Move back from those shutters! They will fire if they think you are at the window," Mom shouts, exasperated, as she looks through the slats from a distance.

"Oh dear God, look, look! Help these young people! They are being taken away. We shall never see these boys again... they will never see their families again! Dear God... help them..." Mom continues praying quietly while we watch young Italian men being pushed into German trucks at gunpoint by Italian Fascists and Nazi soldiers.

Even standing farther away, through the slats we can still make out the soldiers coming out of buildings and moving up via Oriani. A sudden loud spray of machine gun fire hits the outer wall. Ina and I, startled, move farther back.

"Mr. Daccanto's window!" says Mom. "They are firing at Mr. Daccanto's window!"

A loud commotion comes from downstairs. The soldiers are ramming the heavy front doors of the building with the butt of their machine guns. Finally, the doors, with a tremendous explosion, break wide open. We hear the soldiers stomping around downstairs and knocking at the first-floor apartments.

After much shouting coming from those apartments below, we hear the sound of the hobnailed boots coming upstairs to our apartment. There is a loud bang at the door and another bang at Mrs. Daccanto's place.

Mom is frantic as the banging at our door gets louder and louder. She paces back and forth in the corridor looking for some sort of weapon. She first carries an iron security bar. She comes back again with a heavy long-handled brush. She runs to get Dad's jacket and hangs it by the door.

The loud banging scares Vario and Gianni, who starts crying. It feels as if the front door is going to split. Mom has no other choice but to open. Two soldiers violently push the door wide open, hitting Mom in the chest. The rest of the soldiers continue up the stairs, the thumping of their boots resonating up the stairwell.

The two soldiers are well inside our apartment. "*Tuo uomo*! *Tuo uomo!* (Your man! Your man!)," yells one of the soldiers in broken Italian as he keeps on hitting and pushing Mom back with the butt of his rifle, making her stumble.

"Don't touch my mom!" screams Ina at the top of her lungs in terror.

"*Tuo uomo, tuo uomo*," yells the soldier angrily in a strong German accent, still shoving Mom's chest and pushing her back with his rifle.

"Leave my mom alone! Leave my mom alone!" I shout hysterically.

Mom manages to steady herself enough to reach Dad's jacket from behind the door.

"Here! Here is *Il mio uomo, il mio uomo*!" shouts Mom angrily as she shoves Dad's jacket onto the soldier's face.

The soldiers look at Dad's Marshal Major uniform, with the white band of the Red Cross on its sleeve and they leave, their boots clunking up the stairs. Mom slams the door shut with all her strength! She is mad and yelling at the top of her lungs!

"*Maledetti! Disgraziati maledetti*! (Damn you, vile wretches!)," Mom keeps screaming over and over again. She is punching the air and kicking the door.

"Mom... it's okay. Mom… it's okay," pleads Ina, trying to comfort her. Mom sits down on the floor.

"*Maledetto Vigliacco*! (Damn you coward!) How dare you! How dare you do this! How dare you do this to me," Mom keeps shouting, and then she blurts "...*ma va fa ...*&%# a sorata*!"

Ina stifles a gasp. My mom, who never, ever says vulgar words, has just said a very, very bad word.

After a long silence, I look at Mom and Ina crying on the floor and I feel like laughing out loud but I start crying instead, and I break into a long, low sobbing.

After all the soldiers leave the building, there is a great commotion by the stairwell. Everybody is asking if the soldiers caught anyone: "Did anyone get hurt?" "Did they find the men hidden in the underground cantine?" "Did they grab someone out of his apartment?" But there aren't any men in the apartments, except for Mr. Daccanto, and he is too old.

Someone goes down to shut the front doors tightly. The rumbling of the armored cars continues all night long.

Chapter 11:

Florence is Freed | September 1944

The following morning, we wake up to a great silence. via Oriani is completely deserted but soon fills up with people. I open the shutters and can't believe there are actually people walking up and down the street! Children are running everywhere. Neighbors are shouting "Hi!" from window to window.

"Gli Americani, gli Americani," everyone shouts.

It's over. The Nazis are really gone. We are able to walk down the street, we can walk anywhere, and we can go to get water. We can go to the stores for food!

"*Gli Americani, gli Americani!*" Children yell that the Americans are in Piazza Vieusseux and giving away chocolates and "chulimgun" but no one knows what that is.

Ina asks if we can go to Piazza Viessieux to get the chocolate. At the *piazza* Ina mingles with the other children who stand all around the American soldiers. I stand aside and watch, amazed at these young Americans. There are five of them. They are laughing and tossing chocolate bars to the kids. They look different, with hair from blond to light brown. Even their faces are different. They don't have the mostly-oval face of Mediterranean people. Their faces are more open with a sharply-square chin, and when they laugh, laughter fills up their entire faces. An older girl sees me and tries to convince me to join the group. She takes my hand but I resist. She insists and I shake my hand forcefully away from hers. When one of the soldiers holds up a chocolate bar and shows it to me, the older girl takes the bar from his hand and hands it to me. I snatch the bar and run all the way home to show Mom the chocolate. We haven't seen chocolate in years, and I can't even remember what chocolate tastes like.

"Mom," I say, out of breath, "the Americans are very nice. They laugh all the time. They are mostly blond."

We can't believe it is really over. Neighbors visit neighbors from streets nearby. Many have tragic stories to tell of atrocities suffered or witnessed. The neighborhood is finally alive, again.

***

We receive bottled water from the city, but one afternoon, a loud hissing at the kitchen sink startles us. It is like something that was muzzled for a long time finally burst; water is rushing furiously out of the faucet. It stops for a minute but rushes noisily out again.

"Mom, we have water!" Mom runs to shut off the faucets. There is water all over the floor. All day long Ina and I go to open and close the faucet, just to make sure the water is still there. The electricity also comes back, and all of a sudden, just like magic, our apartment, the buildings, and via Oriani are all bathed in a beautiful, soft, pink light.

Schools are still closed in Florence – many parts of the city are all in ruin after the bombing and mines everywhere. Mom and I are walking by the River Arno to get provisions from those stores. We are part of a long line of people making wide turns to try to avoid the rubble of ruined buildings that is completely blocking the road. We are forbidden to climb over the rubble in some roads because there are mines left by the Nazi-Fascists. Even so, we still have to climb over some debris in order to pass. Here and there I see pieces of furniture, twisted steel, and a bathtub lying on its side.

"Look, Mom, look!" I say, pointing at a building. There is nothing left of the place but a flight of stairs with a door at the top leading to nowhere.

Winter is fast approaching and I am glad because Dad will be home for Christmas and I can hardly wait. Mr. Daccanto is very ill and I know he will be glad to see and talk to Dad. In the meantime, the most fun thing to do is to run to visit 'gli Americani' who are stationed at Piazza Vieusseux.

The American soldiers are teaching the neighborhood children a Christmas song in English. I stand outside the circle and listen to the soldiers and the children sing. Ina has a beautiful soprano voice, like Mom, and she sings with the others:

"Singobel, singobel... singo opsele." (Jingle Bells) As the Americans are taken by a fit of laughter, the children's chorus trails down to a murmur and it stops.

"No, no! Canthare, Canthare! Ballow!" exclaims one soldier. Actually, I understand what he is trying to say in Italian, "*No, no! Cantate! Cantate! E' bello!* (No, no, sing! It's beautiful!)." With a wide gesture of his arm, the soldier holds the children's' attention, and they start singing with renewed vigor, following the soldier.

"Singobel, singobel, Singo opsele… eeh!" The Americans roll with laughter, clap their hands, and throw chocolates and 'chulimgun' to everyone. Ina loves to go singing with the children every day.

I run to tell Mom that the Americans speak Italian with a funny accent.

The Christmas holiday is soon approaching, and I can't wait for Dad to come home. I have so much to tell him. Dad never forgets my birthday. Besides, we need to make the Nativity scene really big and beautiful this year.

***

In the first week of September there is a sudden low sobbing outside our door. Signora Daccanto's apartment door is wide open. Mr. Daccanto has left us suddenly last night.

Mom and Signora Fanetti call the people of the *Misericordia* who prepare the body in the sitting room and fill the room with lots of flowers and plants and place lots of candles all around. There as a continuous streaming of neighbors in and out of the place, murmuring and praying. We all go inside with Mom to say goodbye to Mr. Daccanto. He looks very peaceful, almost as if he is sleeping, lying among all the flowers and candles. A Sister from the nearby convent is praying in a corner. We are the last to leave and Mom is comforting Mrs. Daccanto, who is afraid to remain alone in the house.

"No. No need to be afraid, Signora. Where I am from, we believe our dear people are always with us… also, we have the Giorno dei Morti... (Day of the Dead). I will stay with you tonight," Mom says.

"Oh, no thank you. I will be ok."

"Cettina can sleep with you tonight, right Cettina?"

Sleeping in the big bed, next to Signora Daccanto, I think of Mr. Daccanto, looking so peaceful in the other room, among the flowers. I always liked Mr. Daccanto and I felt so sorry for him when he got so upset about the young Fascists. Usually, it takes some time for me to fall asleep, but tonight the scent of the candles and the great silence puts me to sleep immediately and I do not budge until Mom comes to wake me up the following morning.

***

Florence is slowly reemerging from the horrors of the war which is still raging just a few miles north of Florence. Mom feels that things are safe enough now that she decides we need to move again. We need a bigger place to house all of us. She finds a very nice three-bedroom apartment by the entrance of the avenue that goes to Fiesole. We should be moving there some time after Christmas. I am very sorry to leave all our friends there on via Oriani, but most of all, I am devastated because we hear that Dad is not going to be here for my birthday. Christmas Day, 1944, will be the first holiday that Dad is not with us.

***

Florence is bustling again with a tenacious will to live and to bury the nightmare of the war, but the constant news of atrocities committed in the villages north of Florence, still under the domination of the Nazi-Fascists, does not give respite. Florentines have family in the hill just above Florence. The atrocities inflicted on the unarmed civilians inflame the minds of the people in our apartment building and leave them with powerless exasperation.

"Where are the Partisans? Where is the military?" the people shout. "Let's go get those bastards!" The men yell and curse, but there is no Italian military. The only military left is the *Republichini di Salo*, Mussolini's newly renamed army. The Partisans are outnumbered fifty to one. The news of the fighting and the Nazi-Fascists' horrific acts in the newspapers are relentless. As the Nazi-Fascists retreat north, journalists report that 50 or more Italian civilians are executed for every German soldier killed.

> **"The 4th of September, as retaliation for the killing of a couple of Nazi-Fascist soldiers, 35 Italian civilians kept prisoners at Camaiore by the sea, 50 miles northwest of Florence, are escorted to a place called Pioppetti and, there, hanged with wire. Others are killed by spray of machine guns... Around the 10th of September, one of the saddest chapters of the war takes place in the village of Certosa Di Farneta, known for the monastic community, which, since the beginning of the War, has become the destination of many monks from all over Europe, including Germany and Switzerland. The monks are dedicated to helping those in need. As soon as the soldiers of the 16th SS Nazi Armored Division come to the village,**

they enter the monastery with the subterfuge of looking for arms, which the monks obviously do not have... Sixteen monks and thirty-two civilians are taken and killed. In the close villages of Pescia and Maggiona, 34 more civilians are rounded up and killed, some hung with wire. At the end of September, near Massa Carrara, as retaliation for the killing of a Nazi soldier, the SS chase after the men of the village who manage to hide in the woods; the women, the children, and the elderly do not make it in time. The Nazis, together with the Italian Republichini di Salo (Mussolini's Fascist army), round up 30 people in the school building, spray them with machine guns and throw hand bombs through the windows. The building was then set on fire. At the end, there are seventy-one dead. Twenty-eight of them are between the ages of three months and 17 years old. The approximate number of the victims of the Nazi-Fascists massacres in the villages, just north of Florence (Tuscany) was 3,622."

Firenze va alla Guerra - Franca Lanci (my translation)

Chapter 12:

Piazza Edison | Florence, 1945

It's a new year and Ina sounds very happy. She keeps on singing, "*Anno Nuovo Vita Nuova* (new year, new life)" all day long. Our new place in Piazza Edison is bigger and much more elegant than via Oriani, according to my sister.

Our apartment is in a single, turn-of-the-century lovely building with a garden in the back. It only has three floors. Our place is on the second floor, with a beautiful balcony overlooking a small, triangular *piazza*, with benches and grass and trees. All around Piazza Edison, behind some buildings, there are large, rich estates with lots of land and trees and greenery.

I miss Dad for my birthday. He sends us Christmas cards and gifts that finally arrive, after the New Year. To Ina he sends a lovely dress, to Vario and Gianni he sends toys, and to me he sends a doll.

"A doll! A doll for Cettina," Mom exclaims. "I bet *she* has chosen the gifts."

Later that day I dare to ask Ina what Mom meant, and who is this *she*.

"*She* is this Yolanda lady. Mom and Dad are separated… didn't you know? It's been years! What's the matter?" Ina says, staring angrily at my face. "Don't you remember how much they fought? I hated them when they were fighting all the time. I really did! I could not stand all that yelling and screaming, since we were in Tripoli!"

I am astonished at the news. After a long while I yell back at her, "Yes, I remember they fought! I even asked Dad why they fought all the time. But they never yelled or screamed. You lie!"

"*Oca*! (goose / stupid)," Ina yells at me. She shrugs her shoulders and walks away.

I miss Dad even more now because I have so many questions to ask him, like, *what does it all mean*? I liked it when Dad and I discussed things.

Signora Fanetti comes to visit Mom and brings news of the neighbors on via Oriani. Even Giovanna, Mom's friend from Catania, comes to visit us. Her prosthetic arm looks very realistic now. I ask Ina about it but she does not know. The ladies talk about the war that is still raging around Milan and Torino in the north.

***

School starts and I am very unhappy. "I don't want to go to a higher grade," I keep whining to everyone. "I want to remain in the same grade as last spring. I don't know anything, and I don't remember anything from last year!" But it is no use. All students who missed a year off school because of the war are put in higher grades regardless of the circumstances. However, after a few weeks, I realize it isn't so bad. Nobody remembers anything anyway about school, except, of course, the war.

The American soldiers are everywhere, enjoying a mild, sunny April in Florence. They are in buses, in coffee shops, in the streets, and on the road that go to Fiesole by Piazza Edison. I am dying to know what they are saying and I am glad I am taking English this semester. It is a brand-new subject for me and I decide to study hard from the very beginning of the class and follow right along with the teacher. I do not want to remain behind, like I am in math. Mom tells Ina to follow my example.

"Why can't you be more like Cettina? Study more and stop complaining all the time." I think Ina hates me. I wish Mom wouldn't have said anything.

Through Dad's influence, Mom finds a job at the *Comando Del Corpo D'Armata*, in Piazza San Marco. The first thing Mom does is buy a radio, but with four young children, and Dad's reduced allowance, it is hard to make ends meet; we have very little left for anything else. Ina whines that she wants to go to the movies and asks for my help to try and convince Mom.

"All my friends are going to the movies on Sunday. Why can't I go with them! They are playing Meet Me in Saint Louis. It's an American movie. Why can't we all go?" Ina pleads.

To Ina's arguments I add, "All the newspapers say it's a great, beautiful movie. I think we should all see it!" I am surprised Mom agrees. On Sunday we all go to the cinema.

Ina likes to dream about dances and parties. She wants to go places and have fun like the American girls in the movies. She likes to dance in front of the mirror, waving her arms artistically above her head. I follow right behind her, dancing and flailing my arms about, careful not to bump into her. Ina composes a song about Signorina De Martino, the Latin teacher, whom she hates. Ina sings, "Signorina De Martino, *la lezione non sappiamo.* (Miss De Martino, we don't know the lesson)." Around and around we go, singing in front of the mirror and waving our hands like some goofy ballerinas.

***

The news blaring on the radio will not let us forget about the war, which still rages on. The war moved from the Tuscan villages north of Florence to the very northern, industrial cities of Milan, Turin, and Genoa, still under the Nazi-Fascist domination. The northern Italians are ready to snap at the oppressors. From the 25th to the 28th of April, Italy is bombarded by the radio blaring astonishing news.

> **April 25th. "Qui (here) Radio Milano! - Citizens, Workers! A general strike was on against the German occupation, against the Fascist war, for the salvation of our land, our homes, our workplaces. As we have done in Genoa and Turin, we must force the Nazi-Fascists under the dilemma: Surrender or Perish!"**

> Sandro Pertini, Surrender or Perish, YouTube

> **April 26th "Qui Radio Milano – Well informed sources, from the Switzerland frontier, announce the arrest of Mussolini by Italian Partisans...Marshal Graziani has surrendered to the Partisans of Como...the Secretary of the Fascist party, Pavolini, has barricaded himself with a hundred Camicie Nere (black shirts) in a barrack but are strongly besieged by our Partisans..."**

> Sandro Pertini Radio, Cronista, Radio Milano

Italy is happy to hear the Fascists and the secretary of the Fascist party, the Florentine Pavolini, are finally getting their dues. Mom asks to go get the newspaper *la Nazione di Firenze*. People crowd around the newspaper kiosk at the corner of Piazza Edison talking excitedly and cursing, "*Quei Maledetti*! May they receive all they deserve..."

The radio, constantly on, finally announces:

> **April 27th "Qu, Radio Milano – Liberata! In the name of the Italian people, the CLNAI (Comitato di Liberazione Nazionale Italiana) takes control of all civil and military powers. All Fascist military corps are disbanded. The members have to abandon their posts immediately and go to concentration camps... All those belonging to the German armed forces are declared prisoners of war. Tribunals of War are being formed... The members of the Fascist government... guilty of having suppressed constitutional guarantees, having destroyed personal liberty, having created the Fascist regime, and guilty of**

having compromised and betrayed the destiny of the country and thrown it into the present catastrophe, are punished by death..."

Sandro Pertini, Radio Milano

April 27th "Qui Radio Milano – A vanguard of the 5th Army has entered the city of Lody. It's probable that Anglo-Americans will arrive in Milano within the day..."

Sandro Pertini, Radio Milano

April 28th "BBC News – Benito Mussolini, dictator of Italy...has been killed by Partisans along with his mistress, Clara Petacci, and some close associates ...Mussolini was arrested and executed while trying to escape to Switzerland. Their bodies were taken to Milano from the Lecco district near Lake Como, where they were arrested and then killed yesterday."

BBC News, On This Day

April 28th "BBC News – ... the corpses of Mussolini, Petacci and 12 Fascists are on display in Piazzale Loreto with ghastly promiscuity in the open square under the same fence against which one year ago 15 Partisans had been shot by their own countrymen, the Fascists. One woman fired five shots into Mussolini's body, according to Radio Milan, and shouted: "Five shots for my five assassinated sons! Other passers-by spat on the bodies. It was later reported the mutilated bodies of Mussolini and his mistress had been hung upside down outside the forecourt of a Milan gas station."

BBC News - On This Day

April 28th "BBC News – Most British people are shocked at [horrific] Mussolini's end not knowing the full history of Piazzale Loreto... The executions are the first conspicuous demonstration of mob violence carried out by the Partisans who until now have been kept under control by their leaders."

BBC News - On This Day

It's Over
"One of the most gruesome wars in the history of mankind, which has set Europe on fire for years, has finally come to an end. But before dying completely the war has shaken the country in a final and cruel blast; it seems in its dying rage it would exterminate all semblance of human dignity; all hopes and ideals"

MCJ, The Tavern Post

At the kiosk there is a spread of newspapers with gruesome pictures of Mussolini and his people shown in all their gory, bloody details. People crowd in to buy newspapers. They stop to converse with other people and shout, "It's about time, those *figli d'una puttana*. (sons of whores). *Maledetti*, all of them. May they burn in eternity!"

A little boy, three or four years old, holding his mother's hand, looks at the pictures of the bodies hanging upside down and whimpers, "Oh look..."

Mussolini - captured and executed by Italian Partisans, along with his mistress and three other Fascist officials. (Milan, 1945)

There are going to be festivities in downtown Florence today. Ina is happy; Mom says we can go to the movies, but we have to take baby Gianni with us.

Chapter 13:

Sacro Cuore School | Florence, Fall 1948

The Sacro Cuore is an all-girls school run by nuns but not all of the teachers are nuns. This fall semester I dread Signorina De Martino for two classes: European History and Latin.

I get myself deep into my homework and stay pretty much to myself in the classroom. Besides, nobody is interested in my company anyway, especially not two snooty girls, Elena and Cristina, who keep looking at me from the end of their noses. Students have to remain in the same classroom all day long for the whole semester. We can move about, talk aloud, jump up and down for the six minutes or so it takes for the bell to ring and a new period to start, but only teachers are allowed to move around campus from class to class.

When Signorina De Martino enters the classroom, there is an immediate silence. She sits down at the desk and looks into her register for a long time, finally calling on me: "Gargano. Let's see if you are *your sister's sister*! Or maybe *you* do your homework," she says sarcastically. What did Signorina De Martino mean? That Ina doesn't do her homework? No wonder Ina hates her! I stand up and start reading the title of my written homework out loud.

"Pipino Il Breve. (Pipino, the Short) The word *pipino* in Italian means a baby boy's penis, which has nothing to do with the Carolingian King we are talking about in our homework today." There is a sudden burst of laughter in the classroom. Undaunted, I continue, "Pipino Il Breve, 714-768 AD, was made King by the French nobility, was crowned by Pope Stefano II as King of all Franks, and was given the title of *Patricius Romanorum*. The pope needed Pipino Il Breve to defeat Astolfo, King of the Longobards, who had taken possession of papal territories...The Pope even went so far as to invite Pipino Il Breve to invade Longobardia in northern Italy; the Pope would do whatever needed to be done to have his papal possessions restored... Pipino Il Breve, after a long and successful reign became father of the great Charlemagne."

At the end of my homework, I write my own opinion. "Actually," I continue reading, "the Carolingians should have called him Pipino Il *Grande* for all his accomplishments instead of Pipino Il Breve." The class laughs again.

"Well, well, well! We are even using humor, are we?... Nine," says Signorina De Martino after a pause. A nine out of ten is a very good grade. Even Elena and Cristina seem impressed.

The students in my class keep asking me for help after that. "Mom, the students in Miss De Martino's class want to copy my homework."

"What does Signorina De Martino say?" Mom asks. "Does she know?"

"I don't think so. But once she said, 'This sounds like Gargano's work,' after a student read her paper," I answer.

"Absolutely do not let them copy your homework, or you can get into real trouble. Just read it to them."

***

This is the third year that Dad will not be with us for Christmas and I have forgotten all about the doll that Dad sent me for my birthday a couple of years ago. I never play with dolls but it was Dad's last gift to me and I want to find it. I wondered why, at the time we received the gifts, Mom exclaimed, "A doll! Of all things, a doll for Cettina!!"

This year we have a Christmas tree. The Americans brought this novelty to Italy and all the little stores around our neighborhood have beautiful Christmas trees all lit up in their windows. Our neighbor, who lives on the ground floor and has a garden, cuts a branch from his old fir tree. We put it into a bucket with lots of stones around it that we gather from the grassy area in the middle of Piazza Edison and we pour water into it. We adorn the tree with small ribbons and bows and anything that Mom can think of. It looks just as beautiful as the ones we see in magazines and in the stores' windows. I miss Dad's Nativity scene, so I take out the old pop-up paper Nativity scene from the storage box and lay it next to the tree.

***

Ina seems very happy. A school friend from Sacro Cuore, Anna, lives on the other side of Piazza Edison. The two girls are almost fifteen and are always together. Anna is pretty, a little taller than Ina, and has incredibly gorgeous red hair. She has an older sister who is engaged, soon to be married, to a university student of engineering. Anna's house is always full of young people, most of them young men, college friends of Anna's future brother-in-law. Ina longs for the party atmosphere, the laughter and the dances at Anna's house, especially during Christmas time. Mom gets very irritated with Ina and wants her to do her homework first.

"Why can't you be more like Cettina?" Mom keeps saying. "If you want to go to Anna's house, you have to take your sister with you." Ina really hates me and when Mom is not there, she goes around calling me *oca oca* (goose / stupid). I retort with *idiota idiota*.

I really, really do not want to go with Ina to Anna's parties but I can't say no to Mom. The people at the party are fun and polite and the table by a wall is full of delicious pastries. Looking around the room for Ina, I am very surprised at her behavior. She is not at all outgoing or happy. She is shy, hardly talks to anyone, and stays very close to Anna. I don't see her dance at all, even though a few boys ask her.

Ina is very beautiful. She is voted by the Sacro Cuore graduating class as the girl most resembling the Italian actress Anna Maria Pier Angeli, who works in Hollywood. I think Mom worries too much about Ina. Too many people put too many bad ideas in Mom's head, especially her male colleagues, when they come to the house, for work-related matters. "Such a beautiful daughter you have there!" they say. "I bet she has boyfriends galore! Very hard to keep track of a girl like that! God knows where she is when you are not here..."

As soon as I get home from school, I stand by the bedroom dresser to do my homework. We leave the desk for Ina, since she takes more classes and has more books. I need an eraser and go to Ina's desk to get one, when the name 'Cettina' in an open letter by her diary catches my eye. I can't help stealing a peek at a few lines here and there, "I can't stand her... why am I not more like Cettina? I hate her... as soon as she gets home, she does her homework on the dresser, standing up... I am so scared... I haven't been to classes for three days because of Miss De Martino... I stand by the school wall all morning..."

My heart starts beating so fast I can hardly breathe. I move quickly away from the desk. I don't want Ina to find out I am reading her letter. I go back to the dresser, but I can't study.

As soon as Mom gets home, she thunders at Ina, "Where have you been? I just talked to Miss De Martino." Mom is angry and she walks closer to Ina.

"Where have you been for three days and with whom?" Mom is furious and is close to striking Ina as she gets closer and closer to her. "Where have you been? Tell me!"

"Nowhere, Mom, nowhere!"

Mom slaps Ina in the face and continues slapping Ina's arms that she's holding tight to her head. Mom has never struck Ina before.

"I didn't go anywhere, Mom. I didn't do anything," Ina pleads and cries under the blows.

Unable to stand it any longer, I scream hysterically, "Leave her alone, leave her alone! She didn't go anywhere, she didn't go anywhere!"

Mom stops slapping Ina, looking at me at length, then asks me with a glacial tone in her voice, "And how do you know?"

"I know it because… because I know it... because I know it!" I yell, frightened by my courage to yell at Mom, and because Ina might find out I read her letter.

"Okay," says Mom, calmly. "So, tell me where she went."

"She stayed all morning by the school walls... because she's afraid of Miss De Martino," I say without looking at Ina.

Mom looks astonished. She slumps on the bed and looks straight ahead. Then she puts her head in her hands and murmurs to herself, "Dear God, forgive me. I am traumatizing my own children."

After dinner, when everybody is asleep, I lay down between Mom and Ina in the big bed and feel at peace. I hear a soft sniffle coming from Ina. Her hand reaches under the covers and squeezes my hand tightly.

I wondered if Ina misses Dad as much as I do.

Chapter 14:

Mom

Mom has not been feeling well for the last few months. She has a congenital heart defect due to her premature birth. The doctors seem concerned, and they tell Mom she must rest more.

Uncle Frank is back with us. His car rental business in Catania, once thriving, never fully recovered after the war. Uncle Frank decides to look for a job in Florence. He finds one with a promising young man in the shoes and handbags industry. His name is Salvatore Ferragamo. Mom thinks that Ferragamo has a great eye for high fashion and will be famous one day; she says he is a true artist and has already made a name for himself in the fashion world in Milano.

Uncle Frank does not seem to care a whit about shoes and handbags, but Mom seems calmer with Uncle Frank there. He makes everybody laugh with his funny imitations and his dangerous sliding all around the kitchen floor as he tries to be a tap dancer.

The doctors are still worried and want Mom to stay and recover in the hospital for a few days. Social workers and Father Don Vandelli from San Gervasio's parish suggests putting the two young boys, Vario and Gianni, temporarily in boarding school, Vario at the convent of the Franciscan Friars and Gianni with the nuns where he will be a kindergartener. Ina is very upset and doesn't want Gianni and Vario to be put in a boarding school. She tells everybody that she will take care of her brothers. Mom is very appreciative of Ina's love and her help, and proudly tells all her coworkers. I offer my help too but am aware that it is not possible; Ina and I have to go to school, and we are just old enough to remain temporarily alone. The hardest part is at night when we think about baby Gianni and Vario.

It is very hard to concentrate on schoolwork when I am concerned about our home situation. Fortunately, the doctors let mom come home after only a few days.

***

The Marshall Plan, or The European Recovery Program, is asking all students in Italian Schools to participate in writing their impression of World War II. All classes and grades of Sacro Cuore participate. Mom tells me to think deeply and write the best composition I can, and I start; *"Bombs! Alarms! Airplanes! Oh, what horror! Fear was constant! Hunger was insinuating!"*

My composition is only three pages long. Two Italian teachers assigned to correct the students' works debate about my choice of the word 'insinuating,' but do not ask me to change it. Later in the semester the school is notified that my composition has been accepted for a winning prize. Not only that, but I am the only student in the school of Sacro Cuore whose composition has won anything!

Mom is so proud she is in tears, and tells the whole world, and Dad too, about it. I receive a glowing note from Dad telling me how proud he is of me. My happiness in hearing from Dad has no bounds, at first. Then, inexplicably, I tell myself, "Oh, so what? I really don't care anymore," and I ignore the note.

***

It is the end of school and the summer is here. Ina goes to Anna's parties all by herself. Mom doesn't ask me to go with Ina anymore.

Walking around downtown Florence in the summer evening is a great pleasure. With the evening lights flickering all around us, we stop at the famous *Perche 'No?* (Why Not?) ice cream parlor. The boys, Mom, and I all have ice cream cones.

Life seems perfect, except that Mom stops feeling well again. It seems that Uncle Frank is making her nervous, or maybe it is that Mom doesn't have the strength and patience to put up with anything anymore. While Mom is at the doctor with Uncle Frank, Ina asks me, "How long has it been that we have been calling him Uncle Frank?"

"It's been since we left Catania, in 1941."

***

Back from the doctor's, Mom tells us that they want to put her in the hospital for more observation at the end of the summer, this time for a whole month. I understand that to mean that I need to go to a boarding school, too.

Mom finds a store where they sell clothes from America at very reasonable prices. She can buy beautiful dresses for Ina, who is sixteen now, so she doesn't have to wear the same dress over and over again at Anna's parties.

Some Florentines manage to get on their feet fast and fiercely after the war, and sometimes I wish I could do something to help Mom. No matter how hard she tries, it is very hard to keep food on the table for all of us, let alone find nice clothing for two growing teenage girls. I wish I could lighten up her worries.

After another trip to the doctor's, Mom tells us again that the doctors have already decided to put Mom in the hospital for more observations, for two whole months. Vario and Gianni will go to the Franciscans Friars, and I will go to the Suore Calasanziane. I complain loudly and angrily that I don't want to go to that convent.

"Why can't we all stay here in this house? Ina and I can take care of the boys and pick them up from school. We can cook, too!"

"Yes. I know you can. But they are not allowing you guys to stay alone, and you are not fifteen yet. Besides, it's only going to be a month or two."

"But, Mom," I say desperately, "the Calasanziane's convent is for the Daughters of Prisoners! Why can't I go with Ina? I do not want to go to the convent of the *Figlie dei Carcerati*! (Daughters of Prisoners). It's already so sad that we have to go away, and that you have to go to the hospital, but I have to even put up with the *Figlie dei Carcerati*?" I said, almost crying.

"But it's not that kind of place anymore," Mom says, trying to remain calm. "Only the name sometimes is mentioned. Besides, it's only for a couple of months. Uncle Frank will remain here until I come back."

"Uncle Frank, Uncle Frank!" I yell. "What's he doing here? Why is he here?" I look at Mom's pallid face and I immediately realize that I hurt her deeply, and I am very sorry. She points her finger at me and says very slowly and poignantly, "How dare you! How dare you!"

Chapter 15:

Suore Calasanziane | Florence, Fall 1950

The Calasanziane Nuns occupy a fourteenth-century villa and its beautiful surrounding grounds, one of the many properties that once belonged to the Medici Family, Grand Dukes of Tuscany. It has beautiful frescos on most of the ceilings and old inlaid furniture. The convent, a short walking distance away from Piazza Edison, is for girls as young as two, and only up to thirteen-years-old. There are only three girls in the convent who are older: Anna Bank, who is not yet sixteen, Adriana Leban, who is fourteen, and I, not yet fifteen. We are allowed at the convent under special provisory agreement. We have our own sleeping quarters separate from the common dormitory but not too far from the nuns' bedrooms. We are also free to walk alone about the convent; we do not have to walk in line with the rest of the girls to go to the Chapel or the refectory, or the dormitories. I love this arrangement! It makes us feel important. We three are called "the students," and we are the only ones allowed to leave the convent every morning and walk by ourselves to school, to the Sacred Heart.

I like the nuns immediately, especially the Vice Madre, Sister Teresina, and La Madre, who introduces me to the whole convent by my middle name, Concettina. The girls seem very friendly and ask me a lot of questions.

Suor Benigna is the monitor of the students' quarters and she doesn't like me at all. "Do you feel you are better than all the girls here? You sure do put on some airs," she says to me, all the time.

La Madre decides that Anna Bank is old enough and needs her own bedroom. Adriana and I remain alone in our shared bedroom to do our homework.

The cold afternoons are time for melancholic contemplation, prayer at the chapel, and silent studies. Except that Adriana won't be silent. She is always ready to talk and laugh and jump up and down on her bed. She is Slovenian and escaped to Italy with her mom during the war. She has thick, curly, golden-blonde hair and she strikes quite a contrast with us mostly brown-haired Italian girls. Her infectious giggle and laughter reach everywhere, even down the staircase, and La Madre, summoned by Suor Benigna, has already come up twice to see what the matter is.

"And why are we laughing so hard instead of studying? You two will be more comfortable if you have your own place to study," La Madre says. "Concettina, take your books and come with me." I follow silently. "This is going to be your new study area," she says, opening the door of the Grand Salon.

I can't believe my eyes! My study has marble and gilded wood furniture and there are frescos on the ceiling. It is beautiful! I only need to close my eyes and pretend I live in the Medici era. In this great silence, it is easy to get to work.

Suor Teresina comes in often to give me messages from Ina. Ina went to see Mom yesterday and everything was going to be alright. I get the message and go back to studying because I don't dare anger Signorina De Martino. I've just started writing when Adriana comes waltzing into the Grand Salon.

"Adriana, what are you doing here? Are you allowed to come here?" I ask apprehensively.

"La Madre didn't say anything. Besides, I hate that old witch Suor Benigna! She says I'm just like you. She's gone to tell La Madre where I was going. So, it's better that La Madre finds out that I am really here." It is difficult to remain serious with Adriana's weird logic and infectious giggle. Adriana imitates Suor Benigna, and we both laugh.

We hear the jingle of the rosary beads attached to La Madre's belt and soon she comes into the Grand Salon. She tells us we need to study separately and prohibits Adriana from coming to see me again.

***

At the end of October La Madre asks me if I want to go with one of the Sisters to visit Mom in the hospital this coming Sunday. I tell her that I would like that very much. Mom and I are so happy to see each other, and she tells me how much she misses me. I tell her how desperately I miss her! I tell her all about La Madre, the nuns, Adriana, and my beautiful Grand Salon study. The doctors think she should be able to come home soon. As I leave, I look at my beautiful Mom and silently pray, *"Please Dear Jesus, have Mom come home soon!"*

***

November is a very cold month in Florence, cold enough for snow. It is getting dark outside and I gather my books to leave when Adriana comes in.

"Oh no! Adriana, go away! You are going to get us in trouble," I say as I turn the lights off.

"Why? Study time is over. I came to tell you that I made a cake."

"You what? You *made* a cake? You mean you *baked* a cake? How the heck did you do that?" I ask, stunned.

"It's only made with crushed almond flour and whipped eggs, and stuff. My Mom came visiting this Sunday and I asked her to send me the stuff."

Suddenly we hear the jingle of the rosary. La Madre is coming. I point to Adriana to go hide behind the tall-tiered chest by the side of the entrance door and I hide behind the chest on the other side of the door. After a few seconds, La Madre comes in and walks a few steps inside. I am terrified and unable to breathe. My heart is beating so fast I feel it inside my throat. Miraculously, La Madre does not see us and finally leaves. I remain frozen in place, unable to move.

"Come on, let's go!"

"Adriana, so help me, if you do that again, I'll beat you up into a pulp!"

We go upstairs to our bedroom and eat the cake. It tastes very good and sweet, but strange. It feels like having a mouthful of flour except that it is crushed almonds drenched in whipped eggs and fruit. Adriana is happy that I like her cake. She steals my pen and goes back to jumping on her bed. She is tall, and one of these days her head is going to hit the ceiling, hard.

"Give me my pen back!" I command, but Adriana is inciting me to a wrestling match. Adriana is taller and heavier, and I know I have very little chance. I go to her bed and try to wrestle the pen out of her hand but her body is rolled up into a ball and I can't reach the pen!

"Oh, okay! Keep the stupid pen! You are such a child," I say, irritated.

Suor Benigna comes in at that moment and looks scandalized. Without saying a word, she goes into her room and closes the door, which is strange, because she always has some nasty comments for us.

The following day after school, Adriana and I are told to wait for La Madre's call. She wants to talk to us separately and I am starting to get anxious. When it's my turn I walk up the large, long hall where, at the very end, Suor Teresina and La Madre are waiting. I see that Adriana has finished talking and she is walking towards me. She hardly passes me, and she stops. She is crying and she puts her hand on my arm. "Concettina," she says, but she can hardly find her voice, she is crying so hard. "La Madre is angry... she thinks we were doing *le cosacce* (bad things), and Suor Benigna says we were not fighting."

"What? What is going on?" I say, startled.

"Concettina! Come please," calls La Madre. I leave Adriana and walk up to the end of the hall.

"Was Adriana talking to you just now?" asks Suor Teresina.

"Yes," I answer.

"And what did she say?"

"She was crying because La Madre thinks we were doing *le cosacce*."

After a long pause La Madre asks, "And, were you doing le *cosacce?"*

"No," I say firmly. "We were wrestling on the bed and I was trying to get my pen back." I look at Suor Teresina and La Madre and I still can't figure out what is going on. Finally, I blurt out, impatiently and annoyed, "But what are these *cosacce*!"

La Madre and Suor Teresina look at each other. "Concettina, you can go to dinner," says La Madre after another long pause.

That evening we find out Suor Benigna has retired and is not working at the convent anymore. We are delighted that no one is sleeping in the back room as our monitor. Adriana is happy. She can make as many cakes as she wants and jump up and down on her bed as much as she wants.

December is fast approaching and I think about the holidays, Christmas, and Mom, who is still in the hospital.

Chapter 16:

December 7, 1950 | Mom Dies

When we get back from school, Suor Teresina and La Madre try to tell me about it very gently; they tell me, "Mom went to *Paradise.*"

As soon as I realize the meaning of those words I scream, "No! No! Don't tell me, Madre! Don't tell me! Don't tell me! No, you can't!"

Suor Teresina and La Madre cannot make me stop shouting; "No, no! Don't tell me!"

I have completely lost all sense of time and place. The nuns hearing the screams come into the hall to find out what is happening. Some of them are crying and are trying to comfort me. Adriana is quietly crying behind me. Even the younger girls attempt to say something comforting, but I keep crying and shouting to anyone who is listening about how Mom would patch and mend her old undershirts over and over again so she could afford enough money to buy food for all of us, and dresses for Ina and me!

I am given a warm drink to calm me and I fall asleep with the nuns around me, but I soon wake up screaming again.

La Madre asks a nun to take me, that same afternoon, to go see Mom in the antechamber of Piazza San Marco. I stop my hysterical crying.

Mom is all dressed in her best clothes lying on a table, her hands crossed on her chest. A couple of male nurses are tending other tables.

"Concettina, do you want to get closer to your mom?" the nun asks me. I walk over to Mom's table. She looks very peaceful, just sleeping. I stroke her hands and her face gently.

"Mom, I am so sorry! I am so sorry! Mom, look at me one last time," I murmur. *I need to see your beautiful brown eyes sparkling one more time*. I stroke her cheeks and eyelids gently.

Later that same evening, La Madre decides that I should go home to Piazza Edison, where my sister and my brothers are all staying for the night. We all sit quietly around

Ina, listening to her, detailing Mom's last moments. Ina was the last one to see Mom alive. She died in her arms. My sister's face and mouth seem frozen into a grin as she is talking. The young nun, who accompanied Gianni, is shocked and asks me why Ina is laughing.

"No, she is not laughing!" I say, "it's nervousness! She always does that when she is very upset."

Ina hears me. She looks up at me; her eyes fill with tears which stream down her face. With a trembling voice, Ina informs us that Dad will come up from Naples and live with us here in Florence.

***

On the 8th of December I am back at the convent but my mind is still with my brothers and sister and my mom lying in the antechamber.

The 8th of December is a big holiday throughout Italy. We celebrate the birth of the Immaculate Conception. It is also my *onomastico* (name-day) and the whole convent is celebrating my name-day. In the chapel during mass, I am honored with loving words and prayers, cards and gifts. Everyone is so nice to me, trying to comfort me, and I do not know how to say thank you. I seem to remain in a state of silent awareness: I am only able to watch and listen, while my eyes and heart cry.

I remain at the convent until the end of February. I will miss La Madre and Suor Teresina, and Adriana's laughter.

"We will see each other at school!" Adriana assures me.

***

Ina is already back home in Piazza Edison from the Shelter for Young Misses. My brothers and I will be moving back home at the end of February, when Dad and Yolanda move to Florence from Naples. I am apprehensive to tell La Madre that I would much rather stay here, and to please let me stay here in the convent. I haven't talked to or seen Dad since 1944.

Dad was my idol! I thought he looked so handsome in his Marshall Major Uniform. I remembered him leaving Mom and my frightened siblings in the bomb shelter and, holding my hand tightly, we both walked outside the building while the Allies were bombing the marshaling yards of Florence. Dad kept on saying *niente paura, niente paura,* (nothing to fear) while the bombs were exploding nearby. He said it was safer outside rather than to chance being buried alive in the collapsing buildings, and I believed him. When he talked, I used to hang on his every word. I especially loved the Christmases together. But that was such a long, long time ago! I miss Mom so desperately; I feel like crying again.

***

"Are you going to find out if you have the calling?" Adriana asks, waking me up from my reveries.

"What?" I ask, startled.

"Yes, if you have the calling to be a nun," Adriana says.

"No," I answer. "I don't need to find out."

"Today, the young nuns are going to the chapel to find out if they still have the calling. Wouldn't you be much happier knowing for sure?"

"No Adriana. I do not need to know."

"Anna Bank talked to the priest," Adriana continues. "Concettina, suppose you are preparing to get married and then find out too late you have the calling. Wouldn't you rather know it now?"

It is impossible to argue with Adriana's weird logic. "Adriana, why don't you go talk to the priest to make sure?" I say.

"Will you go with me?"

"Of course, I will!" I answer.

Adriana comes out from the Chapel, beaming from ear to ear. She must have found out she does not have the calling! The priest sees me waiting and makes a sign for me to go in.

"Concettina, do you want to know if you have the calling? It's hard to tell for sure but I really doubt it," the priest says, peering and smiling at me.

Chapter 17:

Life Back Home| 1951

I have been back home on Piazza Edison with Ina, Dad, and Yolanda since the end of February. Vario and Gianni will join us later.

Ina is continuing medical school for pediatric nursing and doing an internship in a hospital. She comes home on Sundays and some weekends.

I am the only sibling living at home with Dad and Yolanda at the moment and I am thankful to get deep into schoolwork. Dad has changed. He seems angry all the time. He looks much older and feels like a total stranger to me. I cannot talk to him, even though he seems to want to communicate. To me, his presence here is a constant reminder that Mom is dead. How can I verbalize to him the fact that the only reason I'm seeing him is because Mom has died?

Dad talks often to Ina and me about accepting Yolanda as if she were our housekeeper. She will be cooking for us and cleaning for us and doing chores for us.

"I understand she will never be able to be a mother to you, but accept her as a friend," Dad says to us.

Yolanda comes from a long line of Florentine women. She is beautiful and has the typical light blond-brown hair of the women of Tuscany. Yolanda works as a seamstress and is making a dress for Ina. She likes Ina very much and I am thankful that my sister is a little less unhappy, a little more relaxed.

"I see you are trying to be more friendly with Yolanda," Dad finally says to me one day, which is not the truth.

"Seeing you two here only reminds me constantly that Mom is dead," I answer calmly.

"But don't you know that your mother was a *mala donna*? (bad woman)," Dad says angrily to me. "Don't you know that you have a brother who is your half-brother?"

Dad's words feel like a lightning bolt striking my spine, like the sound of thunder exploding in my brain. I lose all control; an instantaneous furious force throws me against Dad, biting and kicking and screaming. "Yes, I know it! Yes, I know it! *Maledetto*! *Maledetto Disgraziato*, (wretch) I have always known it! I have always known it! *Maledetto*! *Maledetto*!" I scream hysterically.

Dad shoves me away with his hand. I fall on the floor and he pushes me out of the way with his foot. Yolanda hears the commotion and comes out of the kitchen, yelling at Dad. His shirt hangs loose on his shoulders because I have completely torn it apart.

"Are you crazy? Are you totally mad? The child's mother has just died and you call her names in front of your daughter?" Yolanda separates me from Dad, strips of his shredded silk shirt still clutched in my fingers. She takes me into my bedroom, locks me inside, takes the key, and goes back to yelling at Dad.

Locked in the bedroom, I breathe deeply and try to calm down, saying to myself, over and over, "No, Dad! No. Don't push me away with your foot! No. Don't kick me out of the way. No, Yolanda. Don't lock me in. No. Never lock me in, Yolanda."

I go to the window, pull down the cord that rolls the shutters up, and look down. Right below me there is a flat rooftop that belongs to the storage room of the people downstairs. I throw the loose end of the rolling cord outside the windowsill. The cord reaches halfway down but is still six feet or so from the flat rooftop. I take my schoolbag and throw it out the window together with my shoes and sweater. I climb on the windowsill, holding the cord in my hands, and tell myself that I have to hold tight, no matter what. As I go out the window, I feel the weight of my body and a strong, painful tear in my underarms, but I am okay. I quickly slide down to the end of the cord and let myself fall the last six feet curled into a ball as much as possible. I put my shoes and sweater on, take my bag, climb over the little railing, and then am on the street. I run nonstop, all the way down via Baldesi to San Gervasio, then to via Cento Stelle, and finally to the Suore Calasanziane convent.

Our second story window on Piazza Edison.

The nun that opens the door takes a look at me and says, "Wait here, Concettina, I am calling La Madre."

Back in the convent I find myself to be calm and at peace. I walk to the Sacro Cuore School with Adriana and Anna Bank again, but I know I am not allowed to remain there in the convent much longer.

When I tell La Madre what happened, she is sad, but she already knew.

"Concettina, God commands us to honor our mother and father."

"I know, Madre, Dad used to be my hero. He said terrible things about Mom and he kicked me aside with his boot," I say, trying to steady my voice and fight the tears.

"I know, Concettina. He does not see your pain. He does not understand. Regardless, your behavior was reprehensible. You need to write him a letter."

I tell La Madre that I do not really feel like writing a letter. The day after I ran away from home, La Madre contacted Dad to tell him I was at the convent. La Madre explained to my father that it was against the rules of the convent for me to stay there.

In fact, I was not allowed to go back up to the room I shared with Adriana; I had to use one of the guest bedrooms.

I try to get involved in my homework but I can't. I try to avoid La Madre every time she sees me because she keeps asking me if I have written the letter yet, and I keep answering that I have not.

"I'll tell Suor Teresina to help you write the letter. She is a very good writer," La Madre says.

Suor Teresina composes a beautiful letter that sounds like a letter from a romance, begging forgiveness, gushing with love and Christian devotion from a dutiful daughter to her beloved father. I beg Suor Teresina to tone it way down but, after the third try, it is still dripping with love and apologies. I have no choice but to copy the final letter that Suor Teresina is going to send to Dad.

It is the end of the spring semester, my last days at the Sacro Cuore School, and my last day at the convent. I like to think that La Madre and Suor Teresina are just as sad to see me go as I am to leave them.

***

I am back home on Pizza Edison for good. I am happy to talk and laugh with my brothers who are back from the Franciscan's. Ina is doing an internship at the hospital but she is on vacation for a month. She looks beautiful in her nurse's uniform. There is something different in Ina's behavior. She smiles shyly and she seems to always be in the clouds. She is still part of that group of young people who went to Anna's parties. A young man from that group, Franco, comes around often to bring papers and stuff to Ina. He is painfully shy, especially around Dad. He is a close friend of Anna's brother-in-law and also a university student in engineering.

He is not good enough for my sister; I do not think anyone is good enough for Ina, and I tell her that. Ina laughs and tells me I am a nut.

I come to like Yolanda a lot. I especially like her because she understood and took my side when Dad called Mom a bad word. I try to avoid Dad, even though he seems quite friendly; he must have read Suor Teresina's embarrassing letter.

***

Fall semester, for the first time, I am going to a public school, the Insituto Magistrale Giovanni Pascoli, and it is only a little further away than Sacro Cuore.

Paola, a classmate from Sacro Cuore, is also going to Giovanni Pascoli, and I am happy to walk together to this new school.

"You know this school is coed, right?"

"Yes, I know. Unfortunately," I say, making a face.

I am in the same class with Paola in Italian Language and Literature and Latin Language and Literature. In this school, like Sacro Cuore, only teachers walk from class to class. Students remain all day in the same classroom until the bell dismisses them to go home. When I get home, I am totally involved in homework and hardly hear Yolanda yelling at me to take my books off the kitchen table.

In the classroom I keep very much to myself. Like at the Sacro Cuore, students want to read my homework notes.

***

The most interesting professor in school is who everybody calls *Pan Duro* (hard bread). The professor is very proud of that nickname. He teaches philosophy which is the 'hard bread of knowledge,' or in the professor's words, *Il duro pane della scienzia* (the hard bread of science).

Professor *Pan Duro* is a fun person. He is the oldest man on campus and he likes the students. When he enters the classroom, everybody shouts, "Good morning Mr. Pan Duro!"

"Good morning, students. Are you all ready to show me your work?"

The class falls silent immediately; they know *Pan Duro* can be strict. After a long unnerving pause, he checks his grade book and calls on seventeen-year-old Giulio Ferrauto, one of the older students in the class. I sigh with relief because the professor goes by alphabetical order and my name, Gargano, will not be called until the following day. However, this time Ferrauto is complaining that "he worked hard on the written test yesterday and was not ready for the oral test today," and "to please call on to the next student." The professor accepts his excuse and calls, "Gargano." I am terrified! I mumble a little and say, "Professor, I always prepare my oral work with graphs and visuals. So, since I cannot use the blackboard... I can't reach the board and..."

"Oh yes you can," shouts Ferrauto. He goes to the back of the classroom, grabs a small, low chair, puts it next to the blackboard and comes to my desk. With a big flourish, he bows and offers me his hand. The whole class is laughing and clapping. I have no other alternative but to play this game. With a little curtsy, he takes my hand and helps me climb on the chair. Turning my face away from *Pan Duro*, and trying to keep my balance on the chair, I mouth at Ferrauto, *You are going to pay for this!*

Mustering all my brains about me, I read from my entangled notes while writing on the blackboard: "Giovanni Gentile, world-famous philosopher, idealist, pedagogist, born in Sicily. He was Minister of Public Education under Mussolini. He reformed Secondary Schools and to him we owe our strict, very difficult, but beautiful Modern Public Education. Gentile said, 'We do not need to find a place for everybody in school.' The exclusion of a certain number of students from higher public education is our goal and reform. We must steer the student population into more vocational paths, as their wishes and abilities require. Gentile defined the philosophy of fascism as 'the union of the State and the individuals into one inseparable entity.' He was unhappy with Mussolini's interpretation of fascism in 1940, when Il Duce declared war. Gentile was murdered by an antifascist in Florence, April 15th 1944."

When I finish, I jump off the chair while the whole class claps. *Pan Duro* gives me a good grade but I am still fuming. "I will never help Ferrauto with homework, even if he begs," I tell Paola.

At home that evening, Dad asks me how school was.

"It was okay," I say. I feel sorry that I can't be more open towards Dad. I would have told Mom all about Ferrauto and *Pan Duro*.

"That letter that you wrote at the convent, was it your writing?" Dad asks out of the blue.

"No," I say.

"Did the nuns write it for you, and you copied it?"

"Yes," I answer. I see Dad's face sadden and I am sorry.

When I go to my room that night, I am thankful that I do not share Mom's room or the big bed with anyone. However, I am always glad when baby Gianni comes around. He is not a baby anymore but a 6-year-old boy.

He has already started school and made friends. Yolanda is crazy about Gianni. She hugs him and kisses him and constantly combs his curly reddish hair just like

Mom did, even if he gets impatient. She doesn't have any children and Gianni is her baby. Actually, Gianni is everybody's baby.

***

Uncle Frank makes a surprise visit to talk to Dad and Yolanda. Ina is also there for the weekend. The conversation among the four of them soon becomes very animated; everybody is talking at once. Uncle Frank wants to take Gianni with him. Yolanda is very upset and tells Dad, "No you can't! You can't do this. We can't allow it, Gianni belongs here."

"No! Dad, no! We are his family, we are his siblings," Ina is crying, waving her hands and clenching them into fists as she is talking. "He is our little brother!"

I repeat Ina's words aloud with just as much passion. While the argument gets louder in the kitchen, I take Gianni with me down to the *piazza*.

A dog on a leash, that was friendly at first, starts to attack Gianni. I yell at the dog, waving my arms and kicking, trying to scare him while Gianni screams, terrified. Uncle Frank, hearing all the commotion, gives a loud shout at the dog from the balcony, until the owner finally grabs the leash. I hug Gianni until he stops crying and we continue playing. The dog episode, happening just when everybody was talking about Gianni's future, leaves me a little unsettled.

After a while, Dad comes down into the *piazza*, followed by Uncle Frank. Dad walks briskly away from Uncle Frank, who is still talking about Gianni.

"It will also be a help to you. You have a big family to take care of."

Dad keeps walking toward the newspaper kiosk at the end of the piazza and beyond. I go upstairs in the kitchen with Gianni, where Yolanda and Ina cannot be consoled.

For months at night, I keep thinking about baby Gianni and I say the prayer that Mom always said, "Please, dear Jesus, bless baby Gianni and Vario and Ina..."

Chapter 18:

Florence | June 1952

Paola and I take the bus home from school. We do not get home any faster; it is just that we have some money and feel lazy. Paola has passed all her classes and I have just made it through math. That means that I do not have to go to remediation classes and take the math exam in September, before fall semester starts.

"It's not that I do not understand math concepts," I say to Paola. "I do. It's just that I can't visualize numbers. They have no visual characteristics, except the zero, or lots of zeros."

Paola laughs at me loudly. "I know! That's why I always beat you at checkers and chess!"

"No, you don't! Sometimes I win too! Besides, I don't spend the time you do on this game. And having a mother who is a professor helps too."

The bus stops and fills up with people. Paola and I, still standing, are forced to rearrange our positions.

"Do you know it's been almost two years since Gianni left? We hear he is doing well, and will come to see us soon," I say.

"Well, I am an only child," says Paola, "but I can imagine how sad you must have been."

"Yolanda was upset for months. Ina would not stop crying; she practically raised him. She is going with this guy, Franco. I think that he and Anna's parties must have helped her a lot to get over the pain."

The bus fills up with more people and Paola and I are crowded closer and trying to hold on to keep our balance, since there is standing room only. The people are mostly foreign students headed to the Youth Hostel on via San Domenico, or via di Camerata, close to where Paola lives.

"Florence's attitude has changed so much after the war. People are less irritable. Do you realize that more than half the people in this bus are all foreigners? Look!" I say to Paola. "And they all come to Florence! I wonder where they are from?"

"Well, those people down there sound French, and I hear some French words. They are definitely not Spanish," Paola says.

"No, we can tell Spanish right away. What about those guys on the right? In the front of the bus. Those ones laughing all the time."

"They are not Germans. I can't hear any German sounds," says Paola, and I agree with her.

"I hear some English words," Paola continues, "but I can't understand a thing they are saying, so they must be Americans, definitely! Also, they laugh and say 'huao' as they are getting thrown about in this shaky bus! The other people on the right, instead, look very annoyed at being so badly tossed. They must be Italian."

I laugh at Paola and tell her that just because she doesn't understand doesn't mean she is right. Paola is my best friend and I tell her that one day I will be able to understand what those tourists are saying.

I get off at my stop on Piazza Edison but wish I could stop someplace else.

On our way to school, the following morning, I tell Paola that Gianni is coming home to Florence soon. I seem to think about him constantly. I imagine him all grown up and wonder if he misses his sisters and Yolanda hugging and fussing over him. We even send postcards addressing him as, "Gentile Signore Gianni Gargano."

Gianni Gargano. December 12, 1954 during a visit to Florence

***

Ina is seeing Franco, her boyfriend, almost every day now. On a visit home from the hospital she says, "Cettina... I think I am engaged."

"What do you mean?"

"Well, we kissed last night... and I think I am compromised now... and I think that's what it means."

I can't believe my ears! Franco and Ina just kissed! I think about my sister so vulnerable, who felt like she was compromised just because they kissed. I am overwhelmed by inexplicable feelings. My nose feels prickly from the mist accumulating in my nose and eyes.

"What did Franco say?" I ask.

"He said we should be engaged."

"I am so happy for you," I explode enthusiastically, hugging her.

"I thought you said he wasn't... good enough." Ina says.

"What's that got to do with it? Before nothing was sure but now that he's serious, I think he is terrific!" I say.

"You are such a nut!" We both laugh. "I haven't told Dad and Yolanda yet. I am going to wait a while. He has to get his degree. I have to finish my internship." Ina says.

"I shall never get married!" I proclaim loudly. I start dancing in front of the mirror and singing Ina's song dedicated to Signorina De Martino. Ina is very shy but Franco is even more so. I think they are made for each other.

My sister, Ina, engaged to Franco.

***

"This semester has started very badly," I say to Paola as we walk along Viale Manfredo Fanti on our way to school.

"Well, this is it! We have to graduate this year," Paola says.

"I know and I can't concentrate on studying. Ina is back at the hospital and Vario has gone back to the Franciscans. Dad wants Vario to go into the Navy. I am alone again in the house with Dad and Yolanda and I can't stand it!"

"Come and live with us."

"Paola, be serious. I got the first 'F' of the semester. In Latin of all things."

"It's because of the exclusionary rule," says Paola.

"Did I tell you that Ina and Franco are engaged?"

"To be married?"

"Yup! They are so sweet together and they look at each other with such timid eyes and shy smiles. I shall never get married, never!" I say forcefully.

Things are going from bad to worse in school, not just for me, but for everybody. We have all new teachers this year coming from the Commission of the Ministero, in

Rome. The new Italian teacher is returning our compositions this morning and they are mostly F's.

"Did Gargano also get an F?" students ask. "Her compositions are always read in class!" "What's going on?"

"You always get high grades in Italian composition!" says Paola, incredulous. "But I know what's happening. My mom says they are making it harder to go to universities. It's the exclusionary rule."

Paola's mom is a professor of Italian at the Liceo Classico and says that The Ministry of Education is sending commissions of teachers to schools all over Italy for the purpose of redirecting the students. It is still the goal of fascism, as envisioned by the Philosopher Giovanni Gentile, to "redirect the majority of students to vocational and technical schools," but the more the Ministry of Education gets involved in people's lives, the more Italian parents are determined to decide for themselves if they want their children to continue with higher education or not. For that reason, remedial classes spring up everywhere at Giovanni Pascoli, organized and paid for by the parents, where students can attend in groups of five or ten. The parents are so spooked that student are being made to take these remedial classes months before the final exams are due. They have no idea whether students really need remedial classes or not.

Still, knowing my weaknesses, I sign up right away for chemistry, physics, and other sciences.

"It's amazing how much more I learn in closer communication with the teacher," says Paola, who is weak in the same subjects as I am and is taking the same remedial classes.

It is no use. My mind is not focused on studying. I am the only sibling living at home. I come to a point that even seeing Dad's jacket draped on the kitchen chair makes me cringe, and realizing that I dislike it so much makes me even more depressed and unhappy. I cannot communicate with Dad. I avoid him and he knows it.

"Paola, I need to get out of this house. I can't handle it anymore, and this time I can't even run to the nuns. I am going to ask Lisa how she managed to get to England..."

"I'll tell you exactly how she did it. Her father wrote to an agency in London looking for a position as *au pair* for her. The agency wrote back with a couple of names," Paola says as we walk to school.

"What really hurts so badly is that Dad was my hero, he was my strength. During the war I was never afraid, you know? He always used to say to us: *niente paura*."

"Well," says Paola, "I was lucky. I hardly knew my dad. And I don't ever want to know anything about him, either!"

"I suppose I really should help Ferrauto," I say to Paola. "He is begging me for Dante's notes about his exile from Florence."

As soon as we get to the classroom, I sit at my desk and jot down a string of sentences from my notes:

> **Dante Alighieri, born in Florence 1265-1321. Italy's supreme poet, philosopher, politician. The American poet T. S. Elliot wrote that: 'Dante and Shakespeare divide the world between them; there is no other.'**

> **Dante was Prior of Florence during a violent period in the city's history when the two political parties fought bitterly for control of the city. Dante's party, the Guelphs, lost power after the assassination of one of its members. Dante, with many, was exiled under penalty of being burned alive if he ever returned to Florence.**

> **Virgil, the Latin poet who guides Dante during his journey through Inferno and Purgatory, foretells Dante of his own exile:**

> **From Florence then must needs depart...Thou shalt leave everything beloved most dearly..."**

> **Virgil also foretells of the sorrow and humiliation Dante will experience as an exiled, destitute, live-in guest in the richest and proudest Noble Houses of Italy,**

> **"And thou shalt taste how savors of salt someone else's bread, and how arduous a path it is, the mounting and descending of someone else's stairs..."**

> **But Dante has the last laugh; generations of students have read, and will still read forever, the names of Dante's political enemies whom he has thrown into hell. Some of the souls are submerged in crystal clear lakes of ice, some others in rivers of boiling blood, while moaning and pleading for mercy throughout all eternity."**

"I like this," says Paola, who is reading my notes over my shoulders, "but why are you giving them to Ferrauto?"

"I promised him I would. Besides, I have forgiven him since he called me a 'treasure.'" Paola and I both laugh.

Chapter 19:

Graduation | 1953

This is our last semester at the Institute. We have finals in the middle of June and I am very concerned.

The results of the finals are being passed out to the students and there are lots of tears and shouts of anger and grief. A very high percentage of students have failed too many subjects. Passing the exams and graduating from the Pascoli Institute is paramount for students.

I am devastated. I fail six subjects as shown in the first column: Italian, Latin, History, Math, Art History, and Physical Education. Paola tries to be very understanding.

RISULTATO CONSEGUITO DA _Yargano Storia Concetta_

NELL'ESAME DI ABILITAZIONE MAGISTRALE

MATERIE D'ESAME	SESSIONE DI PRIMO ESAME (2)	SESSIONE DI RIPARA- ZIONE (2)	OSSERVAZIONI
Lingua e lettere italiane	–	sei	
Lingua e lettere latine	–	sei	
Filosofia, pedagogia e psicologia	sei		
Storia	–	sei	
Geografia	sei		
Matematica	–	sei	
Fisica	sei		
Scienze naturali, chimica e geografia . . .	sei		
Canto corale	sei		
Disegno e Storia dell'arte	–	sei	
Strumento musicale (_____) (3) . .	–		
Agraria (4)	–		
Educazione fisica (5)	–	sette	

Firenze addì _5 Ottobre_ 19 55

IL PRESIDENTE DELLA COMMISSIONE

"How on earth did you manage to fail Italian?" asks Paola. "The Commission must have on record that you won a Marshal Plan writing competition. And physical education? You always come in second in running and sprint competitions! I don't get it. I tell you, it's the exclusionary rule! They are trying to keep too many students from going to universities." Paola sounds angry. She fails only four subjects.

"Well, look at the bright side," I say to Paola, trying to cheer myself up. "I have not failed chemistry, physics, science, or philosophy, the hardest subjects. I have failed only my easy subjects, except for math."

I have to pass all these subjects in the October session of *Riparazione* (re-takes) and I make a plan of action: I have part of June, July, and August to study for the October exams. I spread all the books of my failed subjects on the desk and divide the pages of the books into four equal parts. I start from the very beginning of the book for two hours and then start another subject for two more hours and so on. For every two chapters, I write a short summary.

Franco, Ina's fiancé, and an engineering student, offers to help me with math. He is very good at explaining things very clearly. We study at the kitchen table while Yolanda quietly gets dinner ready on the kitchen counter.

I am at my desk all day long and do not give up. Sitting for hours makes my back hurt so much that I have to get up and walk about the room. By the end of August, when I can't relieve the pain, I lay on the bed and study like that. Yolanda and Dad walk by the bedroom door to see if I am still alive, but they don't say a word.

Paola comes to see me once in early July. She is going to her family's country house in northern Tuscany for four days, and her mom invites me to join them, but I refuse. I need to study.

Finally, the summer is over and the radio announces that the Commission Examiners have arrived in Tuscany from Rome and are ready to test the tens of thousands of students who failed in the first session.

On the first day of testing, I move like a zombie from one examination table to another through the tests of Latin, Italian, and History. The second day of testing is on the physical sciences – that, thankfully I have already passed – and math.

Math has always been my hardest subject but the test they give me is in algebra. I am happy because I like algebra. Maybe it is because it has more letters than numbers. At the table are seated Miss Emme, my math teacher, and a gentleman examiner. I am given a short algebra problem and I fly right through it. The examiner looks at my math teacher quizzically. I immediately pipe in and tell her that, "as I have been saying to you, I do understand algebra and math concepts, but..." At this point, with a smile on his face, the examiner gets up from the table and goes to another table.

The nightmare of exams is finally over and the results are posted. Yolanda wants to go with me to school to get the results. She is so excited and shouts out loud when she reads that I've graduated. Finally, I've done it!

I do not want to waste time so I go to Lisa's house, which is right across the *piazza*, and talk to her father. He promises to help and writes a letter to an agency in London about a job as an *au pair* for me. I am elated to tell Ina that I am going to England. She is not happy at all and tries hard to dissuade me from leaving but I tell her that there is nothing here for me. She studies at the hospital and will soon be married. Vario is in the Navy and Gianni in Sicily. I can't live here alone with Dad and Yolanda.

***

I do not want to ask Dad for money for the trip, since he has made it clear that he does not agree, but I am over eighteen and, yes, I want to leave. Meanwhile, I find a job teaching a five-year-old to read and write. Her parents are from a well-known, titled, Florentine family with live-in maids. They want their daughter to have an extra advantage before she starts school and I am teaching her how to read.

Her three-year-old sister plays quietly on the floor, in our study room, until one of the maids brings a tray with two glasses of orange juice. One glass is full of blood-red orange juice, the other plain-colored orange juice. When the maid gives the blood-red orange juice to the five-year-old, an immediate burst of loud protests and screams follows from her little sister. The pandemonium is such that the mother comes running down to our room. Scolding the maid angrily, the mother picks up the two glasses of juice and pours the juice back and forth from one glass to the other until the color of the juice is uniformly the same in both glasses. I am stunned for a couple of seconds and feel mortified. *This is a lesson I shall never forget!*

"I am so sorry," I say to Mrs. Al, stumbling for words, "... I should have thought of it."

The little girl learns very fast and her mother is pleased. She compensates me very well and afterwards I have enough money for the trip. The next thing to do is to wait for the British agency.

In the meantime, I get a call from a lady, Mrs. C, also from an old Florentine family. She needs someone to stay with her three children, two girls and a boy, ages six, eight, and ten, two afternoons a week. She received my name from Mrs. Al, the mother of the five-year-old girl whom I taught to read. Mrs. C. needs me to be with the children during their afternoon recreational classes: recital, readings, and classical movies.

The house where they live is one of the estates on the boulevard that goes to Fiesole and it is walking distance from Piazza Edison. The house is huge and beautiful. It is my dream house.

"Mrs. Al says nice things about you. My children go to their 'fun classes' twice a week and they need someone to be with them. Tomorrow they are going to watch Charlie Chaplin in *Limelight*. I would like you to take them," the lady says.

Mrs. C. is not much older than my sister, Ina, and is quite tall and very pretty. I like her immediately and I say, "Yes." The following day I arrive very early but the children are not home from school yet.

I hear Mrs. C. talking and arguing with her-mother-in-law on the other side of the living room. She finally comes to me and after a while says, "Don't mind my mother-in-law. She is angry because I didn't have a conference with her before hiring you. She says I shouldn't hire you because 'you are not even a woman.' Can I ask you a personal question?" she continues, obviously still angry with her mother-in-law.

"Of course," I answer.

"Did you have any problems in school? I mean, did the students pick on you because you look so young?"

"Oh, not at all! My classmates liked me very much, because I always helped them with my homework notes," I answer, with a little pride.

"That's the person I want to be with my children, somebody mature but very young."

As soon as the children arrive home from school, and we all have snacks, the chauffeur takes us to see a private, limited viewing of Charlie Chaplin in the movie *Limelight*.

I like the children, especially Elena, the six-year-old. She has a trusting, beautiful soul and a sincere heart. The job is lots of fun. For two days a week we are chauffeured to their fun classes, or to see the great classic movies.

Chapter 20:

To London, England

Finally, the British agency writes back to me, telling me that a family with two young girls needs a nanny. Lisa's dad takes care of the correspondence and on March 10th they will pick me up at the London main train station. They will have a copy of the February *Time Magazine* in their hands for recognition. I will also carry a copy of the February *Time Magazine.* Dad thinks this is sheer stupidity and very dangerous, and says so to Yolanda.

I tell Mrs. C. that the British agency finally answered. She is delighted for me and wishes me all the best. She also pays me very well and I am grateful.

I make a list of all the people I need to say goodbye to and leave Paola for last.

"When are you coming back?" Paola asks.

"Never," I answer.

"Never"? You are never coming back? You are my best friend. My only friend! You are *never* coming back to Italy?"

"Of course, I will come back to visit. But I will never come back to live here. Look, I need to continue my studies and I don't want to ask Dad. I don't have a home here. Dad and Yolanda want to go back to Naples. Ina is getting married, and my brothers are away. There is nothing here for me. Do you remember Adriana, from when I was at the nuns? Suor Teresina says she is in London also. Why don't you come along?" I say to Paola.

"I would love to but I can't leave my mother alone."

Yolanda wants to accompany me to Milano where I am switching to a train that goes all the way to London. Dad tells Yolanda to definitely accompany me to Milano. Yolanda is very upset that I am leaving and she cries and hugs me at the Milano station as we are waiting for the train to London. She is worried because I do not speak English well yet, and I might get lost.

***

The train trip to London takes 16 hours. We cross part of Switzerland to Geneva, where I am mesmerized by the sight of a cold, lunar light. I remain by the window all night and the following day.

I can't sleep at all; there is so much to see as we race across France. When we reach the channel, a couple of boxcars are detached and are driven on to the ferry. The night is very cold. While we cross the channel, I feel miserable and sick to my stomach and I hardly make it to the sink. People talk to me and I am guessing they are asking me if I feel alright, but I can hardly understand. As I start walking towards the anteroom, I feel like the whole place is gyrating around me and I pass out.

When I wake up, I find myself on the deck, lying on a bench, tightly wrapped in blankets. Two sailors are on the deck asking questions, but I understand English more than I am able to answer, so they smile and give me something hot to drink.

We are back on the train going directly to London's main station and I feel depressed and lonely. I hold on to the *Time Magazine* for dear life, praying that the people will really be there to pick me up. *What if they don't show up,* I worry. An immense sadness and anxiety take hold of me. Dad's words, *this is sheer stupidity,* come to mind, and I start crying. *Dear Jesus! What am I doing?!*

The train slowly stops and I look out the window. A young, pretty face with rosy cheeks and blue eyes is looking right at me. She has black hair and a white complexion. She reminds of Snow White, just slightly fatter. She is excitedly waving a *Time Magazine* and behaving like a person who hasn't seen an old relative in ages. Two young girls are by her side. I walk out of the train in a daze. *Time Magazine* and a small suitcase in hand, I follow my new family out of the station and into a car.

***

Mr. and Mrs. Jacobs live on the outskirts of London with their two little girls, Brenda and Martha. I am trying to learn everything I can about England and British culture as fast as possible. One of the first things I learn is that British people are very polite. They say "please" and "thank you" all the time, even if a "thank you" is not at all needed in context. In fact, when a week earlier I said that the dress Brenda was wearing was beautiful, she said "thank you" so profusely that I left perplexed and wondering why she was thanking *me* so much. According to my Italian culture, no thanks are ever required in this case because I did not *give* her the dress nor did I have anything to do with it. I am concerned because in England, I keep forgetting to say "thank you", especially when my Italian mind tells me I don't need to.

***

Brenda, a sweet ten-year-old, follows her mother around and helps me understand what my duties are: make the girls' beds, do their laundry, get the girls ready for school, and cook their breakfast. Here is the second cultural shock: in Italy we do not cook breakfast. We just have milk and coffee and a brioche or cookies.

It has been almost two and a half months since I arrived in England and I have been running a marathon with myself, trying to learn English as fast as I can, trying to remember everything from the English classes I took in Florence. This conscious obsession distracts me from thinking about Italy, from missing Florence and my family so much.

While I understand almost everything people say, and I can answer accordingly, I realize that people have a hard time understanding me, except maybe Brenda. She knows what I am saying and she repeats it correctly for other people to understand.

Finally, one day Brenda stops me in the middle of a sentence and cups her right hand over her right ear, like someone who was straining to listen. Then, with her hand still cupped on her ear, she makes the loudest sound with her throat as if she was about to spit, "H-h-h-h-hear," she says, and repeats, "h-h-h-h-hear." Then, with her left index finger, she taps her left ear and says sweetly, "Ear, ear." She repeats the whole process a couple of more times.

I remain transfixed, looking at Brenda for a few seconds, and then realize what my problem is; the *h* in Italian is silent, and I forget to pronounce it in *English*. "H-hear and... ear" I repeat correctly. Then, "Thank you Brenda! Thank you so much!" I exclaim, giving her the most necessary thank you that I can muster, "Thank you. You understand what the problem is! Thank you!"

Brenda's parents look at her and seem very proud but I am positive they don't realize how bright little Brenda truly is. She realized that I made the same pronunciation error again and again and she managed to identify it and bring it to my attention. Lisa in Florence had mentioned that it only took six months to *understand* everything, but *speaking* takes a little longer.

***

Mrs. Jacobs needs to go to a clinic for a few days to treat a small skin infection on her arm and Mr. Jacobs is to be out of town. School is over and the girls are left entirely to my care. We play in the yard, read, watch the "telly". We stay up late and we cooked spaghetti with meat sauce. Life is great and soon Mrs. Jacobs comes home.

One Saturday afternoon I am told there is a phone call for me from someone called Adriana. I thank Mrs. Jacobs and am so delighted to hear Adriana's voice that I almost cry.

"Why haven't you called me?" asks Adriana. "I have been waiting for your call and had to ask Suor Teresina for your address."

"I am so sorry! I have your address and phone number but I am still so confused. I am not sure of anything! I don't even know how to make a call, with all those letters in front of the numbers," I say.

Adriana has been in England for more than a year and she knows her way around London. She decides that we should meet at Piccadilly Circus the following day, our day off. Mrs. Jacobs helps me with the directions and what Underground Tube lines to take to get to Piccadilly Circus. This is my very first solo outing in London and I arrive at Piccadilly Circus almost two hours late. I hope to find Adriana still waiting and I start thinking of excuses to tell her, but I have none.

Finally, I see her waving at me with both arms in the air and she yells, "What happened? I have been waiting for hours!"

We are so happy to see each other that we are both in tears. Adriana looks exactly the same, just a little taller and slimmer. Her blonde hair is still tousled around her head. Her laughter is as infectious as ever.

We stop at a cafeteria by Piccadilly Circus Mall and both laugh as we remember our years back with the nuns.

"Do you remember when La Madre came into the Grand Salon and we were hiding by the side doors? You were terrified!" Adriana laughs.

"Of course, I was terrified! How can I forget? I am still terrified just thinking about it," I say. "It was a miracle she didn't see us! You were constantly disobeying her!" I then mention the unbaked cakes she used to make in our room.

We burst out laughing and say how wonderful and incredible it is that here we are, both in London! And nobody is telling us what to do! Adriana lives on Onslow Court in Drayton Garden and is the nanny of the four-year-old son of the English actors Susan Shaw and Bonar Colleano.

"My mom is coming to London next year to be the cook and housekeeper for Miss Shaw."

"This was wonderful," I exclaim.

"No, it isn't. It's an excuse. She is coming to take me back home, but I do not want to go. I do not want to live in that house in Florence."

"Is your mom still the housekeeper for Mr. D.?" I ask.

"Yes, but that's not the reason. I just do not want to live with Mom, she is too austere. Now that I know English well enough, there is no reason for me to remain here according to her," Adriana said.

"What do you want to do with your knowledge of English, Italian, and Slovenian?" I ask.

"I do not know yet. One of my friends is an air hostess with Pan-Am." After a pause Adriana continues, "Concettina, do you have your passport with you?"

"Yes, I do. Why?"

"Can I see it for a minute?"

I take my passport from my handbag and hand it to her. Adriana is reading it very closely and then asks, "Why does it say 'paternity name omitted'? The name of your dad is known and you are legit..."

"Oh that!" I exclaim. "That's the new law that one of the ladies in government pushed through, a few years ago. All the passports are like that now. It's to protect innocent children." I turn to Adriana and she looks as if she has seen a ghost. She murmurs something but I can hardly hear.

"What that means... if you only knew what I went through," says Adriana after a long pause. Then, sobbing, she tells me that every time she has to show her passport, she feels so ashamed it doesn't show her dad's name that she wants to die! She seriously thinks about doing it, she says. She's even made up stories about her life, that she is ill and is going to die. I watch Adriana's face drenched in tears and I can't believe what I'm hearing.

"It's like I am given a brand-new life!" Adriana says.

I try to say something comforting but the only stupid thing I manage to say is, "I am so glad you looked at my passport!"

Adriana is relieved and finally laughs one of her best laughs ever.

I ponder how the previous generation, the Italian-Fascists, were complicit in starting a world war, fomented hatred of brother against brother in a most cruel civil war, and yet, this new generation, my generation, was trying quietly to heal the scars, like this lady in government who wants to protect the innocent.

***

When I get home, I tell Mrs. Jacobs about how wonderful it was to see my friend Adriana again. I tell her that both Adriana and I lived in the convent during our teenage years and next time we meet, my friend and I are going dancing. Mrs. Jacobs is happy for me and she agrees that going dancing sounds very good.

The following week Adriana gets her friends together and we all go dancing. There is Wanda, the girl who works for Mr. Farley, Françoise, a French girl, Julie Nicolau, a girl from Spain, and Adriana and I. Except for Wanda, the Italian girl who works for the CEO of his own company, we all work as *au pairs*.

English-speaking people do not like to pronounce the name Concettina. So, in England I am a brand-new person; everybody calls me 'Tina'.

Everything is so new to me and I enjoy the evening immensely. I dance all night, even though my very high heels hurt. But I never lose track of my goal and I keep asking everybody if they know where I can take evening classes to prepare me for the Lower Certificate in English. Wanda gives me the phone number of an instructor who gives English lessons to foreign students. Her name is Mrs. Blake.

***

Mrs. Blake is a great teacher and suggests that, at the same time, I should also take some classes for foreign students at London University in Russell Square. She also suggests that I start reading English books and she gives me a number of books to choose from. I chose the thinnest book she is offering, *Great Expectations*. She also tells me not to stop looking up words in the dictionary, no matter how much I want or need to.

"Just read right through it. After a few chapters you will realize you understand more than you know," she says.

I obey but find it very difficult not to peek at my dictionary when I find unknown words. Still, perplexed, I continue reading for a couple of more weeks, until I am surprised to find that she is absolutely right! For example, I have never seen the word *briefcase* before, but it becomes quite clear to me when somebody, in the next chapter, puts papers into the *briefcase* and carries it out! I am so excited to have discovered this magnificent secret that I tell Adriana the next time I see her.

Mr. Jacobs helps me fill the registration papers for the University of London evening classes and I start right away. The university is impressive and the foreign students there are much older, mostly from Germany and the northern countries. They are far more advanced than I am, and have better pronunciation. I imagine they are after the Proficiency Title in English. Little Brenda Jacobs tells me that I have learned a lot and speak like a native, and that makes me laugh.

***

Mr. Jacobs, a Rabbi, is being moved away from London to service in the north. We are all very sorry about this but I am most of all, since I have come to rely on them as my family. I am preoccupied and sad. I spend my 21st birthday with the Jacobs and they surprise me with a delicate silver filigree brooch.

"The 21st birthday is a very special day," says Mr. Jacobs. I am very moved and tell them I will cherish this gift forever.

Mrs. Blake, my teacher, who also has a job as an agent for all those *au pair* students she teaches, tells me she has a job for me. It is an *au pair* job in Mr. and Mrs. Lee's home. Mrs. Blake says the Lees live on beautiful grounds in an expensive suburb of London. They have two daughters in their early teens and a boy who is very spoiled by his parents. The little boy, a seven-year-old, has had an Irish nanny since birth, but the nanny is leaving because she cannot put up with the boy's tantrums anymore.

I agree with my teacher to go for an interview and I wear my nicest clothes. The home is very imposing, even more beautiful and much larger than Mrs. Al's in Florence. The place is full of servants and I am received in the living room. Mrs. Lee is a beautiful, gracious lady, and asks me questions about my family. I tell her that my dad was a Marshal Major in the Italian Army, and my mom died a few years ago.

Mrs. Lee wants me to be called 'Miss Tina' by her household and tells me that I should dress accordingly, absolutely be part of the family, and not a nanny. I tell Mrs. Lee that I will do whatever she prefers.

As Miss Tina in London, 1955

"Miss Tina, what are your goals in life?" Mrs. Lee asks.

I answer that at the moment my goal is to continue my education and keep on taking evening classes at the university.

"My ultimate goal is to qualify for the school of interpreters in Geneva and eventually work for NATO (the UN)," I answer.

"This is interesting," she says with a smile. "We will be living in Venice next year for a while, and you will be very helpful to us."

I move in with the Lees and meet the Irish nanny. She shows me my room and helps me with my suitcase. She is crying and I feel sorry for her and tell her so.

"Oh no, I am very happy to go back home, but thank you," she says.

She goes back to her room to finish packing a trunk. I notice her big trunk and am very puzzled. Nobody travels with trunks anymore. I think of my great-grandparents. They traveled with trunks, but they owned the means of travel – they owned the horse and carriages they traveled with! She must have guessed my thoughts because she says, "Mrs. Lee is having it shipped to Ireland."

Peter, the little boy, seems to be a little intimidated by me, and behaves well. I treat him with dignity as I would a teenager and he responds beautifully. My duties are mostly to make sure that all the children get out of bed, are showered, fed breakfast, and chauffeured to school on time. In the afternoon, I am chauffeured around in their Rolls Royce to take care of Mr. and Mrs. Lee's little errands, like going to the post office and delivering papers to the bank and to other important people. Sometimes I shop at the famous Harrods of London for Mrs. Lee.

I am treated very well by the servants and enjoy the luxury of being chauffeured around, as if I am somebody important. This is the easiest job I have ever had in my life and I brag to Adriana and the girls. But I do not feel too guilty because I know I am only paid as an *au pair*.

Mr. Lee is quite a happy person. Every morning he waits for me to go into the girls' bedroom to open the curtains, and then he bursts into their bedroom singing at the top of his voice, "Who wants to be a millionaire, I don't!" I smile and think to myself, *well, guess what – you ARE a millionaire.*

***

Life seems perfect but after five months Mrs. Lee tells me she has to let me go because Peter cries every night that he wants his nanny back. I remain in shock for a few minutes before I fully understand the meaning of the words. I am being fired! I feel rejected and I am devastated. Nothing like that has ever happened to me before. I try to talk to Mrs. Lee but I seem to humiliate myself even more. I call my teacher, Mrs. Blake, and tell her I am being fired. She tells me to come over to her place as soon as I am ready and to stay with her overnight.

It is early evening. The road is deserted and there is no one waiting at the bus stop. I am all alone standing there, only a suitcase with me, which has everything I own in the world. I feel so terribly lonely. A desperate need to cry overpowers me, while I think about how I miss Mom, Ina, and Florence.

I arrive at Mrs. Blake's place and can't hide the fact that I've been crying. She prepares two mattresses on the floor of her study, the same room she uses to give her private lessons.

"I do not want to disturb Mr. Blake. He can be a real nuisance when he wants to be," she says. "He can stay in the bedroom all alone and peaceful. Don't worry about the job and the firing. It happens all the time. Mrs. Lee is going to regret it, which is unfortunate for her."

I understand that Mrs. Blake is trying to cheer me up and I really appreciated it. She comes back from the kitchen with two bowls of stew and we have dinner at her desk. She then takes a box of perfumed talcum powder and sprinkles it on the floor all around the mattresses.

"I hate spiders. This will stop them, in case there is one who wants to crawl on the mattress," she says.

I am tired and exhausted from the silent crying. I feel like I am in a bad dream. The stew warms my stomach and the gentle smell of the talcum powder puts me to sleep. The following morning, I wake up very late. I tell Mrs. Blake that I remembered that today, Saturday, I have a date with Adriana and the girls to go dancing at the club.

"Going dancing is good for the soul," says Mrs. Blake, "and it keeps the body and brain alert."

***

At the club, Julie, Wanda, and Adriana ask me what the problem is with me and why I am acting so strange tonight. I tell them that I have been fired but that I am trying to forget it and have fun. The girls don't seem impressed by my news.

There is a new, *very* tall, handsome American guy on the dance floor tonight. His head floats alone above all others and the girls at my table are making fun of him. Suddenly he is looking at our table and we are all wondering if he is coming towards us. Yes, yes he is. He stops at our table, looking directly at me, and asks *me* to dance. I look aghast around at my friends who start laughing and clapping. *Why me, can't he see I am short?* I follow him to the dance floor and finally he notices how small I am. After a while he asks me if I feel uncomfortable and whether I prefer to go back to the table. I say, "Of course not."

"Great! If you don't care, I don't either. I might ask you again! Let's dance!" he says, with much assurance in his voice.

Then the dance is over, and I go back to the table, where the girls are clapping.

"I must have looked very stupid," I tell Adriana.

"No. You just looked like Concettina who danced with the tallest man in the room," jokes Adriana.

I feel dejected. Yesterday I was fired, today, as the shortest girl on the dance floor, I dance with the tallest man on the dance floor! Why me? But nobody seems worried about my problems in the least. With a heavy heart I go back to Mrs. Blake's place to sleep and with the scent of perfumed talcum powder about me I fall asleep immediately.

***

Mrs. Blake sends me to a family with two boys but they do not need a nanny at all; the boys are teenagers. The parents tell me they need a person to tidy up the house and do light cooking, since both she and Mr. Sims work outside the home.

Mrs. Sims tells me how to cook potatoes and peas and a roast which I cook in the oven, according to her directions. When she returns home early in the evening, Mrs. Sims takes the roast out of the oven, puts it on the butcher block of the kitchen counter and slices it, while its juices and blood splatter all over the counter.

She places the slices on a platter that I take to the dining room table. She takes the peas and potatoes from the kitchen table and distributes them onto four plates that I also carry to the dining room table. She then takes a plate, puts some slices of roast on it and leaves the plate on the counter next to the roast and its spilled juices. "This is for you, you can serve yourself with the vegetables," she says.

I clean a corner of the kitchen table of the spilled crumbs of peas and potatoes and place a clean napkin on it. I then wipe the plate she prepared for me of all the blood and juices splattered on it, put it on the clean napkin, and place a glass of water in front of it. I then free up the only chair in the kitchen, laden with all sorts of stuff, and sit at the table.

What a difference from the Lees home! There, I sat with the whole family in the dining room, served by the maids.

I think about the words of the ghost of Virgil, speaking to Dante as he foretold Dante's exile and the confiscation of all his property by the City of Florence. Virgil warned Dante that he would experience the humiliation of having to eat someone else's food and live in someone else's castle: "And thou shalt taste how savors of salt was the eating of someone else's bread, and how arduous a path it was the mounting and descending of someone else's stairs."

With a pang in my heart, I swallow the roast together with my tears. The lady comes back in the kitchen to cut more slices of roast and stops to look at me seated at the table with my plate on a napkin.

***

The following Saturday afternoon I meet my friends at the club and tell them my sad situation with this new family but Wanda has a much worse problem than mine.

"Mr. Farley is going to Florida and he is taking a secretary along, instead of me," Wanda says angrily.

I don't see why Wanda should be upset at all.

"But that's wonderful," I say, "you are all alone in the house and can do anything you want. We can come visit you and --" Adriana puts her hand on my arm and motions with her head. When Wanda briefly leaves the table, Adriana whispers that Tom Farley is her boyfriend.

"I thought Wanda was Tom Farley's housekeeper," I whisper back.

"That too. He is a creep," says Adriana.

Adriana's mom has been in London for quite a while now as the cook for the British family of actors, the Colleanos, and she is pressuring her daughter to follow her back to Italy. Adriana leaves the club earlier than usual tonight, because her mom gets upset when she is late.

Wanda and I are the last to leave the club and we walk together to the London Tube.

"He never takes me anywhere, just here on the coast, to Brighton. Now he is going to Florida and he takes a secretary instead of me. I hate him," says Wanda with passion in her voice.

"I don't blame you. I would hate him too. I mean, if you are his girlfriend, then fine, he should treat you as his girlfriend," I say.

"Do you think I should go back to Milano?" says Wanda.

"No, I am not saying that at all. I am just talking for myself. If you want me as your girlfriend then treat me as your girlfriend," I say, speaking to an imaginary boyfriend. "But if you want me as a housekeeper, I will be your housekeeper and nothing more. I am not going to be both."

"He used to be so loving and kind before. Did you know his wife left him because he told her he loved me?" Wanda says.

"Oh! No, I didn't even know he was married. So, why didn't he marry you when his wife left him?" I ask.

"Maybe he was ashamed of me. He is very rich. He owns the company."

"Ashamed!" I try to comfort Wanda, who is not even trying to conceal her tears. "Ashamed? You are a very gracious young lady, well-spoken, and you are beautiful, with a very gorgeous figure, to boot."

After a long pause I continue, "Again, I am talking for myself. I remember the last time he had a party at his house for all the people that worked for him. They were all very nice to you. Especially that secretary and her husband. Remember? She had cooked a turkey in a brown paper bag at her home and she brought it over. That evening you should have worn the most luxurious gown you had and…" realizing I am blabbing about nothing but stupidities for the last hour, I finally shut up.

"I am very upset. I told him how much I wanted to go to Florida with him. I hate him." Wanda is still crying.

"I am so sorry you are so unhappy. Frankly, I hate him too," I say.

I hug Wanda good night and leave for the Sim's house.

***

Mrs. Blake tells me to register for the upcoming English tests but I protest that I think I am not ready yet.

"Do it anyway so in a few months you can take the proficiency exam," she says.

I register for the second week of December to take the tests at the university. I study like mad, especially for the translation into English, the hardest part for foreign students because of the need to compose in English.

The day of the exam, however, besides the translation into English, I have to translate an impromptu passage from Agatha Christie into Italian. Everything goes smoothly until I am stumped at the word 'kidnapped'. I have never heard the word before but from the passage I understand it to be something nefarious. Still, I cannot grasp the meaning of the word. After a long struggle, I translate the word into 'sabotaged'. I am elated when the professors give me credit and I pass the tests.

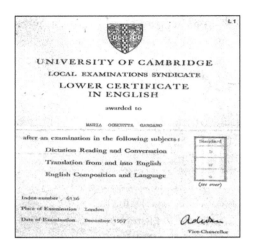

***

It's December, a special month, and I have a list of people to write to and call on the phone before Christmas. It is wonderful to hear from my family and I brag to everyone that I have passed the tests. Ina and Franco are getting married as soon as he gets his degree. His mother won't let him get married sooner and Ina still has one more year to go. She tells me that she would like for me to be there for her wedding. I answer that she can count on me. I will definitely be present at my only sister's wedding! Dad and Yolanda are in Naples and will come to the wedding too. Vario is in the Navy and baby Gianni, all grown up, has sent a photo of himself.

Days before Christmas, I get a phone call and am surprised to hear Mrs. Lee's Irish nanny's voice. She sounds happy and tells me that she has returned from Ireland as Peter's nanny. The nanny tells me that Mrs. Lee would like me to go back to work for her just like before.

"Little Peter improved so much with you and Mrs. Lee is very happy about it. The Lady says that you were a big help to her, and she would like to give you more money and more responsibilities," says the Irish nanny.

I am startled to hear all this but I don't need to think about my answer. "No, I am sorry. I can't come back," I say.

But obviously she has not heard me, because she keeps talking about how appreciative Mrs. Lee feels and how much she needs me back. I feel really sad because it is great to work at Mrs. Lee's.

On Saturday I go to see my girlfriends and brag about my tests. I also tell them that Mrs. Lee asked me to go back but I am not going.

Adriana has sad news. She and her mom are soon going back home. The next time I go to see Adriana, Mrs. Colleano, who is also known as the actress, Susan Shaw, tells me that she would like it if I could work for her when Adriana and her mom leave for Italy.

I tell her that I would be delighted to work for them.

***

Adriana leaves for Italy and we all miss her very much. One of the reasons is her infectious laughter. Even when she is unhappy, she manages to laugh out loud because of some ridiculous thing she's just remembered and makes us all laugh too. Even Wanda manages to burst out laughing and seems to forget her troubles.

I say goodbye to the Sims and start at Mr. and Mrs. Colleano's home. They have a little boy, Mark, and a ten-year-old girl from Miss Shaw's previous marriage. With Adriana and her mom gone, I am the only live-in help at the Colleano's house, with cleaning women and other workers coming in daily. The job is easy. I mostly take care of Mark and his sister when Mom and Dad are busy on-location or at the studios, and take the ten-year-old girl to ice-skating classes on Sundays. I don't want to wait at the bleachers, so I decide to take ice-skating lessons too and I enjoy it immensely.

The three-year-old Mark is a calm, easy-going child and I take him with me every time I need to run errands. Mark loves to ride the bus and squeals with happiness every time he sees cars, buses, and trucks rush by the bus windows.

Every day he asks, "Bus?"

"No, not today, Mark, tomorrow," I answer. I take him on the bus as often as I can because I don't want to disappoint him.

"Bus, bus," he continues. He walks to the garden gate and starts shaking it. "Go bus."

I look at the gate and am thankful that it seems quite safe and strong and the latch is up high.

But today I watch Mark who, standing on his tiptoes on a stone, is determined to reach the latch. He opens the gate and I grab him just as he walks out.

"Oh no you don't! Tomorrow. I promise. We are going on the bus tomorrow," I say as I carry him in the house and make sure the latch is secured and the upper lock is on. The gate worries me because it opens right onto a main road.

As promised, I take Mark for a ride and it is such a delight to watch him. The people on the bus laugh with him because he is so excited.

***

Mrs. Colleano usually comes home from the studio very late, just in time to kiss the little boy good night. But today she is home right after lunch and she keeps Mark upstairs with her. I warn her that Mark can open the gate.

I tell her that I grabbed him just in time as he was walking out of the gate, because he wanted to go on the bus. I repeat my warnings to watch him very closely.

"I heard you. Don't worry," she interrupts me. She sounds tired and annoyed.

Still, I can't relax. Too many people come and go from that gate: the cleaning women, the delivery boys, and the gardeners. I keep telling everybody to make sure to "*please* lock that gate!"

I try to get back to the kitchen to prepare the children's dinner but I am too anxious. I walk back and forth to the gate to make sure the upper latch is locked, while at the same time I sign the delivery boy's receipts and answer the cleaning women's questions.

I go back to the window to look at the gate again and my heart jumps to my throat – the gate is wide open! I rush outside the gate and look at the road in each direction. I then run upstairs.

"Mrs. Colleano, is Mark with you?" I shout.

"No, he is not here. I thought he was with you," comes the answer.

"The gate is open," I shout as I run out of the gate and all the way to the bus stop. Nothing. Mrs. Colleano has taken the car and as she passes me, I shout through her open window, "He loves to go on the bus!"

Mrs. Colleano comes back and, seeing that I haven't found him either, calls the police. Hours and hours go by. It is now evening and sporadic calls – *still looking* – come in. Mrs. Colleano wants to wait to call her husband who is away on-location. Finally, she can't stand it any longer.

"I am going to wait at the police station. I want you to know that I am not holding you responsible," she says in a trembling voice.

I am thankful for her words but I hold myself responsible all the same and I do what my Mom would do. I break into a desperate prayer to God. "Dear Jesus, please, *please* watch over this little boy! I will never be able to forgive myself...please dear God."

I continue praying until finally, very late that evening, there is the call from Mrs. Colleano: "They found him!"

I cry for a long time with relief and gratitude. After a while, she comes home holding little Mark, who is smiling from ear to ear. It took a while for people to realize the little boy was all alone. He was found at a bus depot, miles away. He was having the time of his life getting in and out of buses. As soon as Mr. Colleano comes home, he is told about Mark's adventures, which made the local news.

***

With Adriana my best friend gone, I get closer to Julie Nicolau and Françoise. Françoise is better off than all of us. She has a doting mother who lives on the French Riviera and wants her daughter to get back to France.

Wanda is still very unhappy and my heart goes out to her. I wish I could do something. Mr. Farley is back in England and has very expensive gifts for Wanda but she doesn't seem to care. She says she is going back to Milano but promised she wouldn't leave until Mr. Farley has found a replacement housekeeper. Wanda asks Julie and me if we would be interested.

"You must be joking! Besides, I can't leave the Colleano's," I say.

Mr. Colleano is a fun, very likable guy, just like his son. He takes his daughter and me to the ice rink on Sundays and takes pictures of us skating. Wherever Mr. Colleano goes, he is soon recognized, and people think I must be an important person too. He asks me if I have been on a movie set. I admit that I have never seen one. The following morning, he wakes me up early and Mr. Colleano and I drive to the studio. I am left alone to wander all over the place by myself and the experience is unbelievable. Here and there are small mini parks, sections of streets half-built, and houses with only one front wall. As I wander into a room, someone asks me if I am looking for the make-up studio for extras.

"No, she is with Mr. Colleano. She is visiting," another man answers.

"Mr. Colleano?" says the first man, happily surprised. "Well, have you ever had a cerone put on your face?"

"No." I answer "I don't know what a cerone is."

"Cerone is the special makeup that artists use on the set."

The guy makes me sit and starts plastering my face. "There, you look fantastic. Like you were made of china-glass," he says.

Mr. Colleano is looking for me. He needs to remain at the studio until late tonight and gives me a ticket for the bus. At the bus stop people stare at me. An old lady asks me if I am one of the extras.

"Oh, no," I say. "I am just a nanny."

***

Back home I describe my experience with the cerone to Mrs. Colleano and she laughs and nods knowingly. I also tell my girlfriends when I met them on Saturday about the movie studio and the cerone. None of my friends has ever been on a movie set so I proudly explain everything in great detail.

***

Wanda is leaving by the end of summer and, again, she asks Julie and me if we want to take her place at Mr. Farley's.

I tell her that I would not leave the Colleanos for anything. I am happier there than any other place.

When Mr. Colleano is home, all of us have lots of fun. Tonight, he puts the music on and he and his wife dance the tango all around the house. He then dances with his daughter and pretends to dance with little Mark. He finally invites me to dance too. I have always been told that I was out of tune when I sing, so I try my best to follow him with the music of the waltz.

"What a great dancer you are, Mr. Colleano," I gush.

"You are following pretty well too," he answers.

Pretty soon, Mr. Colleano is leaving to go on location again. This time he is going to be gone for months and everybody is unhappy. Mrs. Colleano is making plans to travel back and forth to her husband's location and will shut down this big house. She is moving to her old London apartment and their grandmother is moving in with her to help with the children. I am asked to come along, but I tell her I do not want to impose, especially if the grandmother is there to help. Mrs. Colleano does not insist and I take it to mean that she prefers it that way. But things do not seem quite right. She has always praised me, telling me she can't have made it without me, especially when we lost little Mark.

The tabloids are full of gossip and rumors implying the Colleanos are in debt or they are separating.

"There are no secrets or scandals but something is wrong," I tell my friends the next time I see them. "Probably a big movie contract that did not materialize for Susan Shaw. I better ask my teacher if she knows of a new position for me."

I then say, "Françoise, tell me when you are leaving for France. I will go to France with you."

"No problem. My Mom can get you jobs in the South of France. She knows a lot of people. Madame Ducarme is the owner of the Hotel Du Cap on the French Riviera. When you are ready, we can talk to her," Françoise says.

"No! Come to work for Mr. Farley," Wanda interrupts, "even if it's only for a couple of months. So I can go back home."

"Wanda, I am not going to live in the same apartment as Mr. Farley. Have you asked Julie?" I say.

"Mr. Farley tells me categorically he does not care for Julie," Wanda says.

"I do not know what to tell you but I am not going to live with Mr. Farley." I say.

"But you will not be living in the apartment. The condos have their private maid's quarters in the basement of the building. Mr. Farley has had the maid's quarters revamped and refurbished with a new bathroom. It's really very nice. Please Concettina, I need to go home," Wanda says.

"So? Why do you care so much? So, go home. I don't understand," I say.

"I promised. I also promised Jeanette, the manager of the retail section. Do you remember the lady at Mr. Farley's last party who cooked the turkey in a brown paper bag? You liked her. She was also begging me to be sure to find a housekeeper before I leave," Wanda says.

***

Back at the Colleano's, I help Mrs. Colleano finish packing the children's stuff. Later we go to the ice-skating rink for the last time. There I meet Arnold again. He is a handsome, young Englishman who I like immensely. We've been to a couple of movies and ice cream parlors over the past few months.

"Tina, I hear you are leaving the Colleanos. What is going on? There is so much gossip, one doesn't know what to believe," Arnold says.

"There is nothing going on. Bonar Colleano is going on a year-long stay on location and Susan Shaw doesn't want to be alone in the big house. Besides, she will travel often to go see him," I say.

"Where are you going to be? I would like to see you again sometime. I would like to remain friends and talk about Italy and Venice. One of these days I will go to Venice," Arnold says.

Arnold asked me to go steady a couple of months ago. Unfortunately, I had to tell him that even though I liked him very much, I could not think of going steady with anybody at the moment because of this goal I have in life, which I must follow at all cost.

"I'll leave you my friend's phone number. You can get in touch with me through her. I have no idea where I am going to live for the next couple of months and I don't seem worried at all. I can hardly recognize myself, you know? I don't seem to have a care in the world! I remember how I cried when I was fired by Mrs. Lee. The saddest thing is that I'll miss the Colleanos very much, especially little Mark!" I give Arnold Julie's phone number.

***

Julie, Françoise, and I are going to see Wanda. She is giving a luncheon to say goodbye to her friends. Some are secretaries and Mr. Farley's employees. Jeanette, the manager of the retail business, is also there. They are all saying how much they will miss Wanda.

"Tina, have you already found a place to go?" asks Jeanette.

"No, I have no idea where I will be." I say.

"I wish you would seriously consider coming to work for Mr. Farley. He is a nice, honorable man and very generous. You would do Wanda and all of us a big favor, too.

Mr. Farley is having the room downstairs painted and furnished. Come and see it," Jeanette continues.

Julie, Françoise, and I go to look at the place. It truly is beautiful with a nice desk and a small settee.

"Françoise, why don't you go to work for Mr. Farley," I ask.

"Me? I am constantly flying to Nice for my mom," she says.

I do not know why but suddenly I say, "Yes I will take the job," and immediately regret it.

Everybody at the apartment is leaving and saying goodbye to Wanda. "Do not let anybody take my place, Jeanette," says Wanda, crying.

"Do not worry. Nobody can possibly take your place and nobody ever will. Tina will be a good person for the company. Her input will come in handy," says Jeanette.

I do not seem to comprehend a single thing they are saying.

What on earth are they all talking about? Also, what does Jeanette mean when she says to me, "You will do all of us a big favor, too"?

I do not get what the problem is. Why does it have to be me?

***

Mr. Farley lives in one of the most beautiful areas of London. It is between the Marble Arch area and Hyde Park. The apartment, on the fourth floor, has imposing views of London. It has two bedrooms, a long dining room, a living room, a bar area, and a large family room. That is where Wanda usually entertained her friends.

My duties are very simple: make sure that his suits are back from the dry cleaning, perfectly pressed, and that his dinner is ready by 7 o'clock. Usually, the dinner consists of a lamb chop or salmon and french fries, a salad, and a dessert. The french fries need to be crispy on the outside and tender on the inside. I achieve this by adding a drop of water at the end of the cooking and covering the pan. Mr. Farley has invited me to join him at the table a couple of times but I always decline, indicating that my uniform does not make it proper.

Since he sits at his desk for hours at his corporate headquarters, he demands that the part of his trousers mostly affected by it be smartly pressed with sharp pleats. Usually, the dry cleaner does an acceptable job and I hardly ever need to redo it.

Edith, an older Welsh woman, comes daily to clean Mr. Farley's bedroom and dust. She is not very friendly. I try to be nice at first but she seems to despise me so I leave her alone, and I use the same tone of voice she uses with me when I speak to her. Today she asks me acidly, "Do I need to clean your bedroom?"

"Oh, no. I don't sleep here. I sleep downstairs," I say, just as coldly. She looks at me, surprised.

"Wanda's room was that one," she says pointing at a door. "Her room was always very neat."

"Yes. Wanda is a lovely person and I like her very much. She is my friend," I say.

"We all loved her. She was the perfect lady of the house," Edith says, in a friendly tone this time. *Finally, maybe we can be friends,* I think to myself.

***

It has been more than two months already since I left the Colleanos. I liked working for them and I couldn't help but think about them often, especially little Mark. The stories about them still fill the tabloids with problems and separations but I know none of them to be true.

Mr. Farley comes in this afternoon, August 18th, and shows me a newspaper with the headline:

"Bonar Colleano Was Killed at 3am Driving Back to His Wife"

I read the headlines and am stunned in disbelief. I slump onto a chair, trying to comprehend, and read the headlines over and over.

"Can I do anything to help?" Mr. Farley asks, finally.

"I do not know."

"Can I help Mrs. Colleano or Mark in any way? Let me know if I can be of any help. I wish I could be helpful somehow." Mr. Farley sounds very sincere and quite upset.

The last time I rode in Mr. Colleano's Jaguar was to go to the movie studio. An immense sorrow overpowers me and I break into silent sobs. I appreciate Mr. Farley's concern but I haven't heard from Mrs. Colleano since I left the house. I gave her Wanda's phone number before I left but she never called me. Perhaps it is better this way. I don't have the spiritual strength to see them or talk to them after this horrendous tragedy.

Meanwhile, falsehoods and stories abound in the tabloids. An article says that Bonar Colleano died a couple of months after his son's nanny left. The article shows a photo of a beautiful, young nanny and little Mark on a boat ride with Mr. Colleano. Except that the nanny in the photo is my friend Adriana, who left almost a year ago.

***

Living in this part of London is very advantageous because it is much easier to get to my university classes. Mrs. Blake gives me another book to read: *The Young Lions*. I tell her that I can't get very interested in this book but she tells me to try it anyway.

I miss the relaxation of the ice-skating rink. Now, I am following the lead of a young *au pair* girl who lives in the same building who is taking horse riding lessons. I buy all the proper gear for horse riding, the knee-high boots, the riding breeches, and the cap. I enjoy horse riding just as much as ice-skating; I try to convince Françoise to come riding with me on our days off, but she is not interested.

When the horse rider needs to cross the short road from the park back to the stables, the riding instructor stops the few cars that travel that way. Mr. Farley's chauffeured limousine is halted at the stop sign. As I ride my horse slowly across the path, I look down and notice that Mr. Farley is looking up at me. He recognizes me right away and motions with his head.

At home that evening, as I serve him dinner, Mr. Farley says, "You were riding the horse well, this afternoon."

"Oh, I am just learning. The coach was helping me cross the street," I say as I put the dishes back in the kitchen. "Thank you, Mr. Farley. Good night, Mr. Farley."

***

Mr. Farley can be quite nice and his concern for Mrs. Colleano and little Mark was very touching. He has a very generous soul and I can see how Wanda would have fallen in love with him.

The following evening, Mr. Farley is constantly under foot. He is in the kitchen looking at what I am doing and following me around the place. He asks me if the room downstairs is exactly what I need.

"Yes, thank you," I say and leave the apartment to go to my room as soon as I am finished serving dinner.

The following day he comes home earlier than usual and follows me around without talking much. As I serve him dinner he says again,

"Sit down and have dinner with me."

"Oh no, Sir. It's not appropriate attire," I say, indicating my uniform.

"Well, you don't have to wear the uniform," he says.

I almost feel sorry for him. For being so rich, he is not very smart and doesn't know how to communicate with a girl. He doesn't know how to tell a girl that he likes her, nor does he know how to woo her. I think about Wanda and feel sorry for her.

I go back to the kitchen to put the shot glasses back on a high shelf on the kitchen wall. I take a chair, put its back against the wall and climb on it, trying to steady myself holding the glasses.

Suddenly he climbs up behind me, on the chair, bumping me slightly.

What in bloody hell! I almost exclaim out loud, nearly dropping the glasses. I hold on to the back of the chair tightly and puts the glasses quickly on the shelf. I feel Mr. Farley's protruding parts against my body and have no room to move. I try to get off the chair and, in doing so, bend down to his protruding body now almost at my neck, and nimbly jump off the chair.

"Thank you, Mr. Farley for... helping me with the shelf. If you don't need anything else... Thank you. Goodnight, Mr. Farley." I look at him still on the chair and can tell he feels awkward and foolish.

***

Mr. Farley has not climbed behind me on a chair again. He has come home almost every night for dinner instead of eating at restaurants with his colleagues. I always try to have everything ready so that dinner runs smoothly. Tonight is no exception.

The phone rings and it's Arnold. I haven't heard from Arnold in a long while. I tell him that I'm glad and that I can see him tonight.

"You have a boyfriend, Tina?"

"Yes," I lied. "Thank you, Mr. Farley. Good night, Mr. Farley."

I am so happy to see Arnold that I hug him tightly and kiss him.

"What was going on? You sound *way* too happy to see me," he says, smiling.

That is what I love about Arnold. He is firmly planted in a real world and does not allow illusion or fantasy to interfere with his life.

I tell him about Mr. Farley and how he does not have a clue about carrying on a conversation with a girl, or how to woo a girl, or love a woman.

***

One evening Mr. Farley comes home with a beautiful, blue eyed, Irish-looking, young woman, her black hair flowing about her head and down to her shoulders. They are just coming back from a restaurant and she behaves euphorically, betraying her recent use of wine and liquor. I stand behind the bar area and see her exploring the place all by herself while Mr. Farley is taking his usual shower. She stops here and there to admire the art on the walls and take exhilarating deep breaths of approval. She double takes when she notices me.

"Oh, sorry," she says, obviously expecting the apartment to be empty. After a long pause, she asks, "Do you live here?"

"Oh, no," I answer.

There is another long pause and then she asks, "Do you sleep here? I mean... are you going to sleep *here* tonight?"

The girl does not know what to make of me and I do not feel like explaining anything but I oblige. "Oh, no. I do not sleep in Mr. Farley's apartment. I am only the housekeeper."

For two more evenings in a row, she comes back to the apartment right after dinner at a restaurant with Mr. Farley but this afternoon she rings the bell and I open the door. She is all by herself. She says 'Hello' and stomps right in, mumbling. She seems quite angry.

"I went to buy something in one of his stores. Does he make you pay, too? Do you pay for anything you buy at his stores?" she asks.

"Whose stores?" I ask, perplexed.

"Thomas Farley's stores. I understood it was going to be a gift and..."

I interrupt, "No, I never go to the stores."

"Well, they made me pay for it! I even talked to a manager. I bought a new radio and he was making me pay for it!"

"Oh, I am sorry," I say.

"Thom makes me pay. Does he make you pay for things, too?"

"Oh no. You see, I am only his housekeeper. I do not sleep in the same bed with Mr. Farley," I say.

***

It is almost Christmas 1958 and it is the end of my classes at the university. The Irish girl hasn't come back to the apartment.

"After the New Year, I need to go France," I tell Françoise next time I see her. "Also, because Mr. Farley said, *Tina must go.*"

"After having pressured you so much to work for him? No wonder! I think it was all a plan," says Françoise.

"What do you mean?"

"Did Jeanette say Wanda was coming back to London?" asks Françoise.

"I don't know. I think so. I do not remember. Why?"

"Maybe Thom Farley learned something. I'll be delighted if Wanda comes back. She was the best thing ever! Listen, as soon as you are ready to go, I'll call my mom and get in touch with the owner of the Hotel Du Cap. She knows a lot of people," Françoise says.

I call my family and friends in Italy and everybody I know in England to let them know I am going to France.

"Where in France?" asks Mr. Farley.

"The French Riviera," I answer. Mr. Farley seems impressed.

Chapter 21:

To France | Spring 1959

As soon as I arrive in Nice, France, I feel like I am in Italy. It looks like Italy and it seems like people speak Italian but with a French accent – the two languages are that close!

For centuries, Nice and parts of the Riviera belonged to Italy. It officially became part of France as late as 1860. I am delighted because I realize how easy it will be for me to learn French.

From the Nice airport, as Françoise instructed me, I go directly to Madame Ducarme, the owner of the Hotel Du Cap, in Cap d'Antibe, on the French Riviera. She knows of an American couple with five children who need a nanny but not until late summer. The job is for more than a year or two. In the meantime, I am allowed to live at the hotel as a *femme de chambre*, cleaning bedrooms.

I like Madame Ducarme immediately. She behaves like a grandmother to me and is genuinely concerned about my wellbeing.

After a couple of days, Madame Ducarme declares, "Nope! You can't be a *femme de chambre*." She is not happy with the way I clean. I do not remove bar-soap residues from the soap-dish of the shower wall.

"I am going to send you to a lady friend of mine for a month. Her husband is very ill and you can be very helpful to her. After that you are going to see Madame de Cervans," says Madame Ducarme.

As I am told, after a month, I go see Madame de Cervans.

Madame de Cervans lives in a small quaint villa called *La Garrigue,* completely surrounded by woods, in the town of Opio in the Alpes Maritimes of Provence (southern France). She takes care of the villas around Opio by sending crews of painters and cleaners to get the places ready for the owners during the summer months.

One of these places is the *Chateau de San Peir*. The owners of this place, the Alexanders, are due to arrive from America with family and friends – mostly friends, about fifteen of them – in two weeks. A cook and her husband, the Maître D, are already hired and are going to arrive at the chateau the evening before the owners.

"That's where you come in," says Madame de Cervans. "I need a French/English interpreter to help make sense, especially with the cook. The place will be empty until the cook and her husband arrive. You are not afraid of being all alone in the place, for thirteen nights, starting tonight, are you? During the day you will come back to la Garrigue. Are you afraid of ghosts, fairies, horror stories?"

"Oh no, of course not," I answer confidently.

"Well then, let's take your suitcases and let's go," says Madame.

I feel very lucky! With Madame de Cervans, I now have two grandmothers!

***

The place is not really a castle but an enormous rectangular building constructed completely of stones. It stands alone among flowering gardens and bushes and trees, with no other visible houses around as far as the eyes can see. It is a refurbished former monastery. In the front of the building there is an Olympic-sized swimming pool.

The first floor is elegantly furnished, with dining rooms, living rooms, and a restaurant-style kitchen. The second-story is made up of mostly bedrooms. A separate, old stairway takes Madame and I to the third floor, the monastery's original third story. The steps are so old and consumed that at some points each lower step melts into the upper in a continuous smooth uphill walk of cement. At the end of the stairway, there is a large hallway with two bedrooms, each on the opposite wall.

"This is your bedroom," says Madame de Cervans, indicating the one on the left. "The other is for the cook and her husband when they arrive."

The bedroom is light and quite comfortable and the window has a180-degree view down the side of the mountains. At the end of the hallway, opposite the stairs, a long dark corridor opens.

"This is an ancient monastery. I do not know exactly how many centuries old. Come and see how interesting the old cells are, where the monks slept," Madame de Cervans says.

A row of cells runs along each side of the dark corridor. The cells are only the size of a bed, with hardly enough room to squeeze around it. Most of the wooden beds are completely disintegrated. Each door has a little window, with iron bars, that opens and shut from the inside.

"This is so depressing," I murmur as I say goodnight to Madame and her Labrador, who are driving back to la Garrigue. The heavy door of my bedroom, like the two outside front doors downstairs, has a large iron bar that slides into a long iron slot in the door, with no possibility for opening or shutting the doors from the outside.

***

My first night alone at the chateau I sleep like a log, with faint sounds and gentle breezes coming from down the mountains right into my open window.

The following morning, I awake to a great silence. The mountains look so serene and peaceful as I take a walk in the shaded gardens among the tall flowering bushes and trees. I am due at Madame's place for brunch, about a twenty-minute walk down a country road, so I have lots of time to spend snooping around the place.

The first thing I do is go back and look at the cells closest to my bedroom. Some of them are open with lots of old papers lying around that belonged to the previous owner. From the narrow windows I can't see very much and I think about the sad lives of those monks. I then go to check the lower floor which has fantastic views all around. The kitchen, a cook's paradise, has a dark staircase in a corner that goes into the cellar. There, I am surprised to see a large red-carpeted room that looks Arabic in style with Arabic furnishings, and paintings on the walls. Streams of light come from windows rising only three feet tall from the pavement. It has a large central table made of cement and lots of papers are strewn about, like the papers in the monks' cells. Something resembling a tall, smoking glass pipe is on the table.

When I arrive at Madame's I tell her about my discovery. She confirms that it was the previous, dead owner's playroom and all those papers belonged to her. According to local lore, she was quite eccentric.

Late that evening, Madame drives me back to the chateau. That night, after locking the outside front doors and sliding the large iron bars across them, I bar myself into my bedroom and start reading, when I hear strange noises in the house, coming all the way up to my floor. I sit up in bed, alarmed, but with iron bars across the doors, I feel confident nobody can come in.

I tell Madame about the noises when I see her the following day for lunch but she disregards them as sounds coming from down the mountain. During the day, the cleaning women at the chateau are shocked that I am living there all alone.

"You couldn't pay me a million francs to stay here at night," one of the women says.

"They can't even find a couple of men to come and check the place at night," another woman adds.

I refer all this to Madame when I walk down the road to see her every day at her house. In the meantime, the noises keep getting louder and closer to my bedroom. I tell Madame that every night I hear noises that sound like iron bars or iron tools scraping at my door. I am getting more and more frightened but am too ashamed to admit it, or ask Madame to let me stay with her, in her house. Madame de Cervans says it is probably rats running up the walls and the doors but the noises continue every night, louder and louder, and I am too embarrassed to mention to Madame the cliché that "it sounds like angry iron chains being shaken and hurled at my door." All the while, I keep telling myself that ghosts do not exist! And yet there it is – this loud, vicious fury of chains rattling right up to a couple of feet from me. After twelve nights of this terror, finally I cannot handle it any longer.

"It's the thirteenth night in this place! Please let me sleep here tonight, even right outside on the veranda on a blanket," I beg Madame.

Madame sees that I am dead serious. "I'll tell you what, I will give you my Labrador to stay with you tonight," she says.

I am thankful. At night I lay with the dog right next to me when the usual screeching of noises starts. The dog jumps at the door and starts a ferocious barking but the crazy clanking of metal gets louder and louder. The Labrador suddenly looks terrorized, his ears down, his head close to the floor emitting a vicious low bark that terrifies me. I comfort myself with the knowledge, from my time back in the convent, that "neither evil thing nor inhuman entity are allowed to hurt God's children." I hug the dog to quiet him down and remain like that until dawn, when finally we both fall asleep.

When Madame comes to pick us up, the Labrador looks ill. I explain what happened and we take him to the vet. The vet says that he probably was poisoned.

"How is it possible? He was constantly with me until we went up to my bedroom last night. He was with me all night. He did not eat anything, or touch anything until you came to pick us up. The noise terrified him," I say.

Madame de Cervans looks at me.

"And Madame," I continue, "I was so frightened and so thankful that he was with me at all times that I wouldn't have hurt him for the world!"

When the cook and her husband get to the chateau, they occupy the bedroom opposite mine. After a couple of days, the maître D. starts complaining about noises like chains shaking at his door.

***

As soon as the owners and their guests arrive, I become so busy taking care of their needs that at night I fell asleep immediately. My nightmare is finally over!

My job is very simple: I take care of all the guests' needs, from getting stamps and mailing their post cards, to finding out what their menus will be for their breakfast and dinners. I give their laundry to the maids, make sure the ironing gets done, help plan their outings, and contact the best travel agencies for local tours.

This job is also fun. I start every morning with a logbook in hand and knock at bedroom doors getting orders for breakfast and lunch, which I then translate into French for the cook. Usually, it is American bacon and eggs for breakfast and, rarely, the French *café au lait* with pastries.

One particular bedroom is interesting. As soon as I knock, a man opens the door. He is hiding another man with his body, who is standing, totally naked, behind him.

"Bonjour Monsieur! What would you like for breakfast?" I ask the dressed man and, just as I guessed I would, I check American breakfast.

The naked man, unaware that I can see him perfectly well, gestures with his hands, trying to get the other man's attention, and steps back and sideways behind the dressed man.

Trying to be as obvious as I can, I cock my head all the way to the right of the fully dressed man and make sure the naked guy knows I can see him, in all his glory.

"And you, sir? What do you desire for breakfast?" I ask him.

Startled by my nonchalant reaction to his nakedness, the guy tiptoes back to the other room.

"He will have the same," the dressed guy says.

"Merci, Monsieur," I answer and leave to go knock on other bedroom doors. I can't help but giggle, You silly! What makes you think I care if you are naked or not? I had two baby brothers! I guessed right. He was worried he would scandalize me.

At night, exhausted, I fall asleep immediately.

At the end of the month, all the guests are leaving. My job at the chateau is finished. I say goodbye to Madame de Cervans and go back to Antibes to see the owner of the Hotel du Cap, as I was reminded to do. The Hotel du Cap is beautiful this time of year with flowering bushes making a magnificent display. I go directly to Madame Ducarme's office.

Madame is happy to see me. I tell her all about my work at the chateau and that the owners paid me very well. Madame Ducarme tells me that my next job should last a year or two, and I need a picture for my *carte de travail* (work visa).

Photo for la carte de travail, 1959

***

"The Michaels have five children. He is the new head of American Express, in Nice. They are not here yet. Meantime, while we wait for the Michaels to come, I am going to send you to Madame Dassant for a month. She needs someone to serve at the table. She already has a cook and a cleaning woman. Do you know how to serve at the table?" Madame asks. Since I have no answer, she continues, "It's very easy. Here, come with me."

We go to the empty dining room and she makes me sit down. She puts a plate in front of me and two forks on the side. "Now, suppose that a guest has finished eating the first course and she lays her fork across her plate. First, get a clean dish from the buffet, then with your left hand you take the dirty dish and fork away and, with your right hand, you immediately replace it with a clean dish and a new fork. Did you see that? Left hand, dirty dish, right hand, clean dish! Never leave the space in front of a guest without a plate! When you serve food on a platter, always approach the guests on their left. Do you see?"

"Yes, Madame. Thank you," I say, remembering how the maids served at Mrs. Lee's table in England, and hoping I would not mess up.

"When Madame Dassant asks you if you know how to serve at the table, you say 'yes'. Also, wear a white dress and closed shoes, with only an inch heel."

***

The chauffeur takes care of my suitcases and Madame says good-bye with a big hug. We arrive at Madame Dassant's villa in the early evening and the cook shows me to my room, which is on the ground floor next to hers.

Things are happening too fast and I am very tired. I hardly have time to reflect. Last night I slept at the chateau and tonight I am sleeping at the villa. I also hope I'm going to remember, *left hand, dirty dish, right hand, clean dish.*

The following morning, the cook wakes me on time to take breakfast trays to Madame and Monsieur Dassant's separate bedrooms.

Madame Dassant is a beautiful lady, elegant and delicate and, at the same time, very sensitive. The cook tells me she is a marquise from an old noble French family. The husband is also a nobleman from French Morocco. Before going back to their home in Paris, they spend the summer months in their villa on the Riviera.

On the left side of the Villa, past the iron front gates and right before the long driveway, there is a small house where the concierge and his family live. The concierge's family also takes care of the many acres of land that surround the property, all planted with fruit trees, aromatic herbs, vegetables, and flower gardens. Usually, I can spot Monsieur Dassant all alone, walking the grounds early in the morning. Further away from the villa, semicircular fields of young wheat stalks sway gently down the hill as far as the eye can see. In the background shimmers the Mediterranean in all its splendor. I breathe in all this beauty and feel like I am living in a different world, a world of long ago, like the world of Mom's grandparents in Italy, in the late 1800s.

***

I have become good at serving at the table and the first nervousness and gaffs have disappeared with Madame's gentle teaching.

"When people are seated at the dinner table, they chat and like to relax. They enjoy the view of the sea, while they sip their wines. No need to rush serving the other courses, Tina. Just relax," Madame reminds me.

Usually there are six to eight people at the villa for dinner, plus Monsieur and Madame Dassant. The guests are friends and family members. They all seem to like me and have nice compliments for Madame, who tells me to nod and smile but to never talk to the guests.

"It will eliminate unnecessary tension," she says.

***

At lunchtime, usually, it is only Monsieur and Madame. He is always the first in the dining room, sits at the table, and reads the newspapers. He very rarely talks to me. He follows me with his eyes, checking that I put the correct items on the table, and then nods in approval. He is a handsome fifty-year-old man who reminds me of the elegant Navy officers who were Dad's colleagues in Florence.

"After lunch go help Madame with her bath. Go to her shower room and wait for me there," he says to me one day.

After lunch I go to the room to prepare the bath as usual. *Why is he coming too? Is he going to help me bathe Madame?*

I prepare the bath and wait for Madame but it is only Monsieur. I hear a light noise in the corridor but nobody else comes in. Suddenly Monsieur is hugging me and it feels like he has six hands roaming all over my body, his mouth slobbering all over my face.

"Oh you delightful little thing… I have an apartment in Nice, you can go there and wait for me there..." he says.

I am stunned! I put my right hand on his chest and gently try to push myself away. *Oh no! A French Mr. Farley! Is that how a French Mr. Farley behaves?* I ask myself as I look at Monsieur slowly, from top to bottom. He doesn't expect my reaction and looks at me as if struck on the face. My stare stops him cold. Like an officer at attention, he steps back and looks at me, his eyebrows in a deep frown.

I am not going to say a thing! I am not going to say a word! I am thinking to myself.

"Pardon..." he murmurs after a long pause.

I'm still not going to utter a word! Madame is right. Not talking eliminates many problems. Monsieur leaves and I am in a panic. Was that Madame I heard in the corridor a while ago? I get busy around the shower and finally Madame comes in.

"Thank you, Tina. I can handle it," she says calmly, without suspecting anything. I go down to the kitchen to see if the cook needs help. She looks at my face, still flustered by my experience.

"Did Madame finally come in to take her shower? She doesn't need your help?" she asks. I answer that, no, she does not want my help. The cook likes Madame and seems very concerned about her wellbeing.

"She is a very intelligent lady. She taught me how to cook fancy dishes for her dinners."

"She knows how to cook?" I ask incredulously.

"No, she doesn't cook. She just reads the recipes to me and watches me making the dishes. She is a lovely lady. She pays for my trips back home to see my family and sends gifts to them." The cook looks at me intently and I can tell that she knows.

"Tina, I do not want to see her get hurt."

"Neither do I. I would not hurt her for the world!" I answer forcefully. I remember how badly I hurt my mom with the cruel words: *What's he doing here!* I regret having so deeply wounded her just before she died, and I wish I could change the past.

***

Monsieur Dassant hasn't spoken a word to me again, nor has he come early to the dining room to read and wait for lunch.

The cook is getting ready for a big dinner tonight and she is making a stand-up cauliflower. The vegetable is steamed whole in a special pot and then gently transferred on a round platter surrounded by cherry tomatoes. The cook drizzles the cauliflower with a special garlic, oil, and herb dressing, as finishing touches to a very showy dish.

Madame asks me to go tell the concierge that there will be fifteen guests for dinner and to make enough onion tarts. She wants puff pastry for the tarts and only a whiff of seasoned condiments. The concierge's onion tarts, called *pissaladiere*, are absolutely the best in all Provence, according to Madame.

The *pissaladiere* is a typical dish originating in Nice that goes back to the Middle Ages when the farmers harvested their best sweet onions at their peak and baked them into pies which were then offered as gifts to their lords.

Madame asks one of the women to carry the heavy platters into the dining room and remain to help.

Everything is ready and the spectacular view of the sea and sky seem to expand the space of the dining room, making its walls almost disappear. The dinner goes off without a hitch and I am glad. The guests include some of the people I already know and, for the first time, the son of Monsieur and Madame Dassant with two male friends, both Americans, who only speak English. The conversation is mostly in French with some broken English from Monsieur Dassant's son. When I serve the onion tarts the Americans are amazed at the taste and they asked questions. Since no one else is answering, I volunteer in my best English, "They are onion tarts. It's an old recipe and a medieval custom. The farmers used to pick the onions at their peak from their Lords' farms, cook them into pies, and offer them to their master as gifts."

Oops! There is a sudden silence at the table. I look at Madame, who was talking to the people next to her but doesn't seem angry that I spoke to the guests. The Americans are surprised and thank me for the information.

Dinner over, I pass out small, crystal finger bowls of water with two rose petals in each. As the guests move to the living room, they are unaware that I can hear snippets of their conversations in French as I stand by the buffet.

"...of course, she is a maid! What else could she be? She wouldn't do this kind of work otherwise," says the son of Monsieur Dassant.

"She speaks French and English," says Madame.

"No, she is not a maid," says Monsieur Dassant. "She is a student."

From the open windows of the dining room, we can smell the flowers and hear the sound of the sea coming from down below.

***

I remain at the villa a few more weeks until the Michaels arrive from America. Meanwhile, since the dinner guests have become less frequent, I spend more time with Madame in her bedroom and I also spend my leisure time with the cook. Madame Dassant tells me she likes her bed with the down comforter laid right on the top sheet and the outer blankets only if needed. I remove the comforter and blankets and call the housekeeping women to come and learn how to make Madame's bed. When the bed is made, I put my hands under the sheet covered only by the comforter and I am amazed at how wonderful it feels! The comforter is puffy and light; it feels like a gentle cloud of air on my hands. I imagine it must feel wonderful on the whole body! I immediately decide that I want the same luxury in my bed.

I go to the kitchen but the cook doesn't need any help. Actually, very rarely does she want people in the kitchen, except for Madame, who is often there. The two women talk about the menus at length and seem to get along perfectly well. The cook is older than Madame and the two women laugh when Madame says something funny about Monsieur Dassant when he was younger.

"It was very different then. And, you know, after my son, he never touched me again," Madame says, looking at me.

I feel touched and a little embarrassed by this confession and can't help feeling that she knows about the pass he made at me. I look at the cook who is nodding and smiling at Madame.

The cook has been with the family for years, and she always travels with the Dassants. When they get ready to go back to Paris, the cook follows them.

Chapter 22:

Visiting Back Home | Italy, Summer 1959

Since I have a few weeks free before my new job with the Michaels, who haven't arrived in France yet, I decide to go back to Italy to visit my family and I manage to coordinate my timing with Gianni's visit to Florence.

I take a plane and am home in a couple of hours. Everybody is very happy to see me and they all treat me as if I am a great world traveler. Ina, Paola, and Franco have never been away from Italy and have never been on a plane before. They consider me quite intrepid and, to complete a thoroughly modern look, I wear pants and a short jacket. Ina can't stop complimenting me.

"However," Ina says, "I could never wear pants myself, no matter how hard I tried."

Gianni is grown up so much I recognize him mostly by his curly reddish hair! It is late summer 1959 and he is 15 years old. I miss Vario, who is in the Navy and is 19 years old.

Ina and I get to do our favorite thing: walk downtown Florence and stop for an ice cream cone at the *Perche'No?* ice cream parlor that my mother loved. Ina wants to know if I'll remain in Florence now that I speak English and French and whether I'll be there for her wedding, September of next year. I assure her again that I will definitely be there for my only sister's wedding!

***

I decide to go to Naples to see Dad and Yolanda. Dad's whole family comes over to the house to see me. There is my paternal grandmother, my dad's sisters, their husbands, and my cousin, Luzzetta, who is one year older than I. I haven't seen this side of the Gargano family since we left Catania for Florence in 1940. They are all happy to see me and they like to hear about France and England. My grandmother remembers me as a young child who refused to be held by the hand whenever we walked down the street.

"I would hold Cettina's hand but she would twist her hand this way and that way and this way again," says my grandmother, twisting her fist right and left.

This is not the first time I hear my paternal grandmother telling this story and I wish I could talk to her openly. I wish I could tell her that I remembered it vividly but I can't explain to her that I wasn't going to run away anywhere, I just wanted to walk right by her side without holding hands. It was simply that my shoulder hurt when my hand was held that high.

My siblings and I were never close to this grandmother. I never remember kissing her or her kissing me. I look at my grandmother and I feel such sadness and regret that at this time in our lives we are such strangers to each other. Dad looks at grandmother and me.

"That one there – see that little girl there?" Dad says, indicating to me and touching his chest, "It's a pang right here, a hurt right here."

I look at Dad and I tell myself that I must ask Ina about Dad's words and what they mean, because this is not the first time I've heard Dad say that.

***

Before going back to France, I visit Suor Teresina and La Madre and go to a couple of parties at Paola's home to meet her boyfriend.

Suor Teresina tells me that Adriana is trying to get a job with Pan Am and at the convent they are praying that she succeeds.

I am sad to leave my family and Florence but at the same time excited to go back to the beautiful Cote d'Azur (French Riviera) and to whatever my future brings.

Chapter 23:

Villa Miami, Juan les Pins, France | Summer 1959

The Michaels have five children; a set of twins, Anna and Sasha, who are eight years old, Patricia, a seven-year-old, and Lloyd, the only boy, a six-year-old. Cookie, a little girl, is still crawling all over the house.

The Michaels return to the French Riviera, to Juan Les Pins, after a few months spent in Beverly Hills, California, Mr. Michael's hometown. Even though the three youngest children were born in France, they are all American citizens and speak both English and French. Mr. Michael has been promoted this year to General Manager of the American Express Agency of the southern regions of France, including Provence and the French Riviera.

Compared to my suddenly-changed, leisurely life at the Dassan's villa, my time with the Michaels is a whirlwind and I am still trying to adjust to it.

My job consists of doing some light cooking for the children and helping them tidy their bedrooms but, most of all, it's taking care of Cookie. One of the more difficult tasks is keeping her in her crib at night; she climbs out of the crib, crawls all over the house, goes downstairs, and cries for help. I ask Mrs. Michael to get a crib strap belt that connects to an infant harness with cloth rings. Cookie can turn over in bed any way she wants to, she can sit and stand up in her crib but she can't climb out of it. We all sigh with relief and the household can sleep in peace at night.

Cookie is a delightful child who is lucky to have four older siblings but she seems to get on their nerves all the time. I am constantly trying to defend her.

When Mrs. Michael starts out the driveway with all seven of us, two adults and five children, Cookies is miserable and cries.

The more dominant twin complains, "Mom, why do we have to take her along? She is just a pain. She just fusses and cries and is a pest all the time."

Soon all the other children chime in and complain that Cookie is a pain in the neck.

The twin is still adamant, "She is always a problem, she gets into everything. Don't let her come, Mom!"

"Perhaps *we won't let you come,*" I say sternly at her.

"But she is always a problem..."

"That's ok! *I am going to take care of her*! Stop complaining," I say finally.

There is a sudden silence in the car. I take Cookie on my lap where she soon falls asleep. Mrs. Michael looks at me with a silent *thank you* in her eyes. The drive to Nice is a long drive.

***

I've started classes at the Polytechnic in Nice where I mostly study French verbs, grammar, and writing. French verbs are even more difficult than Italian verbs and grammar. In Italian, at least, the spelling is always constant with the pronunciation. Not so in French. Still, I am glad I'm making progress. Also, I've bought the book *Le Rouge et Le Noir* by Stendhal. I am going to follow Mrs. Blake's advice, my English teacher in England, and read *Le Rouge et Le Noir* without consulting the French dictionary.

***

Mr. Michael's agency, the American Express, is very involved with the USO and he suggests that I go and help at the Organization's desks in Nice. English speakers are needed to help American soldiers find the correct answers to their questions. They need information on how to connect with family and send messages. Most of them want to know which are the best places to visit on the Riviera and how to get there.

I usually recommend they follow the coast and go to Antibes, see the Cap, and then stop in beautiful Juan le Pins for lunch, and continue to Cannes and romantic Saint Tropez.

Most of the soldiers are stationed in Germany and they travel by car in small groups. Often, they have their own car. When they decide to go to Antibes, I grab the opportunity and ask for a free ride home.

I enjoy working at the USO. It is not a job, actually and I don't get paid for it. I just receive an allowance for the trip home.

It's the first week of July and there are long lines at the USO desks. Many young soldiers are going back home.

"America! Good home sweet home," sing a couple of soldiers. They are just back from England and are complaining about the serious character of the British people.

"Oh no," I interrupt. "I lived in England and I love the British people and their dry humor," I say enthusiastically, but nobody is listening to a word I'm saying and they go back to chatting and laughing.

"My family is from England, from Liverpool, Lancashire," says a young guy standing to my right.

"Oh! That's nice!" I say, surprised.

"My name is David Jackson, what's yours?"

"Oh, just call me Tina."

"Well, Tina, what are the best places to visit around here?"

"It depends. If you want to go to the left, towards Italy, you can visit Monaco, Monte Carlo, San Remo, and the rest of the Italian Riviera. If you want to go to the right, follow the Cote d'Azur to Antibes and Juan Les Pins. You can continue to Saint Tropez where you can find cheap but nice places to stay for the night."

"Saint Tropez sounds good," he says.

"Oh good! Then you can drive me home. You can drop me off at the Route de la Badine in Antibes. That's where I live."

The French Riviera sparkles this time of year and the trip to Villa Miami takes only 30 minutes.

"Do you live here with your family?" David asks, impressed by the beautiful place.

Villa Miami, as an *au pair* nanny (showing off for Françoise)

Françoise and Cookie, Villa Miami

"Oh, no. I look after Mr. Michael's children. He's the Manager of the American Express in Nice. I work as an *au pair*. I study at the Polytechnic. I need to get the Proficiency in French. Next year I am going to Geneva," I say all in one breath, reciting a story that I know by heart and repeat to everyone who will listen.

***

Back at Villa Miami, Mrs. Michael tells me it would be very helpful to her if I had a driver's license and to think hard about it. I tell her that I would definitely learn to drive. Then I show her my sister Ina's newly-arrived letter: she is getting married on the 27th of July! She is working as an assistant pediatrician in a hospital in Florence. Franco has just graduated from the University of Pisa and has great promises of work.

Mrs. Michael suggests I go to Florence on the 26th of July but to make sure I come back on the 8th of August. That night, she has a function at the Grimaldi's castle in Monaco. I tell her I won't forget and I promise I'll immediately start studying for my driver's license when I came back.

I get busy packing and call my friends, Julie and Françoise, to let them know I'm going to Florence. Mr. Michael tells me that he received a call from a young soldier, David Jackson. He called from Baumholder, Germany, and says he wishes to talk to me.

"I gave him your sister's number in Florence. He says he would love to visit that city. I hope it's okay," Mr. Michael says.

Mr. Michael is a WWII veteran. He served as a second lieutenant in the Mediterranean war. As a platoon leader, he keeps a tender spot in his heart for the young soldiers under his care, and for those who visit his office. I tell him that, of course, it's okay.

***

I arrive in Florence early on the 26th to find great confusion in Ina's apartment and I hardly have time to greet everyone who is there for the wedding. Yolanda arrived on the 25th from Naples without Dad, who was not feeling well. My brother, Gianni, could not come from Sicily, and my 19-year-old brother Vario, on leave from the Navy just for the wedding, is having a screaming fight with Yolanda and Ina. He is accusing the family of having abandoned him as a child at the Franciscan's convent and still upset about how desperate he felt when the friars went to see him to tell him Mom had died.

Yolanda is having none of that. She ends up giving him some money, putting him on the train and sending him back to his unit.

I haven't seen my brother since he was 13 or 14 years old and I am stunned by how big and tall and grown-up he looks. I feel sad for Vario and if he stopped screaming for just two seconds, I would explain to him that at the convent where I was staying, the nuns also came to me to tell me that Mom had died.

Meanwhile, Ina is crying desperately. The fight with our brother is a great tragedy that has befallen her just before her wedding day. Franco tries gently to comfort her but she is crying even more uncontrollably.

"Yes, Ina, cry! Cry hard! Cry all your sadness away," I say loudly.

"No, Cettina, what are you saying?" Franco murmurs.

"Cry all your tears and sorrows away," I continue, still loudly "Tomorrow is your wedding and you start a brand-new, happy life!"

Ina is now laughing and crying at the same time, and Franco looks at me, relieved.

***

The following morning the doorbell rings and Anna and Fiorani come into the room giggling. They are ready to escort Ina to church. The wedding in church is beautiful and serene and ends with a delicious candlelight dinner at Franco's favorite place. That evening, just as Ina and Franco are ready to leave for their honeymoon, there's a call for me.

"Cettina, there is somebody on the phone who speaks English, I think," Ina yells. "It's for you. It's from Germany!"

"Yes. Must be from David Jackson," I say.

"Who is David Jackson," asks Yolanda who is getting ready for bed.

"I will tell you all about it tomorrow, I promise," I say to Yolanda.

Yolanda is getting ready to leave for Naples and, to her many questions, I answer that I met David at the USO. He is an American soldier in the Army Corps of Engineers stationed in Germany. I advised him about what cities to visit on the French Riviera.

"Does he like you?"

"Yolanda, he is just a friend," I say.

"So? Why is he coming to see you?"

"Mr. Michael gave him Ina's phone number."

"So? Do you like him?" Yolanda insists.

"Yolanda, he is just a guy from the USO! He is coming to Florence to visit the city and Mr. Michael thinks I can help with the language."

"Is he going to be here long?"

"Just a few days. I will show him Florence, Michelangelo's David, and..."

"So, are you two going to be engaged?"

"Yolanda!" I say, exasperated, "He is not my boyfriend!!"

David Jackson calls to tell me that he's in Florence and I give him Ina's address. I put on the nicest summer dress I have, red, and slightly off the shoulders. As I see his car park outside, I walk down the stairs to meet him. He stops halfway up the stairs, looks up, and says, "You look...beautiful!" I am not sure he recognizes me, and I hardly remember him.

***

Tourists from all over the world come back in droves to this magical city after the long horrors of the war. David has a small tourist book and map that he is consulting.

The first stop is a look at the copy of the statue of Michelangelo's *David*, standing twenty feet tall in front of Palazzo Medici. Many other famous works, among them Donatello's and Benvenuto Cellini's, are tucked inside the arches of the Loggia to the right of Palazzo Medici.

David wants to see the original, so we drive to the Gallery of the Academy where the imposing torso and pensive frown of David's forehead represent a marvel of sculpture. At the gallery David is taking photographs non-stop.

I show David more Michelangelo statues in the corridor. They are called the *Prisoners* or the *Slaves,* because Michelangelo had left them imprisoned inside the marble. David stares at great length at the figures struggling inside the marble.

"I need to take these for my dad. He is a great painter. He also makes great wood carvings, too," David says, taking pictures.

"My very favorite Michelangelo work is the statue, *The Night*," I continue. "It's one of the four statues in the Medici Chapel, in Piazza San Lorenzo: The statues are *Night* and *Day, Dawn* and *Dusk*. In this instance, Michelangelo becomes a poet, and shows his sense of humor."

As we drive to the Medici Chapel, I explain that the statue, *Night,* is one of the most liked works by Michelangelo. The statue is the representation of a woman in deep sleep.

"The longer you look at her the more she looks real. If you look closely, she seems to be breathing, slowly. A poet of that era wrote that *Night* was sculpted by an angel and 'because she's merely asleep, you can tell she's alive. Rouse her, if you don't believe it, and she'll talk to you!' The statue responds – in Michelangelo's words – 'I am thankful to be asleep and, even more so, that I'm made of stone. For while shame and injury endure, not being able to see or feel, is a great fortune. So, do not wake me! Please, speak softly!'"

Michelangelo. Florence, Cappella Dei Medici -The Night

David sounds delighted to hear this bit of history and thanks me profusely.

After a long pause looking at the statues, we stop in Borgo San Lorenzo, close by the Medici Chapel, for dinner. Borgo San Lorenzo is a busy open-air market, a tourist-favorite. Food is very good there since it is frequented by fussy Italian eaters, most of them owners of the nearby shops.

David is very quiet. He is taking in all the noises and lights of a Florentine summer night. He also seems rather shy.

We wrap up the day at Piazzale Michelangelo, where copies of the statue of David, with the four statues by his feet, dominate Florence's famous panorama.

"How far is Naples from Florence?" David asks, taking pictures.

"Florence is about two hours from Rome and there are two more hours from Rome to Naples. What makes you think about Naples as you look at Florence?" I say.

"The guys stationed in Naples rave about the blue grotto and I would like to see it. Have you been there?" David asks.

"Ah, la Grotta Azzura in Capri. No, I have never been there."

"So, how about you coming along?" David asks.

"I wouldn't be of much help. I hardly know Naples," I say.

"You have been terrific here, in Florence! No, really! I mean it! I would have never known so many details. You make me really see Florence. I hope I can take my mom and dad here someday."

***

I haven't seen my dad in a long time and I decide I can spend the night at his house in Naples.

The following morning, David picks me up early at my sister's and we start on the road to Naples for four long hours by car.

The Gargano family is all there. There is Grandma, Dad's sisters, uncles, cousins, and Yolanda. They are all terribly interested in David. They all like David's car and wand to know if he is my boyfriend.

Grandma Gargano, who has hardly said a couple of words to me my entire life, is speaking to me in Neapolitan dialect, *"Che bellu uaglion, Cettina! nun te lo fa scappa!* (What a handsome boy, Cettina, don't let him escape!),"* she says excitedly.

I am mortified and am just thankful that David would never know what she just said. I watch him smile, say *"si"* all the time, and he doesn't understand a blessed word! "He is not my boyfriend! I am not getting married," I say to everyone.

The following morning David comes to get me and we take the ferry boat for Capri. There we switch to small row boats with only two or three people in each. We get in line to enter the grotto.

The experience is unforgettable. The grotto's entrance is so low we have to lie down inside the rowboat to clear the opening. Still, I'm afraid I'm going to hit the top of the opening, especially when the boat bobs up and down with the waves. Once inside, the roof of the cave opens up to 40 feet high. Suddenly, we are inside a completely different, silent world. The water is a shimmering deep blue and the opening to the cave now is just a small bright hole in the distance. There is an eerie yet comforting silence. We are told that we can swim naked if we want. People around us, who are swimming, don't look naked at all, just a bobbing mass of fluorescent deep-blue light. Even the human voice is strange. The words sound as if pronounced, double. I ask David if he is going to swim naked.

"Are you going to swim naked?" he asks me.

"No," I say.

"Neither will I," he answers.

I thank David for this wonderful experience and I agree with him that it would have been a shame if he had missed it.

***

He comes to pick me up at Dad's place the following morning and we get on the road for Florence, stopping in Rome for lunch.

We arrived in Florence early that evening and go to my best friend Paola's house. She has a small gathering of young people I know from school who speak classroom English only. They are all seated around David and want to talk to him to show off their English but they have a hard time figuring out what he's saying because of his American accent. I can tell that David is uncomfortable and he doesn't understand.

He constantly leans forward as if to ask, "What?"

One of the most obnoxious school chums wants to show off how much of a better student he was. He is strong in chemistry and starts asking David chemistry questions! "This should be easy. It's all formulas made of vowels and letters. No language is needed to understand," he says in Italian and spouts off a couple more formulas while we all turn and look at David.

David is silent. He looks dumbfounded as if someone has spoken to him in three foreign languages at once.

"Well," I say in Italian to our 'chemist' school friend, "did you forget that Italian consonants and vowels are hardly ever pronounced the same as English? How is he supposed to understand you? You need to study your chemistry vowels more." Everybody bursts out in loud laughter and call him '*stupido*'.

David gets up, crosses the room to where I'm seated, bends all the way down to my ear, and asks me quietly, "What is happening?"

"A guy was just trying to show off. He asked you chemistry questions, in Italian, and made a big fool of himself. Everybody laughed at him," I say.

"Those were chemistry questions? I never liked chemistry!" David says.

Paola likes David a lot. "Cettina, he is tall and handsome! Are you two engaged?" she asks me.

"No, Paola," I answer for the umpteenth time. "He is not my boyfriend. I am never going to get married!"

But Paola does not believe me. At the end of the evening, when very few people are around, she asks David, in good English, "Is Cettina your sweetheart?"

David looks at me and says, smiling "Yes, I think so."

***

The following day, I meet David at my sister's place, where Ina and Franco are back from their honeymoon. We all decide to go to Fiesole for dinner and Paola and her friend are invited too. We take David's big, American car, so we can all fit comfortably. Franco's Fiat is too small.

Ina doesn't understand a word of English but Franco and David seem to get along beautifully. Franco is delighted to be David's guide; he knows the surrounding hills of Fiesole overlooking Florence well. He tells David that Fiesole is Etruscan in origin and predates the Romans. It was founded in the ninth century, BC. Franco shows David how to distinguish Etruscans walls and ruins from Romans walls and ruins. He points out the medieval castles and the renaissance villas of the Medici.

David is glad to learn all these facts from Franco and so am I. I don't usually remember the history of places very well and am not an expert at telling ancient walls apart. David is impressed by the Roman amphitheater which is still in perfect condition, and by Lorenzo de Medici's renaissance villa, so elegant and serene.

I remind everyone that on the 8th of August I have to get back to work in France. Mrs. Michael is going to a party that evening.

***

David arranges to be back in Germany by the 9th of August so we decide to make the trip back together. The 7th of August, David picks me up at Ina and Franco's place and we say goodbye.

"Cettina, you know this guy really likes you, right?" Ina says without using names. "But he is very shy. Do you like him?"

"Umm...No. Maybe. I don't know." I get annoyed by the same questions over and over again. "What difference does it make? I am never getting married and I need to continue my education."

We leave early in the afternoon of the 7th. The trip from Florence to Antibes by car is supposed to take a little over five hours.

The Tuscany countryside has gentle hills that seem to be swirling all around as we drive. I tell David they are mostly olive groves where the famous olive oil from Tuscany comes from.

As we get to the highway the view of the sea is on the left and stays with us for a good part of the journey.

"I thought your name was Tina. What's Cettina?" David asks.

"Oh that! Well, you see, my name is Maria Concetta, or Concettina, and my family has always called me Cettina. In England and France, they find it very hard to pronounce it, so they all call me Tina."

"That makes sense."

"It's all my great-grand-mother's fault," I say jokingly. "She was the last matriarch of an ancient, titled family and her name was Concettina La Rosa. You know, I remember very well meeting her. I was not yet four. We had just returned to Italy from Tripoli. She wanted to see my mother, who was her granddaughter. She also wanted to meet my siblings but especially she wanted to see me because I had her name. She sent her horse and carriage to pick us up and take us to her palazzo."

David seems fascinated by this story and surprised by the horse and carriage service.

"I remember vividly sitting low in the carriage," I continue, "and the only thing I could see was the tail and the long body of the horse gently moving up and down, like a see-saw. First the bottom would come up and disappear, then the shoulders would come and disappear." David and I both laugh out loud. "Ina remembers meeting our great-grandmother better than I."

"What were you doing in Libya?"

"My dad was a Marshal Major in the Italian Army. When Mussolini declared war in 1939, the military families had to repatriate."

"Italy suffered more than England during the war," David says.

I agree, and tell David that I remember the war years like yesterday.

"The Italians were fighting against everybody, against the German Nazis, against Mussolini's Fascist Army, against the Allies, and the *Franchi Tiratori*. The *Tiratori* were the nastiest," I continue. "The Tiratori were young Italians, mostly teenagers who adored Mussolini and fell for his hateful, screaming propaganda. These kids were made to believe that Italian citizens betrayed their own country, betrayed Mussolini and his precious allies the Nazis, and they wanted revenge. Il Duce demanded it and these young boys and girls were ready to die for him. The *Tiratori* killed many Italian civilians by shooting at them from windows, terraces, and rooftops."

We fall silent, for a long while, as the sky darkens. The only noise we hear is the car speeding on the road with dusk chasing it closely.

As we get closer to the Italian border with France, the scenery becomes hilly and terribly congested with cars. We wait in traffic for hours. It is almost 7 o'clock and we haven't arrived at the border in Savona yet. Word comes that the border gates are temporarily closed. The Michael's place is a two-hour drive from the border and David feels we are not going to make it there at a decent hour after this long delay. He stops the car and I can see he is beat. More than five hours of non-stop driving added to the two late nights out in Florence and Fiesole has taken its toll, and we still haven't recovered from the weekend's seven-hour trips to Capri and back.

There is no other choice; we have to stop in Savona for the night. I want to pay for my hotel room but he insists. David can barely make it across his room before he crashes on the bed, murmuring "good night." I go quietly out of the room and close the door.

***

The following morning, the 8th of August, I am in Juan les Pins by 11 in the morning. Mrs. Michael is frantic.

"Tina, thank goodness you are back from Italy! We have to go to the Prince of Monaco's this evening."

"I know! You have to go to Prince Grimaldi's party. I haven't forgotten Mrs. Michael. That is why I had to be back in France today at all costs." I tell Mrs. Michael about the line of cars, miles long, waiting on the road to Savona, all trying to cross the border into France.

"We had a wonderful time in Florence, Naples and Capri. But I am glad to be back home," I say.

The children are happy to see me, most of all Cookie, the baby of the house. Her four siblings get impatient with her and make her cry. I usually find myself scolding them to protect her.

Cookie knows that right after breakfast the four older children and Mr. Michael all get in Dad's car parked by the kitchen door. After a long series of goodbyes with Cookie, they leave for school. Cookie, still yelling goodbye, runs as fast as she can from the kitchen door to the living room window but she only catches a glimpse of the car as it speeds away. Sad, she stands by the window as her goodbyes slowly die in her voice. I finally ask Mr. Michael to please back up a little farther down by the living room window before making his right turn and taking off. The next morning Mr. Michael does exactly that. As soon as Cookie sees the car backing up, she runs to the living room window still shouting goodbye. Today she is startled to actually see the car stopped by the window and everybody laughing and shouting goodbye. We are making such a racket that Mrs. Michael comes downstairs to hear Dad, four children, Cookie and me frantically waving and screaming hysterically, "Goodbye, goodbye."

"It looks as if we started a new crazy routine," says Mrs. Michael.

***

The five Michaels, attempting to get a decent photo to send to America.

204

Everything is back to normal. Summer is over and I am learning to drive as I promised Mrs. Michael. I decide to drop some classes at the Polytechnic to take more serious, advanced classes in French. I can't keep myself interested in reading *Le rouge et Le Noire,* by Stendhal, so I decide to start reading *Bonjour Tristesse* by Françoise Sagan instead – a very young writer with a compelling story to tell, according to critics.

Suddenly I hear Mrs. Michael singing at the top of the stairs, *"Tiinaa, there is a call for you from Germannyy! David Jackson!"* I run upstairs and she hands me the phone, smiling and making funny faces.

"Hi, Cettina. How are you? I have been thinking a lot about you lately… (*Cettina?* I am a little stunned at being called Cettina. Only my family calls me that.) I had the best time ever in Italy, and Florence was the most beautiful city in the world. I can't stop thinking about it, and you..."

David tells me that he'll be on the Riviera for a couple of days and would love to see me. I need to take the kids swimming these last few, warm days before school starts and I tell him I would be delighted to meet him on the beach at Juan les Pins, the following day.

***

At the beach, the kids are having a grand time running in and out of the water and speaking English with David, especially the twins. In the corner of my eye, I spot a couple of pretty French *demoiselles* sitting close by. They look at David and giggle. They are not aware of me and I walk closer. They are still talking and giggling and looking at him. Since it seems to be a general consensus that David is tall and handsome, I want to find out why they are making fun of him. I get even closer; they are making fun of his paleness. David, lying on the beach under the blinding rays of a watery, late-summer sun, looks very white, and is totally unaware of those girls being there.

"*Oui,*" I say to them and continue in French, "American soldiers are stuck in German barracks for years and unable to go to the beach and tan."

The young girls, startled at my French, look at me, embarrassed and after a while they disappear from the beach.

I don't know why but for the entire evening I can't stop thinking about those French girls making fun of David. I am a little perturbed by the whole thing and I can't help asking myself, what does it all mean? And why I had even bothered talking to them or why I was still thinking about it, even now?

Before going back to Germany, David tells me he will be off for Christmas and asks if it is ok to come see my family and me in Florence. I tell him my sister, Franco and I would be delighted to have him for Christmas.

***

It's the end of November and a cold, sad-looking day on the French Riviera. Françoise is back in France, this time only for a week, and I am happy to see her while I'm alone at home babysitting Cookie.

"Françoise, I never thanked you properly for helping me come to France. Really, I mean it. If it wasn't for you, I would probably still be working at Mr. Farley's," I say, as we both break down laughing.

"I did write to you that Wanda is back in London, right? It seems he is really going to marry her," she says. "You do remember Wanda, right?"

"Of course, Mr. Farley's *housekeeper!* I am so glad! He owes her that much, and more."

"So, who is this David guy?" Françoise asks.

"Who told you about David?" I say.

"Mrs. Michael. The last time I called, you were at the beach with him and the children," she says.

"It's nothing, Françoise. He is just an American soldier in Germany. I took him around Florence and showed him all of Michelangelo's work. Then we went to Naples and Capri and the Blue Grotto. He enjoyed the trip very much and he is still thanking me. I still need to pass my French classes at the Polytechnic. I will be transferring some classes to the school of interpreters in Geneva."

"You are still thinking about Geneva? Are you sure you want to go there?"

"Of course! You know, the Michaels might be going to live in Paris, at the end of next summer. He is being transferred as manager of the American Express there. I told them I need to continue with my schooling. Mr. Michael said if truly I am positive of what I want to do, he will write a letter of recommendation to the Geneva school."

"How nice. You know, Tina, being an interpreter at NATO means you have to be able to translate orally, simultaneously. That's difficult," Françoise says.

"I know. That's why I want to start as soon as I can," I say.

"If you are going to Geneva, I'll go with you. We can rent a room and share the cost."

"That'll be great," I say. I think of how lucky Françoise is to have a mother that can help her with everything she wants to accomplish.

***

In a few weeks it's Christmas and I need to buy a lot of gifts for everyone. Françoise and I decide to go together with Cookie to shop at Vallauris in the Alpes Maritimes, not far from Juan les Pins. Mr. and Mrs. Michael and the older kids are still skiing in the Swiss Alps.

I buy gifts for all my friends and family in Florence. I even have a little gift for Paola. "Do you think I should buy a gift for David also?" I ask.

"Why, are you seeing him for Christmas? Is he bringing you a gift?"

"Yeah, I bet you anything he will have a gift for me," I say.

As we get out of the shop with arms full of stuff, I hear a voice saying, *"Tiiina! How are you? Still babysitting Cookie, I see!"* It is Helmut, a handsome, wavy-haired, blond German. I introduce him to Françoise and we chat for a while.

"Wow," says Françoise as we get back to the car, "he is gorgeous!"

"Yes he is! And he knows it, too!" I tell Françoise that he is a regular on the French Riviera during the summer months. I will introduce him to her again if she comes back to the Riviera next summer.

***

The Michaels are back from skiing and getting ready to go to Monte Carlo with Mrs. Michael's mother, Princess Kourakine-Ouroussow, for Christmas.

The Princess and her husband escaped from their country during the Russian revolution and were exiled on the French Riviera. They supported themselves by working in managerial capacities at the Casino in Monte Carlo.

Mrs. Michael is so proud of her mom that she tells everybody, "My mom is a princess." I sympathize with her and understand perfectly.

***

I pack all my gifts for my family and friends and leave for Florence. I am going to ask Ina to help me find a gift for David.

In Florence I find an express letter and 20 red roses from Germany.

"You told him that it's my birthday?" I ask Ina.

"Sorry, but he asked."

I read the express letter and put the red roses in a crystal vase that Ina hands me. In the evening there is a call from Germany and I thank David for the beautiful roses. I feel quite emotional and can't remember ever having so much attention for my birthday in Italy, France, or England, except from the first family I worked for as an *au pair*. Ina promises she'll help me find a gift for David.

David arrives in Florence early on the 25th and Ina's place glows with soft, subdued lights all around. The Christmas tree sparkles in a corner and candlelight is everywhere. The dining room table looks beautiful. As David comes into the apartment, we all welcome him warmly.

By the wall there is the piano my mother used to play. After a while David asks, "May I?" He then starts playing a lovely melody.

"Did you know he plays the piano?" Ina, very surprised, mouths silently to me.

I am just as surprised as Ina. I have never heard him play before. I translate for David, word for word, exactly what my sister is saying: "...we finally received the piano back many years ago, and a few more household goods too, from the Italian Government after we repatriated from Libya. Nobody here knows how to play it. It has never been tuned, so it probably sounds terrible to you."

"It's not that bad at all," David laughs and continues playing some fast music, some American Christmas carols, and Silent Night.

We exchange gifts and David hands me a small jewelry box. It is an exquisite gold chain with a heart-shaped, precious topaz stone.

"Like the color of your eyes," David says.

I get emotional but I don't want anybody to know it. Paola and Emilio come to visit us in the evening and we all have a great time. I ask Paola to help me with the translating.

Before David goes back to Germany, we have long conversations. We sit at the table and as he talks, he takes my hand between the palms of his hands. He cradles my hand in his, as if praying. He continues asking me what I want to do in life and if I would be open to coming to visit California. He tells me that he thinks about me constantly.

Almost like in a reverie, David says, "What small, beautiful hands you have!" Absent-mindedly, he keeps holding my hand and talking.

When David leaves, Ina wants to know what was said.

"Well? What did he say? Do you like him?" Ina insists. "He was holding your hand very lovingly, all the time."

"He asked me to go visit California. He said he cannot stop thinking about me and that he loves me and he wants to marry me, and would I want to marry him?" I say, aware that I sound irritated.

"Why are you so nasty?"

"Because... be realistic! He lives in California. As soon as he gets home, he will get back to his life, his work, and his friends. And that will be it! Of course, I like him. So?"

***

A week later I see Adriana in Florence! In Piazza Della Repubblica. I cannot believe my eyes! I haven't seen her since she left the actor Mr. Colleano's house and I took her place as the *au pair* nanny to little Mark. She is holding the arm of a young man and they are both running and laughing. I want to yell and run to meet her, but it's too late. They disappear.

I get a little teary eyed as I remember our time with the nuns and all our escapades. Before I leave for France, I go to see Suor Teresina and she tells me that Adriana works at PanAm as an airline hostess and that she is married to an attaché to the American Embassy in Indonesia. I knew she worked for PanAm, but I didn't know she got married.

***

It's January 1961. I'm happy to be back and promise myself to take time to register for the tests in French and pass them.

At the end of January, I receive an express letter from David. He is leaving for America and gives me his address at Signal Missile Support Agency, in White Sands, New Mexico. He will be out of the Army in October. He ends the express with, "See you then." I refuse to think about what these words mean. Instead, I intentionally wrap myself up in the present, and whatever is happening around me. Spring is a quiet, sleepy time on the French Riviera. I do not need to take the children to the beach and I use this opportunity to study. Besides, I have decided to take the French tests anyway, even if I feel I'm not quite ready. I just want to be done with it.

***

The Michaels are having a dinner party with 16 guests. They hire a professional cook. Mrs. Michael and I will serve and clear dishes. The guests are mostly American couples from the military, the American Embassy, and diplomats. Mrs. Michael's parents, Princess Ourrossow and her husband, are also guests. The dinner has a relaxed atmosphere with people walking about to the buffet and bar and chatting.

One of the topics of conversation is Mr. Michael's new job as Manager of the American Express in Paris, where he is to start in the fall.

When Mrs. Michael passes around a chiseled crystal bowl of shaved ice, with a smaller, hand carved crystal goblet full of caviar inside of it, Madame Ouroussov's face lights up and she gently claps her hands. Not many guests help themselves to the caviar and Mrs. Michael takes the bowls back to the refrigerator in the kitchen.

Dinner is over and I am glad that everything has gone so well. Mrs. Michael did a great job. I think she was the prettiest lady at the party and I say so to Mr. Michael who is still rearranging the dining room chairs.

"Oh, definitely! You are absolutely right. Not only the prettiest but the smartest, too!" Mr. Michael says with a smile.

In the morning, when the cook comes back to finish cleaning the kitchen, she asks, "Tina, would you like some caviar?"

I wrinkle up my nose, "That's fish eggs, isn't it?"

The cook takes two slices of toasted French bread, spreads two teaspoons of caviar on them and gives one to me. "Mm mm..." she murmurs with closed eyes as she eats the toast.

I start eating my toast and am surprised, "It doesn't taste like fish at all!"

"Of course not! It's caviar. This is the first time you've tried it, isn't it?"

"Yes. I have never eaten anything like that before... it tastes like whipped..." I can't find the word to describe this delicious flavor.

"It tastes delicious! That's what it is! You want another one? I know there will be lots of it left over. Only a few people familiar with caviar were here last night: the Michaels, the Ouroussows, and the diplomat," the cook continues. "If you find caviar in grocery stores, don't buy it. It's not good. Never order it in restaurants either. The real caviar is very expensive. Just think! How much money are we actually eating with these toasts, eh?" the cook laughs out loud.

We eat two more pieces of toast with caviar and I'm so glad. If it wasn't for the cook, I would never have known how delicious caviar was.

***

The Michaels are moving to Paris this fall and I call Françoise to let her know. She will be looking for a room for the two of us in Geneva. Before transferring to Paris, the Michaels have to go to America and they'll leave Cookie with me. We'll both stay with Princess Ouroussow in Monte Carlo for the whole month of August.

At the moment, though, Mrs. Michael is putting all problems of traveling and moving, all thoughts and anxieties aside, and for the whole month of July the children and I have fun at the beach in Juan Les Pins. When Mr. Michael gets out of work early, he runs to the beach and runs right into the sea with all the children following. He is having a blast, meeting old friends and making new ones. Mrs. Michael joins us whenever possible.

***

I haven't received mail from David in months. Suddenly, I receive five letters in a row. He scolds me for not writing! He cannot wait to be back in California and sounds unhappy. He misses me. I do not want to get too involved and I just write light nonsense to him.

The beginning of August, just before the whole family leaves for the US, Mr. Michael packs for Cookie and me to go to Monte Carlo. Cookie doesn't seem to mind at all that she is not going with the family to America.

"As long as you're there, she'll be happy. We are going to miss you in Paris this fall, Tina, especially Cookie, and I don't know what we'll do," Mr. Michael says. He hands me a copy of a letter that he sent to the School in Geneva. It is full of praise for me and I blush a little.

Larvotto Beach in Monte Carlo is small but quite beautiful. They say it's man-made because in its natural state it is all rocks and pebbles. Tons and tons of rocks had to be removed and replaced with sand and espaliers of flowers.

I take Cookie with me everywhere I go in Monte Carlo, sometimes just walking the Larvotto sidewalks. Here, I meet Helmut and Morgan, two beach-friend guys from Juan les Pins. I tell them I'll be starting school in Geneva in the fall.

Helmut points to Cookie's nude feet on the sidewalk, "Tina, still no shoes? You have to do something about that."

"I know! Cookie absolutely refuses to wear shoes in the summer. I asked the family for help, but they themselves all go shoeless, even Mr. Michael," I say, carrying Cookie's shoes tied with a string. No matter where we are in Monte Carlo, people comment about Cookie's pretty dress and then laugh at her bare feet and at me, hand-carrying her baby shoes. French children never walk with bare feet on a sidewalk.

***

Back at the house, Mr. Ourrossow is upset because he likes homemade mayonnaise but it always separates when he adds lemon.

"Do you know how to make homemade mayonnaise, Tina?"

"Yes, do you want me to make you some?"

"No, I just want to know how to make it." Mr. Ourrossow gets all the ingredients and starts anew. When he adds lemon, everything curdles up.

"See what I mean?" He flings his arms up in the air.

"Don't quit! Don't stop beating!" I shout. "Don't stop, beat harder, faster… faster… See?" The mayonnaise finally looks beautifully whipped.

Mr. Ourrossow is happy. "I know, don't quit," he says, looking at me.

***

It is the first week of September and the Michaels are back in Juan Les Pins from America. They need to be in Paris by September 14th, the start of school. For a few days the house is in a big uproar. We pack, we all say goodbye, we cry, and we all promise to write. Mr. Michael wants me to write to him about the school. I am sorry to leave Cookie.

The following day, with a heavy heart, I say goodbye to France and leave for Florence. I am enjoying the peace, the silence, and the complete relaxation at my sister's place. Franco, my sister's husband, comes into the apartment bringing the mail. He has two letters for me. The second letter is from David. I open the first and am surprised – it looks like court papers.

"What have you got there Cettina?" Franco asks.

"I am not sure. It's just a copy. It's from the State of California."

"Who is sending it? Look at the signature."

"Jacqueline Samuelson, Notary Public in and for Orange County, State of California."

Franco takes the letter and reads: "Henry E. Jackson, residing at 1108 West McFadden, Santa Ana, California, permanent resident of the United States, does hereby wish to sponsor Maria C. Gargano. Edith Jackson, sponsor's wife, does here by…"

State of California)

County of Orange

Henry E. Jackson, residing at 1108 West McFadden, Santa Ana, California, being a citizen of Great Britain and permanent resident of the United States, having the occupation of Sales Clerk, does hereby wish to sponsor Maria Concetta Gargano, Viale Manfredo Fanti 101, Florence, Italy, born in Naples, Italy and citizen of Italy, as a visitor to the United States for a period of 6 months. Said sponsor will see to alien's departure from the United States at the end of the six-month period.

Attached is proof of sponsor's ability to assume the burden of expenses entailed in this visit.

Edith Jackson, sponsor's wife, does hereby concur in this affidavit.

DATED: February 14, 1961.

_____
Henry E. Jackson

_____
Edith Jackson

Subscribed and sworn to
before me this 14th day of
February, 1961.

Jacqueline Samuelson, Notary Public
in and for Orange County, State of
California. My Commission Expires Dec. 4, 1963

Dated February 14, 1961.

"Well, I think it means that you are going to California and that David's parents are waiting for you!" Franco says, sounding triumphant.

Suddenly my stomach folds in painful knots and I take deep breaths. After a while, I open David's letter and give a quick glance at the writing: *"My darling Cettina, enclosed please find plane tickets to LA. I will be in Los Angeles on that day..."* The knots in my stomach multiply. Franco takes the airplane tickets and reads, "...Departure date, Friday, October 13th from Rome to London, London to LAX... that's Los Angeles. You have a whole month's time!"

***

September 14th is Ina's birthday. I suggest we have a fancy cocktail party. Franco invites his university buddies and some of Ina's friends from the School of Pediatrics. The topic of conversation is mostly *Ina's little sister is leaving for California. He even sent the tickets!*

We have lots of liquor for cocktails but do not make enough finger foods. Renato and Franco are in charge of making the drinks but they do not know much about them. They are measuring the hard liquor as if it's wine. While the music plays and everybody has fun, they are also getting a little drunk. Ina is worried. I tell Ina that a cocktail party is only for drinks, then they all go out to dinner.

"We need more food! Giorgio is getting plastered already!" Renato yells from the corridor. We want to make more appetizers but there is nothing left. Renato and Franco ransack the cupboards and grab as much pasta as they can. Franco puts two big pots of water on the stove and soon Renato and Franco are serving huge plates of spaghetti all around. The sophisticated cocktail party I envisioned ends up as a spaghetti dinner. I should have remembered Italians are more connoisseurs of wines than cocktails.

Yolanda, my stepmother, wants to know if I've decided, finally, to go to California. I tell her *yes* and if I cannot handle it, I can always come back. She wants to make sure I visit Dad before going to America. I tell her I've set aside the last five days for them.

I call all my friends to say goodbye and write to Madame Ducarme and Madame de Cervans. I also write to Mr. and Mrs. Michael in Paris. The hardest thing is talking to Françoise. She has already found a room for us in Geneva and is very disappointed. I am truly sorry and I tell her to come visit me in California anytime.

The day of the departure for Naples, Paola, Franco, and Ina drive me to the train station and I say goodbye to Florence.

***

In Naples, Dad's family, his sisters, their husbands, and my cousins, all come to say goodbye to me.

Dad is worried. "She is so young, and she is going so far away all by herself." Then, there come those usual, sad words. Dad turns to Yolanda and almost inaudibly among the chatter and the noise in the room, he whispers, "That little girl there, see that little girl?" he says, indicating to me, "She is a pang right in my heart, a thorn right here!"

Dad always says that, ever since I can remember. I wish I had the nerve to ask him just what it all means. I wish I had the same rapport with Dad that I had as a child – that period of time, when he was still my hero! He used to say to us, *Niente paura, niente paura,* (nothing to fear) during the war in Florence. I remember he used to hold *my* hand – not my siblings'– as we ran to the shelter with the bombs exploding around us.

Chapter 24:

Leaving for California, USA!

Early in the morning on Friday the 13th of October, I leave Naples for the Rome-Fiumicino airport. It is a three-hour trip, by Train-Italia, of total relaxation, as we speed through the Campania region and the Roman countryside. I admire the beautiful hills dotted with unmistakably Roman ruins and Roman walls. I also realize that I might not come back to this place for a long time.

At Fiumicino airport I board the Alitalia plane for London. From Rome to London, it is only about two hours and forty minutes by air. As soon as I get in my seat, I breathe deeply. All the tension and anxieties of traveling disappear. I did my part to get there on time, now it is the airline's turn to get us there. I settle in my seat, happy and relaxed. I close my eyes and doze off. When I wake up I look out the window and it seems as if we are still over the French Riviera. I look at my ticket and see that the connecting flight in London with British Airways is in one hour. Very anxious, I call the hostess and show her my ticket.

"Oh, no Signorina, we won't be in London for at least one and a half hours, or more. Let me talk to the captain," she says when she sees the horrified look on my face.

She comes back and asks if the captain can see my ticket. When she returns with my ticket, she tells me that the captain called British Airways, who confirms Gargano's connecting flight to LAX.

"Am I going to miss the plane?" I ask, terrified.

"I hope not, Signorina! Do you want me to talk to the captain again?"

"Yes, please. If I miss the connecting flight to LAX, I don't know how to get in touch," I say.

The hostess comes back yet again, "The British Airways captain says they will try and wait for the passenger, as long as possible. Our captain says he will do the very best he can."

After what seems like an eternity to my frail nerves, we land in London with the early evening lights. As soon as the door of the Alitalia plane opens, the hostess asks everyone to please let me speed ahead first. At the bottom of the stairs, I see an officer and he is calling my name. "Miss Gargano. Miss Gargano." He is driving a limousine with flashing red lights. He helps me get in quickly and we race across London airport through the cold evening air, all the way to the steps of a British Airway plane, its headlights flashing, its engines roaring, ready for takeoff. At the bottom of the stairs a British Airways hostess meets me, grabs my hand and my luggage and we ran up the steps.

"We have been waiting for you, Miss!! Welcome aboard." Once inside, the Hostess says to the passengers, "She's here. The Miss from Rome has arrived!" A big explosion of clapping hands startles me as the plane lifts into the air. I feel emotionally drained and murmur, "I am sorry," as I return a hand-wave. *Wow! They are all clapping just for me – they knew about the problem!*

I settle down for a long 16-hour flight feeling completely exhausted and hungry. I welcome dinner being served and fall asleep for a few hours until the sunlight wakes me up. The night is short and I have no idea what time it is, for I have never experienced crossing the time-zone. I look out the window and what impresses me most is the expanse of the landmass down below which, when the clouds temporarily disappear, looks immense. We have been flying for hours and we are still over the US, regardless of which way we look towards the horizon.

I will soon meet David in LA and I wonder if I'll be able to recognize him. The last time I saw him was in January and I can't remember the last time I talked to him on the phone. Or, will he recognize me? We land and as I go through customs, I hear loud and clear, "Cettinaaa!" He is behind the railing, waving and smiling. He gives me a big hug, gets my luggage, and we get into his big American car.

"You are finally here! I didn't think it was ever going to happen!" he says, turning his head quickly to glance at me.

"I almost didn't make the plane. Alitalia was late..."

"I know. I have been calling British Airways, and they told me. I had to make sure you were on that plane," he says as he drives onto the freeway. "I still can't believe you are really here, Cettina," he says as he quickly turns his head again to look at me.

I can't believe I am really here! We drive in silence for a while.

"COD," says David suddenly with a big smile.

"Uh... what?"

"Oh, it's just an idiotic thing young people like to say, nowadays," David says as he puts his right arm across my shoulders and pulls me next to him across the one long seat in the front of the car. "They tell me it's supposed to mean, *Come Over Darling.*"

***

Before arriving at David's parents' house, we stop to have dinner. I'm thankful because I'm starving and can't see straight.

As we sit in the cozy dining room, David is making plans – we will get married next month and get our own place. I am still dazed and I can't answer anything. It is late evening when we get to his parents' house.

West McFadden Ave is a large, quiet street with rows of lovely cottages with colorful flower beds and plants on each side of the street.

Mr. and Mrs. Jackson are friendly and happy to meet me finally! They offer me a hot drink and ask how long I've been traveling.

"Well, from Naples, at my dad's house, to Rome, from Rome to London, from London to Los Angeles."

"You must be exhausted. Here, let's show you your room," says Mrs. Jackson.

We say good night and I crash on the bed.

I revisit the same feeling of loneliness as when I first arrived in London from Italy, a nineteen-year-old who hardly spoke English and didn't know a soul. Mercifully, I am too tired to feel too lonely and fall fast asleep.

***

Today is Sunday. David is not working and he plans to go out for dinner with a married couple that has two babies. We meet them at their big house and they are a lot of fun to be with. George and Moira are close friends of David's and ask me a lot of questions.

"He is like a younger brother to me and seems very happy to be with you. You guys are coming to the company picnic next Saturday, right?" Moira says, putting her cocktail glasses away.

"We think the world of David and we love to see him happy," says George, who is one of David's bosses at the engineering company where they work.

I get the same kind of message from Hal and Lois, another couple, friends of David, who invite us for dinner. They also have children. I get busy helping Lois with dinner.

"Have you already picked a date?" Lois asks me.

"Yes, we have. It's definitely, absolutely, sometime at the end of November or December, right Cettina?" David laughs.

"You know, I haven't seen David, so happy and laughing in a long time," Hal tells me confidentially.

Ina and Franco call from Italy and ask me so many questions. How was I? Was I happy? Was I going for it? Did I like my in-laws? Ina tells me that she is having the dressmaker make the wedding dress we liked, and she will ship it right away. I tell Franco and Ina that this is a completely different world. There is a feeling of great, open spaces everywhere, with expansive, unlimited horizons. Also, the social interaction between Americans is quite different. For example, we went to the home of one of David's bosses and the relation between them was like two equals, friendly. There was not much difference between boss and employee. I tell them that I find it difficult to explain and I will write soon, and that David sends them hugs.

***

After a very delicious dinner one evening, I tell Mrs. Jackson, "Truly, this is the best roast beef I have ever eaten. Even in London!"

Mrs. Jackson says thank you, and she wants to know if we have decided on a date.

"Yes, Mother, it is December 30th," David says.

"That's only three weeks away," Mrs. Jackson says in an alarmed voice.

"Yes, tomorrow we are going to decide on one of the apartments I told you about. They are both very close."

"Where will you have the wedding? Is it going to be in a church?" Mrs. Jackson asks me.

"I am not sure," I say, looking at David. "Yes, I think so. I am Catholic. So, probably there."

"Oh, well! Then I will definitely not be able to attend," she says, walking out the room.

I look at David and he shrugs his shoulders. From my room that evening I hear them arguing and I understand most of the conversation.

"Well! If you want to go, please yourself. But I will not be there!" Mrs. Jackson says, I imagine, answering Mr. Jackson.

"Mother, what's to worry about? There is no problem," David says.

"Yes, there is!" Mrs. Jackson says.

"Like what?"

"You are getting married! That's what!"

"So?"

I don't want to hear any more and I move as far away as possible from the closed door and tell myself that I must talk to David tomorrow.

***

The following day after work, David and I are looking at the same apartments, again. He is very happy and talkative.

"This place is ok. Only temporary, one year or two. We can then get a better place and we might even be able to buy a house. I am just so thankful that you are here with me, Cettina."

Gently pushing myself away from his embrace, I say, "David, I don't know how to say this... and I don't know where to start. Your mother is not very happy with me. Perhaps... we should reconsider..."

"What? What? What are you saying!" David takes a step back and looks at me. His strong reaction totally overwhelms me.

"I can't be the cause of... discontent in your family," I mumble, trying to find the right English word.

"No, don't say that!" David yells.

"It will be okay...I will go back to Italy, and..." I say as calmly as possible.

"Don't say that! Please, do not say that!"

"We hardly know each other and we are both so young," I start to cry a little.

"Please, don't. Please don't even think about it!" David is very upset.

"But she is so unhappy that you are getting married," I say, in tears.

"No!" he yells. "Dear God, No! Please don't!" David is repeating the same thing over and over. "Please... don't go."

His sorrow seems to come right from the depth of his soul. I recognize the same cry of despair from when I was 15 and Suor Teresina came to tell me my 'mother had gone to Heaven that night.'

David's pleading is heart-breaking. He is down on the carpet, half down on his knees, crying.

"Please don't go, Cettina! Don't leave me," he repeats over and over.

Unable to stand it any longer, I say, "Okay, I won't, I won't," embracing him and crying.

We both cry. Then we both stop crying, for a while, then we laugh, then we make plans, and we start by putting a down payment to rent this place.

***

The day of the wedding, Saturday, the 30th of December, David's friend Hal comes to pick me up and take me to church. There are only about six people in church – just a few friends of David's. I walk to the altar all by myself with a very shaky step. Mr. and Mrs. Jackson are nowhere to be seen. After the wedding we go to a party at George and Moira's house. There is music, some dancing, and laughter until late into the night. I decide I am going to be quite happy there and will become friendly with my in-laws. I will have to win them over. I have no other choice. I will have to win my in-laws' friendship.

Ina and Franco call again and want to hear all about the wedding.

"How are you? Are you happy?"

"Yes, yes, I think so," I answer.

"You *think* so? What do you mean, 'you think so!' Cettina, what's wrong?" Ina sounds upset. She wants to know everything. I tell her I'm going to write them a letter as soon as we hang up. Here is the letter I ended up writing to them:

> **Dear Ina and Franco,**
> **I can't stress enough how everything is so different here! When you come to visit, you'll see that this is totally another world! A completely different planet!**

If you were here, you would have seen me in an empty church walking by myself, all the way to the altar. There, a priest and David were waiting, with four of his friends that I hardly know. But <u>you</u> were not here! No one in my family was here. My friend, Paola, was not here, and not one of my friends was here. The only thing I had from home was the dress that was made just for me. It's an elegant, short dress that I will be able to wear also in the summer. I thank you so much. I will cherish it forever. I have no idea when I will be able to see you again.

If I had known his parents were so unhappy about the church, I wouldn't even have mentioned it. Of course, they were not at the wedding. There was no wedding reception but a party that George, a boss and friend of David's, gave that night, at his house.

David and I have a nice place here. He stops by his parents' for a couple of minutes, almost every night after work, before he comes home, which is the right thing to do. This tells you what a nice person he is and I love him very much.

Hope to see you soon.
Bacioni,
Cettina

***

For dinner I am making a fancy dish that I learned from the cook at Madame Dassant's, in France. It's called *vol au vent* (flight to the wind). It is puff pastry shaped into small round bowls filled with pan-toasted shrimp and bits of lobster, in a creamy béchamel sauce. I know that David loves shrimp. The table looks as beautiful as I can make it, considering that I do not have much, but at least we have candles.

"Wow! Candles! And shrimp! What's the occasion!" David asks.

"It is our two-month marriage anniversary," I say. After dinner, we feel relaxed by the scent of the candles and their soft light. I ask, "David, what is it that you really, really would like to do?"

> Carissima Cettina,
>
> Thank you so much for such a wonderful dinner last night
>
> Love you always.

"You mean as a job? Well, I have always been interested in learning how a small engineering company like ours can retain its ability to prosper financially and even become extremely successful."

"And you would be what, then?"

"I would be a Financial Analyst, Manager of Finances, and work directly under the controller of the company."

"Well, you need a college degree of some kind, then. We received a catalog in the mail from Santa Ana College. You might still be on time to register. They have evening classes, too!"

We talk excitedly for a couple of hours while David makes plans. He is going to talk to the college counselors, take as many units as he can, and then transfer to California State University Long Beach.

"And what are you going to do, Cettina? You have always wanted to be an interpreter at NATO since I met you at the USO, in France. Don't you want to be an interpreter?"

"No, I changed my mind. I will go to college and take foreign languages and English Literature. I will also look into that job at Farmers Insurance," I say, looking at David and thinking, *you come first now, David. Your job and your success have priority now. I will be quite happy with Santa Ana College.*

***

I remember that I promised Franco I would keep him informed about David's and my progress with our studies, or he would scold me again, so I write another letter.

1964 / Dear Ina and Franco,

You will be happy to know that David has finished his B.S.B.A and has registered at Cal State Long Beach where he is working on his M.B.A. I have a part time job with an insurance company. It does not pay very much, because I do not do very much. I keep papers and files in order but it helps pay my college tuition. I am taking Foreign Languages and English Literature and I am enjoying myself a lot. I submitted a short story to the Santa Ana College Literary Magazine and won the second prize.

The professor told me to make sure to be at the Awards Banquet. My in laws are coming to the banquet, also. They are quite friendly now. I told the two men of this Jackson family that I will always take Mother's side, if my input was ever desired. I am sending you a copy of the story, because you will have to have it translated.

Bacioni,
Cettina

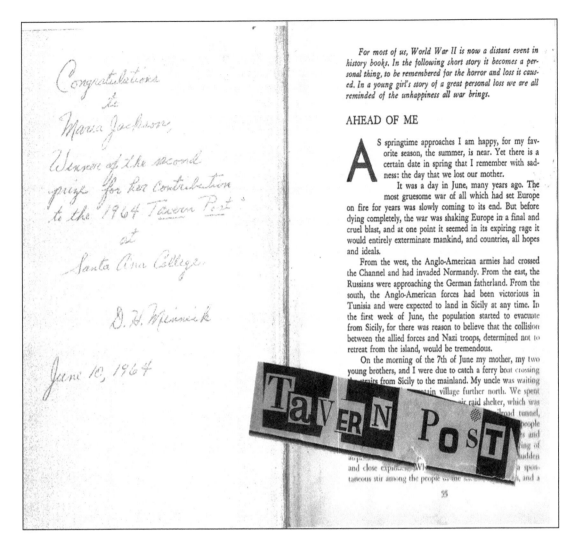

Congratulations
to
Maria Jackson,
Winner of the second
prize for her contribution
to the 1964 Tavern Post
at
Santa Ana College.

D. H. Minnick

June 10, 1964

For most of us, World War II is now a distant event in history books. In the following short story it becomes a personal thing, to be remembered for the horror and loss it caused. In a young girl's story of a great personal loss we are all reminded of the unhappiness all war brings.

AHEAD OF ME

AS springtime approaches I am happy, for my favorite season, the summer, is near. Yet there is a certain date in spring that I remember with sadness: the day that we lost our mother.

It was a day in June, many years ago. The most gruesome war of all which had set Europe on fire for years was slowly coming to its end. But before dying completely, the war was shaking Europe in a final and cruel blast, and at one point it seemed in its expiring rage it would entirely exterminate mankind, and countries, all hopes and ideals.

From the west, the Anglo-American armies had crossed the Channel and had invaded Normandy. From the east, the Russians were approaching the German fatherland. From the south, the Anglo-American forces had been victorious in Tunisia and were expected to land in Sicily at any time. In the first week of June, the population started to evacuate from Sicily, for there was reason to believe that the collision between the allied forces and Nazi troops, determined not to retreat from the island, would be tremendous.

On the morning of the 7th of June my mother, my two young brothers, and I were due to catch a ferry boat crossing the straits from Sicily to the mainland. My uncle was waiting [in a] tain village further north. We spent [the night in an] air raid shelter, which was [a railroad tunnel,] ...people ...and ...ing of ...udden ...and close expl... Wh... a spontaneous stir among the people ...and a

25

***

David and I are invited to my mother-in-law's for dinner tonight. I am always glad because she is a terrific cook, especially with roast beef. She wants to know about my visit to the obstetrician that morning and what the doctor said. I tell her that it is what I thought it was and give her the news that the baby has stopped growing, but the doctor wants to wait one more week.

Ina is also expecting her second child and is already four months along. When she calls me the following day, she wants to know how I am doing and how far along I am. Sadly, I say to her, "This baby will never be born, Ina, because…"

"Why? Did the doctor say that it is not growing? Well, sometimes things happen and are quite normal. The baby grows slowly in the womb, the first couple of months. I encounter it often at work." Ina is a pediatric assistant so she knows a lot about this kind of thing.

"No, you see, I think I know what happened…"

"But did the doctor say the baby is not growing?"

"Yes. The baby is not growing. But let me explain. I think I know what happened. I was crossing the street, when I heard people in their car scream "run, *run.*" I ran like mad and cleared by inches a heavy truck that was speeding towards me. The tremendous blast of air from the truck burned my face and a horrific jolt hit my body from my legs to my head. I stood there paralyzed with fear for a long time trying to breathe normally. The driver, trying to beat the red light, never saw me, never knew I was there."

Ina is silent, then she tries to cheer me up. She makes me promise to call as soon as everything is back to normal from the doctors.

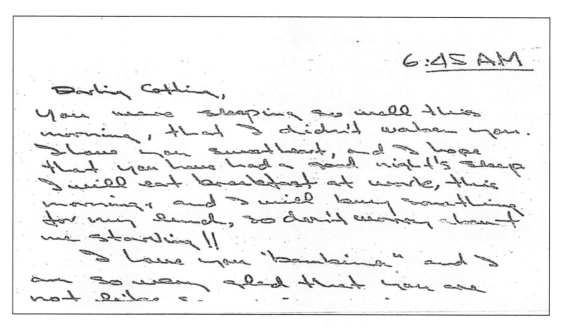

I tell Ina that David is studying very hard and twice a week he drives from Santa Ana to Long Beach State for his two evening classes. Sometimes he spends the night there when the classes end too late at night. The GI Bill pays for his hotel. I take care of running the household to let David have as much time as he needs to concentrate on his work and studies.

***

I involve myself more and more in my schoolwork. In my health class the professor wants the students to give a speech for our final grade. The speech will be pro or con, about the topic *freedom of choice*. We all have to partner with a classmate. The first half hour my partner will be speaking and then I will pick it up for the conclusion. We do not know which side the professor is on but we will be graded on our ability to be persuasive and convince others to agree with us. I tell my speech partner that I think the professor is definitely pro *freedom of choice*.

The afternoon before the day of my speech, I go to the university medical library and check out two fetuses in jars of formaldehyde with a leather carrying case. The babies are in different stages of growth. The youngest baby has legs and arms, well-formed but still tucked under a ballooning belly. The second is an already perfectly-formed miniature baby, with his head in a downcast position.

I tell David that I feel a little spooked carrying these with me, or even just having them in the house, so I leave them on the table by the front door.

"Please, don't show them to me," David says, walking away.

I think about my sister Ina who is a pediatric assistant and I try to get a little more courageous.

Tuesday, the day of the finals, I have all my notes with me and since I am not very good at making speeches, I decide that mine is going to be more like a question-and-answer presentation.

My classmate is at the end of her speech and lets them have it, thundering, "No! You can't do what you want with your body if it means killing a person."

As my classmate goes back to her seat, I gather all my notes and the square carrying case from the university medical library. I say a quick mental prayer, go to the professor's desk, and face the classroom. There are about fifty students in this class, boys and girls, mostly in their early twenties, just a few years younger than I. I introduce myself and begin, "My major is Foreign Languages and Literature. I would like to start my speech by mentioning the tremendous power of words. As a student of literature, I find language is particularly adept at putting people into a beautiful state of mind. It can charm the reader into being aware of something quite sublime that the author has written, only for us. Shakespeare, in particular, was a master of the English language. Iago was weaving a horrific, tragic plot while showering Othello with reassuring words." As the class is listening intently, I address the students more specifically. "For example, when you say, *I want freedom of choice,* nobody could disagree with you. We all want freedom! It conjures up the idea of pure, exhilarating liberty. Just think, *true freedom!* Freedom from my parents' oppressive house rules, freedom to come home anytime I want to at night. But most of all, *rebellion!* Rebellion against society! Against imposed regulation!"

At this point the class becomes noisy, readily agreeing with me. I continue, "I want the freedom to choose whatever rules I want to follow. From my professors I want the freedom to choose whatever exams I want to take, whenever I want to take them, whether it's a speech or not!" The class is laughing and snickering.

"Words flatter us into an alluring sense of wellbeing. I have '*the freedom of choice* to do whatever I want with my body!' Let's see. Can I become a blonde or a brunette? Can I use lime color for my makeup and black-charcoal for my lipstick?" Students are having fun answering yes or no.

"I can exercise my body. Can I lose all the weight I want? Can I change my eyes to blue, naturally, without using colored contact-lenses? Can I choose to make my body grow to an acceptable fashion-size-model height, like 5'11"? The class, looking at me, answers with laughter and a big no. I continue asking more questions in the same vein.

"But I do have the freedom to cut up my arm if I want to! I can do whatever I want with my body! The chances are doctors will think I am crazy, though, and would want to put me in a mental institution." The class suddenly turns quiet.

"If a terminal, incurable disease is growing inside my body, do I have the choice to destroy *it* before it destroys me? Or, supposing I have a baby growing inside of me, can I keep nourishing and breathing life into that little body to prevent it from dying? Or better said, can I please have the '*freedom of choice*' to be able to bring life back to a little person that has suddenly died in me?" I take the two jars out of their case and hold them up high for all the students to see. The classroom yells with a long eeewwww! The students look at me, aghast, their eyes filled with hate for me!

"The words *'freedom' of choice'* are deceiving. *'Freedom to do whatever I want with my body'* is a lie," I continue. "The brutal reality is that *freedom of choice* means a baby in formaldehyde…" The bell rings.

The class starts to roar out of their seats but the professor halts everyone and announces he is stopping all speeches from continuing. We will have a final test, instead. Those who have already given the speeches are done. The class streams noisily out. The professor tells me my grade is an A-. I return the jars to the medical library right after class.

"How did your speech go?" David asks later that day.

"It was a total failure," I say, dejected. "Not only did I gross out the whole classroom, but the story of the jars went all over campus and they all got grossed out. And now everybody knows me and they all hate me. The professor cancelled all the speeches. The bell rang too soon and I could not explain the most important thing…"

"What's that?" David asks.

"Women are being seduced by the words, *freedom of choice!* It's not like they are really fighting for freedom from tyranny, or for liberty, or something like that… They are deceived by the false meaning of the words of *freedom of choice* here…"

"And it's not like this is our great-grandparent's era, when they were ignorant of stuff!" David says forcefully.

***

Ina now has two gorgeous babies, a little girl, Flavia, and a baby boy, Simone. She calls me often to tell me that she is going crazy and asking about how I am coming along, and what the doctor says. I tell her that the doctor is very pleased and my baby is due in March. Franco gets on the phone and asks what is happening in California in Berkeley.

"We hear the students are demonstrating by the thousands. It sounds like anarchy to me, and some students are getting arrested. America just went through the assassination of President Kennedy last year. What is going on in America, Cettina?"

"Ah yes, I remember that morning well. I was driving to classes when they mentioned on the radio President Kennedy had been killed. We all sat in the classroom in a state of shock. The professor was stunned. She told us to go home. Only one student was angry, 'just because this happened, I don't see why we must cancel classes!' Would you believe it? Her question shocked us even more. Yes, but there is no anarchy at the university, Franco. Students are protesting because they want freedom of speech. It's the first amendment of the Constitution and for Americans these are sacred words."

Franco is asking a lot of questions and I try to answer as best as I can, as ignorant as I am about many things. "The university is not forbidding freedom of speech, as such, they forbid political speeches and political activism on campus. That is what I understand. David's father believes that a university should be a place for studying only, period."

"We saw a young student being dragged away by the police and all the students yelling around him. That was pretty scary," Franco says.

"You saw Mario Savio, the leader of the protest. He makes terrific speeches."

"Sounds Italian," Franco says.

"Actually, yes. His father was Italian, born in Sicily. He is an American citizen now."

"Another Sicilian troublemaker," Franco laughs.

I smile because Franco adored his father, who was born in Sicily. He was a highly-respected Colonel during World War I and World War II and a prominent member of the local government.

The next time I have the chance to talk to Franco I tell him not to worry. The faculty has relented and allowed some political speeches on campus. Franco wants to know what party they belong to. I don't understand much about politics in general, especially the American kind.

"Franco, I do not see much difference between the Democratic and the Republican party. They sound very much like 'Americans' to me. The veneration they have for their Constitution, and the First and Second Amendment is what cements all the people together. But I need David to tell me more about this."

Chapter 25:

Children

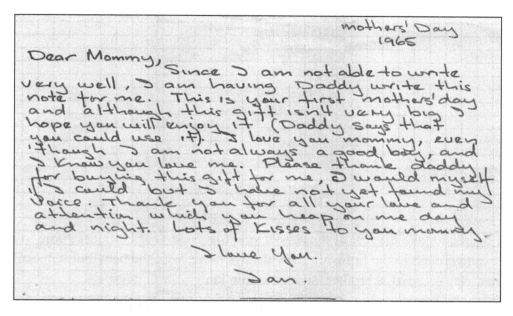

mothers' Day
1965

Dear Mommy,
Since I am not able to write very well, I am having Daddy write this note for me. This is your first mothers' day and although this gift isn't very big I hope you will enjoy it (Daddy says that you could use it). I love you mommy, even though I am not always a good boy, and I know you love me. Please thank Daddy for buying this gift for me, I would myself if I could but I have not yet found my voice. Thank you for all your love and attention which you heap on me day and night. Lots of kisses to you mommy.
I love You.
Ian.

I am so proud of having a son like Ian that I feel like running back to Florence to show him off. I tell David that a professional photographer asked if he could keep Ian's photo in the window of his shop because he thinks he's that handsome! I tell him of course he can.

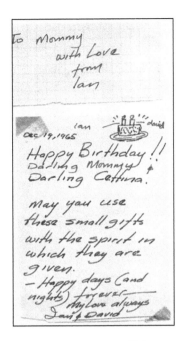

I decide to take the rest of the school year off. Next year I am just going to attend one evening class in the fall while David stays home with the baby but it doesn't turn out that way – Lloyd, a brother, arrives to join Ian.

"I think you should go visit your family in Florence," says David one evening.

I don't wait to be told twice and make immediate plans. I think he is just as eager to show off as I am. I get passports for the babies. Mine is still valid. I am almost packed and as the trip approaches, I think about David who is going to remain here all alone. While David is out shopping for a couple of things, I write him a little note.

When David comes home and reads my note, he gets very emotional and says, "I have been thinking of going too. You go ahead and I will join you in Florence."

"Really? This is so wonderful! It's going to be a beautiful summer in Italy!"

We change plans; the kids and I stop first in Naples, to see Dad and Yolanda, then go to Florence.

In Naples, my parents can't do enough for us. I tell David on the phone that Dad has built a crib for Lloyd and Yolanda has an inexhaustible number of hugs and kisses for the babies. It brings tears to my eyes to see Dad and Yolanda enjoying the American babies so much that I wish we didn't live so far away.

Dad is having fun with Ian, talking to him as if he is a grown-up, showing him how to make things and laughing with him. They seem to understand each other very well. My dad does not speak nor understand a word of English, and two-year-old Ian, though he does not talk very much, still understands me perfectly in English and seems to understand his grandfather perfectly in Italian, too.

When it is time to go to dinner, Dad tells Ian to go wash his hands. Ian comes back and Dad notices Ian's hands feel too *asciutta* (dry). My dad asks Ian again if he washed his hands.

"*Si,*" Ian says.

"*Con acqua e sapone*? (With water and soap?)" Dad seems to enjoy himself.

"*Si, con acqua sapone,*" Ian answers.

But Dad is not giving up. He explains to Ian, as if he is a grown person, that his hand feels too *asciutta* (dry) for being just washed. Dad asks Ian again if he washed *con acqua* (water).

"Si, *con acqua,*" Ian says.

"But your hands are too *asciutta*!" Dad pats Ian's hands again, and shows him, "See? You see what I mean? Feel! Feel! It's *asciutta!*" Dad asks Ian again, "*Con acqua*? (With water)?"

"Si, *con acqua asciutta!* (Yes, with dry water)!" Ian says triumphantly, throwing both his arms in the air. Dad and Yolanda explode with laughter. I have never heard my dad laugh so hard and so long my entire life. With tears running down his face, he hugs and kisses Ian and for days keeps on telling everybody about his grandson washing his hands with *acqua asciutta.*

When the time comes to meet David arriving from the States, Yolanda convinces me to leave Lloyd with them and pick him up on the way back to the US.

"The trip to Florence and the island of Elba will be much easier for the two of you. We can take Lloyd to the beach here, in Naples. It's even more beautiful than Elba," Yolanda says.

"Besides, Nonna Yolanda will be that much happier, too! We have already talked about it," Dad says.

Lloyd is such a calm baby. He is so peaceful, snuggled up in Nonna's arms. Maybe because her arms are bigger than mine.

***

In Florence it is wonderful to see Franco again. Ina and her kids are already at the island ahead of us. I can't believe how much I miss it here! David wants to roam around Florence and see all the things he remembers. After three days in Florence, we finally pack everything in David's rented car, and Franco, David, Ian, and I race on the Autostrada del Sole toward the city of Piombino, on the Mediterranean coast.

"It's similar to the road we took a few years ago, when you had to go back to work, in France, do you remember?" asks David, smiling at me.

In Piombino we embark on the Torremar, the ferry that takes us to Porto Ferraio, the main city on the island of Elba. The trip takes an hour and a half and we decide to go to the upper deck. David is enjoying all this. He has a half smile permanently painted on his face and deeply breathes in the salty air. He enjoys the view of the receding hills of the Italian coastline and the calm lull of the Mediterranean. With his hands on his hips, he exclaims, "Aah! Now, I feel like I am really on vacation!"

***

Ian and his older cousins, Ina's children, get along well. Flavia is only 3 years older and is very maternal. She hugs and kisses Ian and wants to take him by the hand. Flavia and Simone are good swimmers and have a great time running in and out of the water. The sea in the Gulf of Procchio by Ina's house is as calm as oil. We can walk out to sea for 50 yards or more and the water is still only two to three feet deep. Just "like an immense bathtub," tourists say. Ian learned how to swim the previous year through the Neighborhood Swim Classes for Infants and he loves the sea.

"Mommy *isto bello mai?* Mommy, *vuoi mai?* (Mommy, see the beautiful sea? Mommy you want the sea)?" Ian says in broken Italian, pointing at the water.

"He is two years old and the first sentences are in Italian," Ina says. Delighted, she hugs and kisses Ian.

"Actually, he has already conversed with Dad at length in Italian!" I relay to Ina the conversation with Dad and the *acqua asciutta.*

***

Seated at the edge of the water, under a sun umbrella, I watch Ian dive in the three feet of water. The water is so clear that I can see him down at the bottom, among lots of minuscule fish, grabbing sand and stuff in his hand. He is having lots of fun going down to the bottom and up again holding sand and pebbles. I do not like that he is taking longer and longer to come up each time and I tell him so. Franco and David are seated close by, having a serious discussion and watching me and Ian, while my sister Ina is distributing snacks.

Ian does down again and I start counting silently… Ok! Now, he is down way too long and I tell Ian to come up, right now! I look toward his direction and I see he is floating, face-down, motionless. I yell his name and I jump into the water, while a searing pain strikes my foot as I step on the sharp edge of a submerged rock. I continue to walk, grab Ian from the water, and lift him up in my arms. He turns around to look at me and says, "Guarda, Mommy, pesci. (Look Mommy, fish)." A bruised, tiny fish escapes from between his tightly-pinched fingers.

On the beach David and Franco look at me, not understanding what is going on.

"Come and get him," I say to David.

David takes Ian back to the beach. I try to walk back, but I can't, and I remain in the water.

"What's wrong, Cettina?" David asks, extending to me his hand.

"I can't walk," I say.

Ina, who is following the conversation, asks, "You thought Ian was in trouble, didn't you? Can you put any weight on your foot at all?"

I shake my head and Ina says, "Well, let's go everybody! We are going to the Emergency Room."

At the ER, x-rays show two shattered toes. The young doctor puts a cast on my left foot that goes all the way up to my knee.

"There! You mustn't move your foot, at all. Well, vacation is over and you need to go back home and heal," says the doctor as he hands me something for the pain. "Do you live far?"

"San Diego, California," I can hardly find the voice to answer.

"*Accipicchia*! (I'll be darned)! In California? All of you?" asks the doctor, surprised.

"No, only my sister and her family," says Ina.

***

We go back to Naples to get Lloyd earlier than planned and decide to leave earlier for the States. With me in a wheelchair we don't feel like doing much.

Dad and Yolanda did such a great job that Lloyd is unrecognizable. He's grown so much! David has a hard time believing it. "This is Lloyd? This is Lloyd?" he keeps repeating as he holds the baby above his head and talks and smiles at him. I have missed the baby a lot, and now that I am stuck in a wheelchair, I tell Lloyd he can remain seated on my lap for a long time.

At the airports of Rome and London people ask me if I have broken my leg skiing in the Swiss Alps. "No," I tell them, "no such glamorous event happened! I just broke my toes on a rock, dashing into the sea on the island of Elba, because I thought my baby was drowning. But he was only grabbing a tiny, bitty fish from the bottom of the sea."

***

The 1970's start with a recession in California and in most of the U.S.. The company where David works has gone out of business and for three long weeks, he, like all other Californians, has been looking for work. He is very worried and can't sleep at night. He is home all day now, researching and looking at all the possible companies, and getting very discouraged.

"How are we going to manage?

"David, I have gone through World War II. I can handle this! Besides, I remember all the tricks my mother had and how to make delicious meals for the whole family. I have a reserve of beans, rice, and canned milk to last a long time. My mom had nothing. I can make lentil soup with noodles, split pea soup with noodles, and bean soup and noodles with rosemary from our yard. The children are going to love it. And you will too!"

David smiles and I continue, "You'll see! It's a good thing, because you will finally get the job that you really dreamed of, and you will get more money! Soon you will get your master's from Cal State. Just concentrate on the job that you really want."

"I know, I know," he says and goes back to add all the companies that he plans on visiting to his list. I am glad that I encouraged him a little bit. Alone in the kitchen, I call our mortgage company to advise them that our situation has not changed. The young secretary is very understanding.

"Mrs. Jackson, you are only one of thousands of families in the same situation. I really feel for all of you, but I read things are getting better…"

"You know what also worries me?" I tell the young lady, "I am expecting my third baby in four months!"

***

The doctor gives David some valium for his anxiety. I do not want him to have a nervous breakdown and I try to help him as much as possible. I take care of everything by myself – the house, the shopping, the bills, the kids – and keep telling him to have faith and pray that it will happen. And it does happen! He finds a job with the Solar Turbines Division of the International Harvester Corporation in San Diego, California. That is the job that he really wants, working as a chief financial analyst right in the company's comptroller office. David moves to San Diego ahead of us while the boys and I pack.

"You know what boys? Very soon we are going to have another baby in the house."

Ian and Lloyd look at me in amazement. "Is it a boy or a girl? Please, please Mommy make it a boy. Make it a boy!" says four-and-a-half-year-old Ian.

"Well, we do not know what the baby is yet." I say. "It could be a boy, it could be a girl, it could be any…"

"It could be anything," interrupts three-year-old Lloyd "It could be a boy, it could be a girl, it could be a Mickey Mouse…"

"Lloyd, you dummy!" Ian exclaims. "Mickey Mouses come from mommy Mickey Mouses."

I hug and kiss Lloyd who looks sad and mortified.

The following Friday, when David comes back from San Diego, I tell him that Lloyd is hoping for a Mickey Mouse.

***

It's 1971 and we are moving to San Diego. "Well, we bought the house!" yells David coming in the front door of the apartment.

"We bought the house? What do you mean we bought the house! Which house?"

"The one that you liked so much! The one with the sunken living room and 4 bedrooms. The one that you liked the best in University City."

"The split level one? But that one was so expensive!" I say, horrified.

"No, No! Not expensive! The builders sold it to us for the same price as the cheaper ones. Believe me, they were really motivated to sell!"

"Really? Wow, you are so clever! You are so wonderful!" I say, really impressed.

My mother and father in-law are helping us with the moving and I am thankful because, with three babies, I can use all the help I can get. Grandma loves Mark.

"The most beautiful baby I ever saw! Looks like his Daddy when he was a baby!" she says.

This beautiful house has four bedrooms and I immediately plan to furnish one bedroom for my in-laws when they came to San Diego to visit us. But the nicest thing of all is that my next-door neighbor has three children just a little older than mine, a girl and two boys, and they get along beautifully. The six of them run from my house to theirs, back and forth.

Chapter 26:

College

As soon as I can, and have the time, I look into San Diego State University and I apply. I want to impress the admissions office with all the school papers I have from Florence, London, France, and Santa Ana College. I register for two classes only.

"I am accepted," I yell at David and show him my acceptance letter. He tells me how glad he is and how sorry he felt that I hadn't been able to go to school more full-time like he did.

Baby Mark is almost two years old now, and SDSU accepts him at the University Children's Center as long as he is potty trained. I am thankful for this because now I can get to my classes. The only thing they want from me is participation two afternoons a week at the school.

I get myself as organized as I can. After Ian and Lloyd go to school, which is just a couple of blocks from home, I get Mark ready and we drive to San Diego State. My classes are late in the morning and it is hard to find parking. Mark likes to help. He stands on the car seat and looks for parking spaces.

"Here, Mommy, here!" But I am too late. Someone gets there just before me. Besides, it is too hard to guess if Mark means "here" or "there".

"There, there, Mommy, there," Mark says, holding on to the dashboard of the car. This time I see the space and I get it. We both run to the Childcare Center and Mark soon disappears through the doors yelling, "Bye, Mommy bye, bye." I follow him and realize that he must really love this place and I say so to Rene, the lady at the desk.

"Maria, did you talk to Mark about the rules that children must not bring anything to school? Yesterday he had his pockets full of toys."

"Yes, I checked his pockets, he doesn't have anything today," I say. Mark makes lots of friends and seems to be the center of everything. The following morning as I take Mark to the Childcare Center and I check in at the desk, Rene is annoyed with me again.

"Maria, you said you checked Mark's pockets, but he had little toys inside his socks, and was giving them to the children. I am sorry, Maria, we can't allow that, for the safety of the kids and everything, or we will have to let him go."

"Oh, I am sorry! No, no, I agree with you. Absolutely!" I tell Rene that Mark has never been disobedient or defiant. He is very easy going and always does what he is told. I go to get Mark at the main classroom and I see he is surrounded by children.

"Look, that lady is Mark's mom," someone says and pretty soon I am also surrounded by children. I didn't know I was a celebrity. I tell David about the problem that I have with Mark and he talks to our son.

The following morning, I make sure that he understands that he mustn't have anything to do with bringing toys to school. I check his pockets, his socks, and even his underwear, and pat him all down before he goes to class. When I go back to get him after my classes, I am greeted at the desk by Rene and two other ladies.

"Maria, we are sorry but we do not know what else to do…" she says.

Oh, no! What did Mark do now? I think to myself. Rene shows me a three-foot long cord that I immediately recognize as the cord that I keep above the dryer in the garage. When Mark is brought to the desk, he is all smiles.

"Hi, Miss Rene. Hi, Mommy," Mark says.

"Mark, this morning before you came to the Childcare Center, I checked well. I did not see the cord. Where was it?" I ask him in front of the two ladies.

"Here!" Mark says and touches the inside of his leg.

"But I patted you down! You mean, the cord was inside the leg of your pants?" I ask.

"Yes, here," Mark answers, touching the inner side of his leg again.

"But how? It didn't fall out as you walked?" I ask.

"No, I put it here," Mark says and he shows with the gesture of his hand that he had tucked one end of the cord inside the elastic of his underpants. At this point I fall silent. I really do not know how to react. I am flabbergasted.

"It looks like Mark's need to connect with his peers is stronger than any fear of being punished," I agree with Rene.

Mark Jackson at the Childcare Center

Renee agrees. "Yes. Social interaction at this moment in a child's life is paramount." Like the other ladies working at the Center, Rene is majoring in child's psychology.

The following evening, I am delighted to tell David that the ladies at Mark's school have come up with a solution: "The first hour will be Show and Tell for the whole class!"

"That sounds very logical to me! Why didn't they come up with that sooner? Good job, son! He told them to change the rules!"

***

David Jackson and Mark

I am going to classes, cooking, and taking care of the house. The boys take every bit of my time. I cannot seem to get enough sleep. What is more, I am forgetting to pay attention to David.

"Come with me and meet my work buddies for a drink at the bar down the street," David says.

"David, I have a final tomorrow. How can you ask me such a thing!" I say. I am getting my bachelor's degree at the end of the semester and I can't mess up. Still, I know something is bothering him. He tells me the company's CEO is very rude.

"I say 'Good morning, Mr. Cooper' when I meet him in the hallway and he totally ignores me. I am the newest person hired there!"

"Well, maybe he's just had a fight with his wife and he didn't see you. Maybe he was worried about the company losing millions during the recession. Maybe his wife was cheating on him," I say to David who is now laughing. "Please, do not take this personally. Just ignore it. Just keep on saying 'Good morning, Mr. Cooper' in a nice strong tone of voice." I tell David that many times I've found myself in the same situation in my jobs in England and France. I just had to ignore it, too. Of course, things are much different at this new job. David was a close friend of his bosses at the old company.

***

The boys are doing very well in school, especially in reading. I use the same method with Ian that my mom used with me, and he reads well and fast. I am doing the same thing now with Lloyd. His favorite books are Dr. Seuss'. I make him read one page and circle the words he doesn't recognize right away. If he circles only one word, he has to reread the whole page only once. If he circles three words, he has to reread the page three times.

"It's amazing how well it works," I tell David. "Lloyd reads it over and over again, more than he is supposed to. He loves it. He is learning some passages by heart. I am so thankful to my mom for this. You would have liked my mom. She had incredibly strong willpower."

***

David finally gets his master's degree and I call Franco to tell him about it because he cares immensely that we both finish our education.

"Well, Cettina, it's your turn. Do not give up now!" Franco says.

I tell Franco that I am working on my master's very slowly. Unfortunately, I cannot take more than two classes per semester. My sister comes to the phone and has bad news from Naples. Dad is very ill. He has advanced lung cancer and only 5 to 6 months to live. The doctors and the family have decided not to tell him. He has only one chance in thousands to improve with the cures. Doctors think that knowing he only has 5 or 6 months to live will not help his mental outlook and his will to fight the disease, but they will use cancer treatment anyway.

"My dad smoked all his life. He was a chain smoker," I tell David. "He lights up a match only once. I used to watch him bring the butt of his cigarette, with hanging dead ashes, to the new cigarette in his mouth, breathe deeply, and then briskly brush the falling embers and ashes off his shirt sleeves. I would like my dad to know his grandsons." David agrees.

"It's also very important for the boys to know their grandfather," he says.

We need to take time to talk very seriously about this, so I get busy doing all the chores that he usually does at night, like watering the orchids his father gave him, to help bring them back to life. David's father is the manager of the garden section of a department store.

We talk it over with David and he can make it happen. It will be Christmas soon. We will spend the 25th and 26th of December here with the Jackson grandparents, leave on the 27th for Italy, and celebrate the new year, 1977, with Dad, then stay as long as possible in Naples and then a few days in Florence.

Chapter 27:

Nonno's

At Dad's place, the whole family is there, my grandmother (Nonna Gargano), Dad's sisters, their husbands, and Yolanda. They are all delighted to see us but most of all my dad. Ian remembers Nonno well and runs to hug him.

The boys get to play a game of Stiks with Nonno. It is incredible how quickly and easily the boys like to hug and kiss their grandparents.

Naples. My dad's house. December 1976. The boys closely watching Nonno's next move.
Grandpa laughing, knowing he is being watched.

Dad's place, like almost every other corner of the city, has a great view of the sea with the omnipresent volcano, Vesuvius, and its constant thread of smoke slowly rising from the top. It is New Year's Eve and one can feel the excitement bubbling up from the Bay of Naples. In Italy there are not many restrictions about fireworks, especially in Naples, where they are manufactured. However, many Italian cities think Naples exaggerates a little with its display. The Most Beautiful City by the Sea counters that "it's all envy!"

Truly, the spectacle of New Year's Eve in Naples is something to behold. The night of the 31st of December at around midnight, the whole city is ablaze with fireworks. Neapolitans have firework displays in every window, every balcony, every rooftop, every condo's entrance gate, in the streets and in the piazzas. The city's official fireworks display starts at 1 a.m. at the *Lungomare* and lights up the sea. It is an unforgettable sight. The lights of myriads of fireworks change the deep blackness of the night to a dark blue afternoon sky.

Wikipedia: The Lungomare of the Bay of Naples. January 1st, 1am

Dad makes crowns of pinwheels that are whirling around by the balconies. The boys screech with happiness and hug and follow their grandpa around (who is busy making more and more pinwheels) and constantly call him 'Nonno'. We all go to bed around 4am.

The boys love all the attention and the hugging they get from their grandparents. It breaks my heart to look at Dad, knowing that he is so ill.

***

In the afternoon, Dad needs to go shopping and wants to use the *funicolare*. "Go with him Cettina, go with him. Leave the boys here," Yolanda says.

This is the first time I use the Naples cable-car system, the *funicolare*, which inspired a famous song, *Funiculi Funicula.* Italians call Naples "*La piu Bella Citta' dell Marine*" (the Most Beautiful City by the Sea). I've never seen this city from this point of view before but the sight is spectacular. The Bay of Naples, the sea, and Mount Vesuvius all at my feet. I tell Dad how beautiful it all is. Dad nods silently in agreement but I sense that he wants to speak to me.

I wish we could talk to one another freely the way we used to such a long time ago. Leaving the cable car, I almost have a heart attack watching Dad getting down the steps.

"Dad be careful!" I scream. He is skipping two steps at a time going down full speed. He finally stops at the landing and turns to look at me. "Please wait for me. Be careful," I hardly have the breath to utter.

On the way home we stop at a church and he gives me a small book of prayers and songs that he got from a pew. I am touched by the unspoken meaning behind it. I want to say *thank you for giving this to me, Dad,* but I say instead, "Am I allowed to take it?"

"Of course. The priest keeps on telling us to take them home and pray," he says.

At home, I tell Yolanda that Dad scared the heck out of me when he went down the stairs. It seems as if he was barely touching the steps, as if he was gliding from one step to the other.

"Please watch him very carefully, Yolanda," I tell her.

***

In the kitchen, Grandma Gargano is cooking for everybody. She is ninety-five years old, and I explain to the boys that she is my dad's mother. My aunts and Yolanda are busy helping everywhere. They are cooking *capitone*, a traditional dish for the holidays.

The boys love it and think they are little round pieces of chicken. I explain to them that it is a long skinny fish instead.

After dinner, while Dad leaves the table for a few minutes, Grandma Gargano bursts out in Neapolitan dialect, crying, "*Pigghiami a mia Signuri, Pigghiami a mia!* (Take me! God, take me)!" I look at my grandma and I share her heartbreaking pain. But I don't remember her ever talking to me when I was a child, or as a grown up, nor do I remember us two ever hugging each other.

Dad asks me if I am still in school. I tell him I am working on a master's degree but very slowly.

"She is like her mother," Dad says to Yolanda. And then there are those words again, "That little girl there, see her there?" Dad says, nodding towards me across the table, "She's a hurt right here, is a thorn right here," he whispers quietly.

I look at my dad and I so desperately wish I could ask, *Why, Dad? Why am I such a thorn in your heart?* But I am not able to, and I am painfully aware that I will never see my dad again.

***

We take the train back to Florence and the boys, who have never been in one of these European trains before, love to open the door of our private compartment, run in the corridors, come back, and slide the door shut again. Mark, who is four and a half, never gets tired of it.

The trip takes about 5 to 6 hours. In Florence we get a call from David. He misses us. I tell Ina that I should have insisted he come with us and that I mentioned to him how lucky we are that we have a good, sound marriage.

During a visit to downtown Florence, Ian is the one who is most impressed with the statues in Piazza Della Signoria and the paintings at the Uffizi Gallery.

"Mom, I want to start on this floor and see everything! Everything!" Ian says.

We leave Ina's children and Lloyd and Mark outside the Gallery with Franco. Ina and I stop for a moment to see our favorite paintings by Botticelli, *The Birth of Venus* and *Primavera*. I explain to Ian that the lady in the center of the painting represents *Primavera* (Spring) and that all the ladies around her are dancing and are so happy because it's springtime. Ian is listening intently but by the time we walk halfway around the room he disappears out the door and runs and slides up and down the corridor. So, we all decide to go for ice cream at the *Perche'No*.

I enjoy this last day in Florence and realize how much I will miss it.

Back at Ina's house there is a call from David. He wants to know if we are all packed and ready for the trip back home.

"Please come back soon, I miss you so much," he says.

"David, you know we are leaving tomorrow morning! We all miss you so much too, darling."

After a couple of seconds Ina calls me to the phone: "It's David, again," she says.

I talked to David briefly and Ina wants to know what happened.

Very emotionally I tell her, "He said he forgot to tell me that he loved me, and he loves the children."

Chapter 28:

Back to a Changed Life | January 1976

San Diego looks splendid from the air as we get ready to land in the early afternoon. The boys are excited to be back and David is so happy to see us! We all pile in his car and he stops at the bar restaurant which is his favorite spot before coming home from work. We decide to have dinner there and the kids are happy to order their own meal and dessert. David goes to the bar and wants me to meet some of his friends. I wave at them from our table while one of the bartenders comes with a drink for me.

"From your husband," she says. She then proceeds to wipe our table and with urgency in her voice she whispers to me, "Stay with him, Tina! Stay with him." I am surprised at her tone, like almost an admonishment: "Stay with him, Tina!"

***

Life forcefully grabs me back to reality – the boys, the housework, the cooking, and school. I am taking post-graduate classes and want to hurry up with my master's degree even though I can't handle more than two classes per semester.

Since we are back home in San Diego, David seems irritable, especially with the children. I notice he is taking Valium and I ask him why. "The doctor suggested it," he says. Maybe he is worried about his mother who is in the hospital and very ill, according to my father-in-law.

I try to be more understanding of his needs and ask my next-door neighbor, Diana, to keep an eye on the children while I go with him to the bar to meet his friends. "You? You are his wife?" There is the same intensity in this guy's voice as there was in the bartender's voice who said, "Stay with him Tina, stay with him!"

David is half an hour late from work tonight which is very rare. At 6:30 I am always ready with dinner on the table. I receive a call from my father-in-law from Santa Ana Hospital. He is crying. My mother-in-law died this afternoon. I tell him, "I am so sorry! I am so sorry! David is not home yet but we will call as soon as he gets home. I am so sorry!"

The boys, who are ready to get in the shower, hear about Nana's death. They are very upset and crying. I am trying to comfort them.

"Nana was very ill…"

"No, No! Mom! Why…" Lloyd is upset the most.

"Nana was very old, and… when we get very old…" Lloyd is sobbing and does not accept my explanations.

"NO, NO, MOM! WHY, WHY she died…?" The intensity in Lloyds' crying voice alarms me, his staring eyes burning inside my brain.

"Well," I say, desperately looking for the right words, "we don't really… really die… You see, the soul, our souls, never die… they go to heaven, and… the body …" I continue in this vein for a couple of minutes more.

"We remove our body, just like we remove our clothes for the shower." Lloyd says calmly, and for that I am very thankful.

***

Three months after the funeral we are still all devastated, even though David doesn't say a word about it and never talks about his mother or her death. I am trying to do my best to comfort him but I make him more irritable. He tells me he wants to sell the house which has more than doubled in value.

"Are we going to buy something else? Another house?" I ask.

"No. You are going to get half of the money and so will I," he says.

My neighbor, Diana, notices something is bothering David and when I tell her that he wants to sell the house, she asks, "Does he have a girlfriend?"

"I don't think so, he is always home at 6:30."

"Do you have any family here, Tina?"

"No, my family, my sister, my siblings are all in Italy."

"See? That's very hard! I have my mom and dad and my sisters here. Do you know Little Italy? You need some friends, Tina, that you can talk freely to. Tomorrow is Saturday. Let's take the kids and go visit Little Italy."

Little Italy is a great place. The boys immediately recognize Italian words and phrases and I feel as if a breath of fresh air is blowing from Italy. I am immediately asked to become a member of the Little Italy Club, and I make many friends. One lady in particular, Francesca Brown, is of Italian descent and I can tell from her accent she is from New York. I am delighted to find out she lives in University City, two blocks from us, and we meet often at my house. I tell Fran that my husband wants to sell the house.

"It figures! He's a bastard!" Fran is 10 years older than I. She is divorced with a grown daughter who lives in San Francisco. For her, all men are bastards. I try to explain that he is not like that.

"We have a close relationship. He shares everything with me, all his problems at work, things like that. I do the same thing with him about my problems at school. He wrote an article a couple of years ago that was published in a financial magazine. His bosses were very impressed, and he got quite a promotion! We celebrated with champagne and a fancy dinner," I tell Fran Brown.

***

It has been almost 5 months now that we are back from Italy and things seem to be getting worse. I miss the closeness, the sharing of our days' problems, and his loving notes. After dinner I asks David, "How was your day?" But he does not want to talk. I tell him that I've thought about it and I feel we should not sell the house. I don't want half of the money. He gets irritated and tells me, "It has nothing to do with you. This is strictly a money arrangement."

A money arrangement? I wish I knew what was happening and how to get back to my life as it was before we went to Italy to see Dad. I ask him if this means we are separating. He says 'yes' and that we'll have equal time with the children. I feel like I am living in a nightmare and I confide in Fran that the night we left Florence for the States, he called me back on the phone because he had forgotten to tell me he loved me. That was only about 5 months ago. We hadn't even had a fight!

"What a bastard! I tell you! But how is it going with the house?" Fran asks.

"He is selling the house. I told him he will have to force me to sell. The house is the symbol of my home and family and I feel I am just being tossed out! He asked me 'Do you want me to go? Do you want me to go?' I said 'Yes, go! The sooner the better.' So, he left."

"So, what happened?" Fran asks.

"So, he left, and he took me to court. I thought 'feminists' were pro-women, but the lady judge feminist was definitely against me. She scolded me for making such a fuss about the house, said that women must be self-reliant and that I do not need a man to take care of me. I can be just as good a head of the household. I tried to make this stupid judge understand that I do not have any desire to compete with my husband as head of the household. She asked me, 'You have moved many times before, haven't you?' Yes, but we moved all together, as a family, I told her. She turned to look at me as if I were something really weird. She did, however, let me stay in the house for two more years until I finish school."

I tell Fran I only have 5 more units to go for my master's degree but I need to find a job soon to be independent, so the best thing I can do is study for a teaching credential instead. I have to do it in two years. So, I throw myself into the books and then notice my two older sons are doing the same, copying me.

At the end of August, I get a letter from the Italian embassy in Los Angeles telling me that my family is very worried about me because I have not answer their letters or their phone calls.

"So? Why don't you call home?" Fran asks in one of her visits.

"I can't. I would start crying and I can't do it. They would keep on asking me question upon question and I can't do it. It has been only a little over eight months that we came back from Florence and I am still in shock. They will want to know why. I know there is no other woman, or he wouldn't look so unhappy and miserable."

"It figures! Busy bodies, family people." I am thankful that Fran is always around to help me and make me laugh.

***

David comes to see the kids often but the boys do not act as excited to see him as they used to when he came home from work. I notice their indifference and feel sadness. I feel sorry for my sons. My dad, too, stopped being my hero.

***

Fran Brown tells me of a big sale at the grocery store and comes to pick me up. I leave the house open so the children can come and go from the house next door. I tell Diana I should not be more than an hour. Just a little over an hour later, Fran helps me quickly bring all my groceries in the house and leaves.

I am on the way next door to tell the kids I am back, when I realize the car is not in the driveway, where I am sure I left it. I go to the garage, and it is not there either.

I am dumbfounded! My big Chevrolet Impala is nowhere to be found! I start panicking and tell myself I should call the police – I definitely do not want to call David. I cross the driveway to Diana's house to call the kids when I see my Impala come down the street and slow down slightly, in front of my house. It then makes a perfect right turn into my driveway, continues up the little incline at the end, and stops gently just before the closed garage door. I am stunned! Ian is driving!

Lloyd, Mark, and two of the neighbors' children get out of the car, laughing as they run into Diana's house. Ian follows them. (He is 12 years old.) Diana's husband has watched all this from his front door.

"When did you teach him to drive?" he says.

"Oh, no!" I say, still horrified. "I never, never again..."

"He learned just by watching you? You know what that means, right Tina? You have a very bright young man there."

***

I am halfway through my teaching credential and am sent to get experience at an elementary school in the San Diego School District. My job is teaching struggling children how to do their homework. I enjoy drawing little birds on the children's notebooks and asking them, "Okay, now cross out ten, how many birds are left?" I do this just in case there are students who can't visualize math. That was also my problem as an elementary student, back in Florence. The supervisor, in one of her rounds, stops to look at what I'm doing, smiles, and nods. Unfortunately, though, this is not a paying job.

The divorce settlement gives me and the children enough money to survive but I hardly have enough left to pay the mortgage and utilities.

"Tina, I'm more than happy to lend you money for food."

"It's not the food that worries me, Fran. I have enough to make bean and lentil soup with noodles for months, and just watch the boys gobble it all up. No, what I am worried about is paying for the mortgage," I tell Fran.

I let my lawyer know that David is almost two months late in paying. I do not want to give the judge an excuse to immediately put the house up for sale. I want to remain in the house until I finish school and get my teaching credentials, as the judge promised I could.

I haven't felt anxiety about money in a long time and my mother and the horrors of war come to mind. At night, as I say prayers with the boys, I tell myself how lucky I am compared to what my mother went through, and I pray quietly, "Dear God…"

The following morning, as I look at my bank account, I see that a thousand dollars was deposited two days before. I am in shock: *a thousand dollars.* It did not come from David, and it shows just numbers. I call my lawyer and read him the numbers. He is also in shock and shouts incredulously that it is a rare bank error, and to go ahead and pay the mortgage. "They would never be able to trace the originator. Might just as well be you who keeps the money!"

I am speechless and fall into a silent prayer of gratitude. My older boy, Ian, looks at me.

"What happened, Mom? Are you Okay?"

"The bank made an error and deposited a thousand dollars in my account. All throughout my life, God has always been there," I say.

"A *thousand dollars?"* marvels Ian. He is more aware than Lloyd and Mark of what is happening to our family.

I feel relieved and so much happier that I decide to call Florence and talk to Ina and Franco. Everything that is happening to me must be for a higher reason and I can talk about my separation from David and answer all the questions, calmly.

***

Form N-414
UNITED STATES DEPARTMENT OF JUSTICE
IMMIGRATION AND NATURALIZATION SERVICE
(Edition 12-15-44)

ACKNOWLEDGMENT OF FILING PETITION FOR NATURALIZATION
(This card is not to be regarded as evidence of U. S. citizenship)

Name and location of court: U.S. District Court
Southern District
San Diego, California

The Oath of Allegiance

"Fran, I have applied for American citizenship! If there is a job opening for me as a schoolteacher, I want to be ready," I say, carrying the Naturalization Papers. "Stay for dinner, I am making pizzas. Big flour tortillas with cheese and tomatoes, and all other stuff on top that the boys like."

"But you can still work even if you are not a citizen, as long as you are legal," Fran says.

I read out loud to Fran the Oath of Allegiance, over which I have agonized for months.

"I hereby declare, on oath, that I absolutely and entirely renounce and abjure all allegiance and fidelity to any country of which I have been a citizen. See? This part is easy to understand, I do not like the old countries and their governments, anyway. There is too much contrast between the rich aristocrats/elites and ordinary citizens."

"Well, we don't have titled aristocrats/elites here, that's for sure! So, why have you agonized for months?"

"Because I know, I will always have a special spot for Italy and Florence in my heart, and I want to make sure that it will not interfere with the allegiance and fidelity oath of the United States."

"That's the same way I will always feel about New York, my hometown!" says Fran.

"The second part of the oath says, 'I will support and defend the Constitution and the laws of the United States...' How long does it last?"

"How long does what last?" Fran asks.

"The part of the oath to defend the laws and the Constitution. I mean, how long is it valid for?" I ask.

"If you are born here, you are an American citizen and you should know the oath and... I don't know," says Fran.

"That's what I don't understand. For example, take the underground movements and their bombing and all those protests that caused so much harm. They are people born here, but they want to 'fundamentally' change the Constitution! Have they taken the oath to defend the Constitution?"

"Ooohh! I know what you are getting at! You think American-born citizens should take an oath, and renew it as we renew our driver's license?" Fran bursts out laughing.

"Yeah! Why not?! School teachers, lawyers, and doctors all have to renew their credentials!" I join Fran in a loud laughter. "I don't know what I am talking about Fran, but I know positively that I did not like the students that trashed the university so violently and viciously. Don't you think all citizens should take an oath to protect the Constitution? I like it here in America. I don't want it to be a victim of propaganda and bullying like Italy was during the war. It never quite recovered from it!"

Chapter 29:

Fran Brown Looks for a Job

Fran Brown is looking for a job. She has worked at a ladies' boutique for years but the owner of the shop, "Evie, the greatest lady you would ever want to meet," died early this past year. Fran wants to work in the boutiques of the Princess Cruises cruise line and is asking Evie's widow to give her a good recommendation.

"Can I tell him to come over to your house? He is bringing the resume and we are going to talk about it at a coffee shop. I do not want him to come over to my house."

"Sure! Is he coming now?" I ask.

While Fran is getting ready in my bedroom, the doorbell rings and I meet the gentleman in the hallway. We chat for a while as we stand by the stairs that go down to the sunken living room. He is a 59-year-old man and I notice his hair has barely any grey at the temple, and I think about how lucky, at his age, he is to still have a head full of dark hair. Fran tells him that I am getting a divorce and am forced to sell the house.

"It's so very hard when we have children. Do you have children, Mr...?"

"Bill. Just call me Bill. Yes. Yes, I do. Two grown sons, and a beautiful grandchild, Amie."

"I have three boys. The youngest is going to be six soon," I say, barely keeping my voice steady, and keeping myself from almost stumbling down the first step.

"Oops! I've got you, I've got you!" Bill grabs me by the hand and after a while he says, "Are you alright?... What a crying shame! A nice little lady to have to go through all this! Such a crying shame! Can I do anything for you?... A cup of coffee? Anything?"

"No, thank you," I smile. "Wait a minute. Yes, a cup of coffee. I have to go back to court tomorrow morning. Those lawyers are nasty. If I know that I have something to look forward to after court, I shall not be so upset. I can remain calm and uninvolved when they yell at me."

The following morning the lawyers are merciless. I am told to sit at the witness bench to the left of the judge's desk.

"Mrs. Jackson can speak four languages," David's lawyers tell the judge, "and she should have no problem at all finding any type of job, pretty fast. She is vindictive and obstinate. Her vengeance and her behavior are very harmful to Mr. Jackson and his work. We need your honor to order her to sign the agreement to sell the house."

I don't dare look in David's direction. He is sitting facing me in the courtroom and I cannot make the judge understand my sorrow. The only thing I can do is manage to keep myself from crying and answer the judge with a shake of the head. "No, I cannot sell my home. It's also the children's home."

After court I meet Fran's old boss for coffee. I tell him the judge ordered my lawyer to sign the papers in my place, so the house can be sold.

"I am sorry! I am truly sorry! I thought death was the worst thing that can happen in a marriage, but I guess divorce must be even worse than my wife's death, isn't it?" he says, deep in his own thoughts. "Come, let's go and have lunch."

***

Fran Brown, who has been waiting for the Princess Cruises answer, comes in all smiles. "He wrote a fantastic recommendation and I need to thank him. All his employees love him." Fran says.

"You mean, at the boutique?" I ask Fran.

"Oh no, the boutique belonged to his wife. He is the West Coast General Manager of the Fox Theaters. He is a World War II veteran. He is from the greatest generation! He is like a grandfather to all these young kids who work at the theaters. They all adore him," Fran says.

"Yes, he seems very nice. I had coffee with him after my court date. He comes across concerned about people. He reminds me of Mr. Michael. I worked as an *au pair* for him in France. He was a WWII veteran and part of the greatest generation also! He was so concerned about all those young soldiers who came to the USO, asking for help. Well, this is it, Fran! The judge ordered my lawyer to sign the papers to sell the house. David will have to take care of the kids until I have a full-time job."

"It's a good thing you have your teaching credentials. What does it look like, let me see it?" Fran asks. I showed Fran all the papers I have: the degree, the teaching credentials, the Phi Kappa Phi, and the Phi Beta Kappa, for good measure. Fran is impressed.

"You will soon find a job."

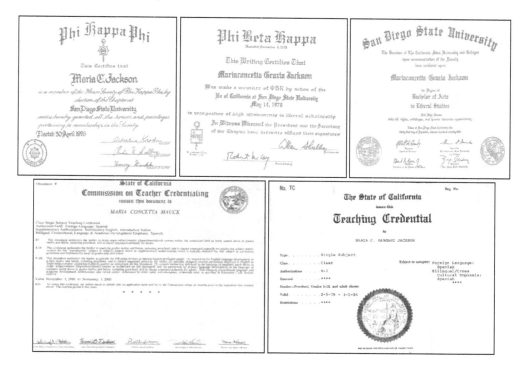

"You think so? I am scared stiff, Fran! And I still have lost my home!"

***

Fran starts her new job with Princess Cruises at the end of the month. Today, we are both invited to a big promotional dinner party given by the Fox Theaters and the big cinema industries. We are both excited and Fran even more so because she likes the big band that is playing during dinner.

There are fifteen people or so sitting at our round table. Fran knows some of the people at the table and points to two young men sitting opposite us.

"They are the boss's two sons, William and Robert Mauck. That stunning lady next to Robert is his wife, Stephanie. Some of the young men are childhood friends of theirs."

Soon the boss comes in to join us and sits to my right, the only empty chair left at the table.

"Hello Fran, hello Tina, I am glad you ladies made it," he says, but he hardly sites down before two ladies and a gentleman come running to him.

"Sir," says the gentleman, "you are needed at the office..."

He gets up in a hurry, saying, "I'll be right back!"

When the band takes a rest, the conversation at the table intensifies and people ask me about Italy. As I talk, the boss comes in quietly and sits down. The conversation now turns to "who are the most important US presidents?" followed by, "Who are the men we admire most in history?"

"The man I admire most in the world is my dad," says William, the oldest son.

"I absolutely agree, the best man in the world is my dad," says Robert, the other son.

Some young men around the table agree that, yes, he is the best man in the world and they start telling their personal experiences. I am astonished at hearing all this being said right in front of the boss, whose name I now realize is Mr. Mauck! I turn to look at him sitting silently, as if he isn't even there, as if he isn't even the person everybody is talking about.

Finally, it is William's turn to tell his story of when, at the end of their graduating year, he and some of his buddies were drinking beer, singing and having fun late into the night, until they ended up at the zoo. The noise they were making caught the attention of the guards and the police were called. From jail he called home and, terrified, asked Dad to come and get him. William holding his fist at his right ear, as if holding a telephone, relays the conversation as thus:

"When are they going to let you out?" my dad asks.

"They say the day after tomorrow," I answer.

"Oh, okay. I'll see you then. Call me, I'll come and get you," answers my dad.

There are gasps and laughter all around the table. Robert, the younger son, when asked if he got caught too, answers, "Heck no! I wasn't getting into trouble the way he did! I saw the messes he always got himself into! Officer Dan, who walks shifts at the theater, called Dad and said they had him and his friends. They let them out the following day."

As the band starts playing again, I turn to Fran and say softly, "What an incredibly beautiful story. When my boys have children, I'll tell them: *Be the dad that when your sons are grown up, they can say, 'The man I admire most in the world is my dad'.*"

At the end of the evening Mr. Mauck asks me if I have ever been to the city of Solvang, in central California. I answer that I have not.

"I am flying there on Saturday for work," he says, addressing himself to me and Fran, "and I think you two ladies should come along. We leave in the morning and we should be back by five. It's like being in Europe, Switzerland, or Norway. I'll come and get you both with my car."

***

Friday, Fran tells me that Princess Cruises called. They need her to start right away and to meet them at the port of Long Beach. She called Mr. Mauck and told him but I can still go to Solvang if I want to.

We drive to the Gillespie Field airport in El Cajon where lots of small airplanes are housed in hangars. We walk to a hangar where a young man is preparing a 6-seater Piper Cherokee, ready for flight.

"Good morning, Mr. Mauck, the plane is ready."

"Thanks, Chuck." Suddenly I realize *he* is the pilot!

Bill Mauck

"Oh, you are a pilot?" I ask. "How wonderful," and I immediately feel stupid about my silly question. I should have guessed it sooner. After a short exchange with the tower, he has a conversation made of hands and finger signs, a sign of two fingers, forcefully extended forward, must mean we are ready to roll.

As we ride slowly away, a string of more signs keeps coming back and forth from the hangar.

"What is that?" I ask.

"Oh, you noticed, huh?" asks Mr. Mauck, breaking into a laugh. "Don't mind Chuck, he is just a kid and needs to feel important!"

Soon we are in the air. Without the walls of a big airplane surrounding us, the view is wide open and I feel like I am sitting right outside, as if in the middle of the air! At a higher altitude it looks even more beautiful.

"Are you okay?" he asks.

"Oh yes! I love it. I have never been in a small plane before. Were you a pilot during World War II? Did you ever fly over Florence?"

"No, Uncle Sam did not want pilots who needed glasses in those days. My unit was stationed in Badneuenahr. We flew over France, Germany, and Belgium during the Battle of the Bulge. I never flew over Florence. How old were you during the war?"

"I was five when Mussolini declared war to the world."

"You can't remember much, then."

"Oh, but I do! Some things are quite vivid in my memory. I remember the bombing, the Germans shooting at the people hiding behind the window shutters, and those sirens! They seemed to wail inside my brain for an eternity. I remember events and complete conversations of people around us. It's only the sequence of events that sometimes is not clear," I say, trying to make him understand.

Solvang is a beautiful peaceful city, without many cars in the streets. It is like being in northern Europe. It reminds me a little of Switzerland.

We have lunch in one of those typical coffee shops that are also bakeries. I enjoy walking along the main streets looking at the shops until Mr. Mauck reappears from one of the business buildings.

"What a shame that Fran could not make it and missed all this fun," I remark.

"Yes, but she has come many times before to help my wife," he says.

The sky is a beautiful blue and the dense clouds below seems to cling to the airplane. We are half way to San Diego when Mr. Mauck asks me to look for a hole in the clouds.

"A… what?" I ask incredulously.

"Yes, a hole in the clouds. You see, we are now above the clouds and we need to descend below the clouds," he says, gesturing with his hand. "Tell me if you see an opening so I can descend underneath the clouds." I look at him, puzzled.

"Yes, see if you can see an opening. Do you see anything down below? Land, or mountains? Anything?" he asks.

Oh no! He has to be kidding! I look and look but I see nothing but clouds forever and I get a little panicky.

"Do you see anything? Houses, trees?" he asks again.

"No. No. I don't see…Yes! There! There!" I yell.

"What do you see?"

"The, the…trees, I mean… the hills! The houses!" I answer breathlessly.

"Where, on my right or left?"

"There! There on your left!" I say, pointing it out.

"Ok, I am going to make a left turn and a U-turn."

We descend, making a U-turn to the left, and continue making a U-turn until the airplane makes a complete circle. We are now above the opening. We descend more, going down right through the hole in the clouds and continuing the flight to Gillespie Field. I feel relieved and turn to look at Mr. Mauck. He looks at me, smiling from ear to ear. He seems to really be enjoying himself. He looks at my worried face and breaks into a small laughter. He was teasing me! A hole in the clouds indeed!

"Are you making fun of me, Mr. Mauck?"

"Who? Me?" he says, breaking into laughter again, "Never! Never make fun of cute little ladies! And call me Bill!"

He turns to look at me and breaks again into laughter. We leave the plane at the hangar and Mr. Mauck decides we still have time for dinner at a fancy place and orders champagne. He leaves me at my front door and says, "Tina, do not forget there is the opening of the *Star Wars* tomorrow at the Fox Theater. Bring the boys. I'll tell the manager to watch out for you. I had a great time tonight."

San Diego. Mr. Mauck and Maria

***

Mark, Lloyd, Ian and I are waiting in a long line outside the Fox Theater. The boys are very excited, most of all Lloyd, when a man in a theater uniform spots us.

"This way, gentlemen," says the man. He takes us out of the line, opens the golden cordoned-off entry doors to let us into the still empty theater, and closes them again. The boys, impressed by the looks on the people's faces standing in line, follow the man, who opens a series of closed-off carpeted sections to let us walk through, until we reach a special cordoned-off section inside the main hall. He shows us to our seats and then cordons off our section.

"Enjoy the movie, gentlemen!"

"Whoa! Whoa!" says Lloyd. "We must be really important people, huh!"

The boys are truly blown away by the special treatment and all the attention.

The long movie is over and Mr. Mauck comes looking for us, engaging the boys in conversation.

"Do you boys think we should show this movie again? Was it good enough?"

"Yes, again and again and again!" exclaim Lloyd and Mark. Ian behaves more reservedly but he loves it too.

"How about you, Tina?" he asks, putting his arm across my shoulders. "Were the boys impressed with all the VIP treatment? I told Lawrence to lay it on thick, all the way."

"Yes, I am still speechless…"

He walks us to my car and says, "I'll call you tomorrow. There is a Kiwanis Club picnic coming up and a sack race for the boys."

The End

Sources

Books:

- **Firenze: Gli Anni Terribili** – Bonechi (dal 1940 all'emergenza) as expressed by Piero Pieroni p.15, 29, 35, 39, 69, 92, 94. Sopra Intendenza alle Gallerie di Firenze

- **Florence, Cradle of the Italian Art** – Giusti di Becocci Via Canto de' Nelli, Firenze. p.117, 86

- **Firenze Va all Guerra** – Franca Lanci p.116, 114, (photos)

- **Firenze "Citta' Aperta"** – Ugo Cappelletti, Editrice Bonechi. p.111, 62, 43, 40, 16, 38, (photos)

- **Firenze Com'era**

- **Firenze, 1943-1945** *Anni di Terrore e di Fame*, Alberto Marcolini – p.45

- **BBC Home. On this Day – April 27th 1945**

- **L'Armir – Le origini della Radiodiffusione in Italia. Cronistoria della Radio dal 1923 al 2006**

- **EIAR - Ente Italiano per le Audizioni Radiofoniche. 14-23 Gennaio / 20 Dicembre 1944**

- **LA FONDAZIONE DELLA R.S.I.** Republica Italiana Sociale. (Liberated by the Germans from Gran Sasso Prison) *"Il Duce parla in diretta…from Radio Monaco"18th Settembre 1943*)

- **America in Chains.** Dictators and gun control. The Death of Freedom

- **Battaglia del Mediterraneo.** Wikipedia, L'enciclopedia Libera

- **Firenze. Storia** – 25 Settembre 1943 I **Bombardamenti** di Firenze

- **Aproffondendo. I bombardamenti di Firenze**

- **Sergio Lepri. Firenze, 1943 – 1947**

- **Giovanni Gentile. Wikiquot**

CPSIA information can be obtained
at www.ICGtesting.com
Printed in the USA
BVHW090339171121
621781BV00004B/94